BIOTERRORISM: PREVENTION, PREPAREDNESS AND PROTECTION

BIOTERRORISM: PREVENTION, PREPAREDNESS AND PROTECTION

J. V. BORRELLI
EDITOR

Nova Science Publishers, Inc.
New York

For permission to use material from this book please contact us:
Telephone 631-231-7269; Fax 631-231-8175
Web Site: http://www.novapublishers.com

NOTICE TO THE READER

Library of Congress Cataloging-in-Publication Data
Available upon request.

ISBN 13 978-1-60021-180-5
ISBN 10 1-60021-180-1

Published by Nova Science Publishers, Inc. ✦*New York*

CONTENTS

PREFACE

A bioterrorism attack is the deliberate release of viruses, bacteria, or other germs (agents) used to cause illness or death in people, animals, or plants. These agents are typically found in nature, but it is possible that they could be changed to increase their ability to cause disease, make them resistant to current medicines, or to increase their ability to be spread into the environment. Biological agents can be spread through the air, through water, or in food. Terrorists may use biological agents because they can be extremely difficult to detect and do not cause illness for several hours to several days. Some bioterrorism agents, like the smallpox virus, can be spread from person to person and some, like anthrax, can not. This book presents new analyses on the prevention of, preparedness for and protection from bioterrorism.

The recent anthrax attacks, though small in scale compared to the scenarios envisioned by bioterrorism experts, strained the public health system and raised concern that the nation is insufficiently prepared to respond to bioterrorist attacks. Improving public health preparedness and response capacity offers protection not only from bioterrorist attacks, but also from naturally occurring public health emergencies. In December 2001, the House and Senate each passed legislation (H.R. 3448, S. 1765) to improve the public health system's capacity to respond to bioterrorism. This legislation builds on the programs and authorities established in Title III of the Public Health Service (PHS) Act by the Public Health Threats and Emergencies Act of 2000 (P.L. 106-505, Title I). While the two bills are similar in many respects, there are several key differences that are being addressed in conference. The Senate bill (S. 1765) would authorize a total of $3.25 billion in FY2002 to increase the public health system's bioterrorism preparedness and response capability, including $640 million to expand the National Pharmaceutical Stockpile (NPS), $509 million to purchase smallpox vaccine, and $1.46 billion for grants to state and local health departments and hospitals. S. 1765 would also strengthen regulation of domestic and imported food by the Food and Drug Administration (FDA) and give the U.S. Department of Agriculture (USDA) new authority to safeguard the nation's agricultural industry from the threat of bioterrorism. The House bill (H.R. 3448) would authorize almost $3 billion in FY2002 for bioterrorism preparedness, including $646 million to expand the NPS, $509 million to purchase smallpox vaccine, and $1 billion for grants to states and localities. H.R. 3448 does not include any of the agricultural provisions that appear in S. 1765. Unlike the Senate bill, however, H.R. 3448 includes provisions to protect community drinking water supplies from bioterrorism and it places more emphasis on upgrading facilities at the Centers for Disease Control and Prevention (CDC). As discussed in chapter 1, while lawmakers work towards final passage of new authorizing legislation, Congress has appropriated $3 billion to the Dept. of Health and Human Services (HHS) for FY2002 to increase bioterrorism preparedness at the federal, state, and local levels. HHS anti-bioterrorism funding was included in the FY2002 Labor-HHS-Education appropriations bill (P.L. 107-116, H.R. 3061) and in the $20 billion emergency spending package (P.L. 107-117, H.R. 3338). HHS is dispersing the funds according to existing authorities and the broad spending parameters set out in the appropriations bills.

The purpose of chapter 2 is to aid public officials in communicating more effectively during a biological security emergency. Experience suggests that officials need to find out in real time what Americans know and believe, whom they trust, and what actions they are taking in response to the crisis. Using examples from four years of research by the Project on the Public and Biological Security at the Harvard School of Public Health (HSPH), the chapter examines the role surveys of the general public can play during a biological security crisis. The HSPH project has conducted twenty surveys of the general public for the purpose of advising the Centers for Disease Control and Prevention (CDC), national security officials, and state and local health officials on how to improve communications with the public in the event of a bioterrorist attack or a widespread attack of a newly emerging infectious disease. These surveys have been used to assess public knowledge, attitudes, and behavior in response to threats of bioterrorism, such as smallpox and anthrax, and emerging infectious diseases, such as SARS, and in response to the shortage of influenza vaccine in 2004. The authors' results suggest some overarching conclusions for those planning to respond to such events. Different publics will trust different information sources. In addition, the public's response to attacks and their need for information is likely to differ according to the type of attack in question. It is important to know whom these different groups trust as a reliable source of information. Because of the high level of public trust of physicians, it is important for public health authorities to develop ongoing communications with primary care and emergency room physicians. It is also necessary to know and address the public's specific beliefs about a biological threat. In the face of a threat, the public will make decisions based on what they believe to be true, whether or not these beliefs are true. Many times, they may be acting based on incorrect information. Likewise, it is imperative that the behavior of public leaders be consistent with their advice to the public concerning the threat and what the facts suggest should be done.

Future war/terrorist attacks may include invisible hazards such as a variety of deadly poisonous chemicals without prior warning. Materials responsible for chemical vapor/gas decontamination in existing respirators are activated carbon impregnated with metal oxides (such as copper, zinc, molybdenum and silver). For additional protection against blood agents, triethylenediamine (TEDA) can be incorporated. Biological weapons are characterized by low visibility, high potency, substantial accessibility, and relatively easy delivery. These can be eliminated only through simple filtration by virtue of their size. So far, there is no protection system, which is both breathable and highly efficient for biodefense. Recently, there has been an increasing attention of researchers throughout the world to improve the protection from chemical and biological warfare agents. Here, the authors have discussed how nanotechnology comes into potential use for protection from the various warfare agents. It is extremely essential to improve the protection spectrum and decontamination capacity of existing personnel protection devices without compromising on the user friendly traits. The importance of nanomaterials for effective performance has been highlighted. Various approaches for decontamination of the warfare agents through fabrication of catalytic nano-filters have been described. The major requirements for supportive material for catalyst are high specific surface area, high number of binding sites which are also selective and continuous porous structures to minimize the transport limitations and increase the user comfort. Nanofibers have intrinsically high specific surface areas namely surface-to-volume or surface-to-mass values. They can be easily produced at a large from various polymeric materials by the popular method of electrospinning. The different functional modifications (both chemical and biological) of the nanofibers are explained in detail in context with the detoxification mechanism. These techniques discussed in chapter 3, include both polymeric and non-polymeric nanomaterials fabricated by electrospinning. Two main strategies viz. pre-spinning and post-spinning functionalization are discussed and compared. With future advances in biotechnology and material science, the authors can expect these "smart materials" to play an integral role in personal protection with advanced sensing abilities.

In chapter 4, the Centers for Disease Control and Prevention's (CDC) activities to prepare the nation to respond to the public health and medical consequences of a bioterrorist attack. are presented The country is now dealing with anthrax exposures resulting from the agent being sent through the mail and the consequences of dealing with even limited exposures have proven to be quite significant. Prior to the recent anthrax incidents, a domestic bioterrorist attack had been considered to be a low-probability event, in part because of the various difficulties involved in successfully delivering biological agents to achieve large-scale casualties.

Among terrorist events in general, those that use chemical and biological weapons disseminate panic among the populations of both developed and in development countries. This fact was evidenced in the bioterrorist events after the fatidical September 11, 2001, especially those that concern letters with anthrax. It also has attracted attention to the fragility and vulnerability of people exposed to the risk of terrorist attacks with chemical and biological weapons. All of the countries, independent of their political and ideological orientations or international relationships, are at risk of a terrorist attack. Some countries are already worried about the formulation of safety protocols, answer programs to disasters caused by man and prevention of terrorism. Terrorism represents a danger for public health and it is a challenge for the epidemic surveillance of the systems of health and for the professionals that work in them. Explosions of bombs as well as chemical or biological attacks resulting in victims produces a great impact in the community and the epidemic data collected after the occurrences of such attacks have great importance in the formulation of prophylactic measures, treatment and control of diseases and others consequences of bioterrorism. The health professionals need to be trained to identify and assist people with diseases caused by biological and chemical agents. The health systems should have effective epidemic surveillance, laboratories prepared to identify noxious biological and chemical agents, trained human resources, medications, materials and equipment adapted to face several types of menaces. Chapter 5 offers updated information about epidemiological actions to be taken on the imminence of and/or immediately after biological terrorist attacks. The main goal is to collaborate with health professionals in the formulation of prophylactic protocols and measures of control of diseases through recognition of infections and intoxications. The epidemiological aspects of old and uncommon diseases are also considered, as those caused by *Bacillus anthracis*, *Clostridium botulinum* toxin, *Yersinia pestis*, *Variola major and Ferver hemmorráfica-Ebole* which are easily cultivated - as well as the chemical agents, which are easily manipulated and transported. Care precautions, infection control and occupational risk measures are also presented. The nurse's role is well described, because these professionals have special importance in hospital or community attendance of patients and therefore need to be trained to act in different situations. The cooperation among the countries is an important element to improve the knowledge and the information on how to deal with bioterrorism consequences towards world safety.

The September 11th attack and subsequent intentional release of anthrax spores via the U.S. postal system have focused policymakers' attention on the preparedness and response capability of the nation's public health system. The anthrax attacks put a tremendous strain on the U. S. public health infrastructure, an infrastructure that many experts argue has been weakened by years of neglect and under-funding. To better understand the preparedness gaps that exist, as well as the disparate functions and agencies that define public health in this country, the Congressional Research Service (CRS), in conjunction with George Washington University's National Health Policy Forum (NHPF), convened a seminar on October 26, 2001, entitled, *The U.S. Health Care System: Are State and Local Officials Prepared for Bioterrorism? How Should the Federal Government Assist?* Chapter 6 was supported, in part, by a grant from the Robert Wood Johnson Foundation. Speakers included William L. Roper, M.D., M.P.H., Dean, School of Public Health at the University of North Carolina; Georges C. Benjamin, M.D., Secretary, Maryland Department of Health and Mental Hygiene; Amy Smithson, Ph.D., Director, Chemical and Biological Weapons Non-Proliferation Project, the Henry L. Stimson Center; and Janet Heinrich, Dr. P.H., R.N., Director, Health Care–Public Health, U.S. General Accounting Office. The panelists presented a detailed overview of public health and the difficult choices the country faces in preparedness planning and rebuilding. The speakers made clear in their remarks that while immediate needs must be met, the importance of planning for the longer-term must not be overlooked. They suggested the need to recognize the multitude of returns on initial investments in public health. For example, if some drug-resistant bacteria were to emerge, independent of any terrorist activity, the capabilities developed to combat bioterrorism would be invaluable. Based upon their varied experiences, there was general consensus among all the speakers that public health preparedness, while dependent upon federal financial and other assistance, was largely a local matter. They argued that mending the gaps in the current public health fabric will require significant long-term commitments from the federal government, including investments and improvements in: laboratory capacity, regional planning, workforce training, epidemiology and surveillance systems, information systems, communication systems, and media relations. The panelists stressed that as priorities are set and resources committed, it is imperative that all preparedness efforts be coordinated at all levels of government–federal, state, and local.

Throughout history, humankind has battled infectious microorganisms that cause outbreaks of disease and death. As if the microbes weren't formidable enough in themselves, man has often employed some of these pathogens as weapons against other humans. The use of biological organisms or toxins to incapacitate or kill (biological warfare), or to cause civil disruption, chaos, and terror (bioterrorism), is documented to have occurred over the past several hundred years, all building to the anthrax mailings in the United States in 2001. The new paradigm of protecting the public from natural and man-made biological threats has rapidly transformed the public health and national security infrastructures in the United States. The nexus between basic research and applied research focused on protecting humans from pathogenic organisms has been termed biodefense. Biodefense is not a discipline *per se*, but a concerted application of other disciplines (immunology, biochemistry, pharmacology, microbiology) to the protection of human health and the enhancement of national security. One major component of biodefense is the rapid detection and identification of pathogenic or toxic materials that may be the etiological agents of a biological attack. The public health infrastructure must be able to rapidly detect (i.e., rule-in) these agents, as well as agents that cause more common, natural diseases with similar clinical presentations. This rule-in/rule-out algorithm is essential for an effective, rapid response, enabling initiation of appropriate medical intervention. An optimal diagnostic test would be able to rule-in any causative agent, while simultaneously ruling-out (i.e., determine not to be present) all of the others. Validating assays that are used to identify pathogens like anthrax- or plague-causing microorganisms are complex and costly, but absolutely necessary to ensure a quality diagnostic with near-zero false-positive and false-negative results. A rigorous, quality-controlled, and statistically robust process must be followed, to validate these methods. As an initial development of a broad-spectrum diagnostic platform, the authors have employed a real-time PCR (rtPCR) array detection approach to rule-in or rule-out many of the NIAID categories A and B priority pathogens. Also discussed in chapter 7, parameters for assay sensitivity, specificity, accuracy, and robustness are defined and established prior to assay development, to ensure the quality of the method. Approaches, achievements, and obstacles encountered along the path to assay validation are discussed.

In the wake of the September 11 attacks, federal, state and local governments have become increasingly aware of the need for an effective response to future terrorist activities. Of significant concern is the government's ability to respond to a biological attack, including the introduction of an infectious or contagious disease into a population. An effective response could include the isolation of persons exposed to infectious biological agents or infected with a communicable disease as a result of the attacks, as well as the quarantine of certain states, cities, or neighborhoods.Currently, state and local governments have the primary authority to control the spread of dangerous diseases within their jurisdiction, with the federal government's role limited to interstate and foreign quarantine. However, many states have inadequate procedures in place for isolating individuals who are infected or believed to be infected and quarantining areas that are or may be infected. Generally, the laws currently in effect do not address the spread of disease resulting from a biological attack, and for the most part only address specific diseases that were the cause of past epidemics. In light of recent events, many states are reevaluating their public health emergency response plans and are expected to enact more comprehensive regulations relating to isolation and quarantine in the event of a biological attack. Public health experts have developed a Model State Emergency Health Powers Act to guide states as they reevaluate their plans. Chapter 8 provides an overview of federal and state quarantine laws as they relate to the isolation or quarantine of individuals, as well as a discussion of the relevant case law. The Model State Emergency Health Powers Act is also discussed.

In: Bioterrorism: Prevention, Preparedness and Protection   ISBN 1-60021-180-1
Editor: J. V. Borrelli, pp. 1-41   © 2007 Nova Science Publishers, Inc.

Chapter 1

BIOTERRORISM: LEGISLATION TO IMPROVE PUBLIC HEALTH PREPAREDNESS AND RESPONSE CAPACITY[*]

C. Stephen Redhead, Donna U. Vogt and Mary E. Tiemann

ABSTRACT

The recent anthrax attacks, though small in scale compared to the scenarios envisioned by bioterrorism experts, strained the public health system and raised concern that the nation is insufficiently prepared to respond to bioterrorist attacks. Improving public health preparedness and response capacity offers protection not only from bioterrorist attacks, but also from naturally occurring public health emergencies.

In December 2001, the House and Senate each passed legislation (H.R. 3448, S. 1765) to improve the public health system's capacity to respond to bioterrorism. This legislation builds on the programs and authorities established in Title III of the Public Health Service (PHS) Act by the Public Health Threats and Emergencies Act of 2000 (P.L. 106-505, Title I). While the two bills are similar in many respects, there are several key differences that are being addressed in conference.

The Senate bill (S. 1765) would authorize a total of $3.25 billion in FY2002 to increase the public health system's bioterrorism preparedness and response capability, including $640 million to expand the National Pharmaceutical Stockpile (NPS), $509 million to purchase smallpox vaccine, and $1.46 billion for grants to state and local health departments and hospitals. S. 1765 would also strengthen regulation of domestic and imported food by the Food and Drug Administration (FDA) and give the U.S. Department of Agriculture (USDA) new authority to safeguard the nation's agricultural industry from the threat of bioterrorism.

The House bill (H.R. 3448) would authorize almost $3 billion in FY2002 for bioterrorism preparedness, including $646 million to expand the NPS, $509 million to purchase smallpox vaccine, and $1 billion for grants to states and localities. H.R. 3448 does not include any of the agricultural provisions that appear in S. 1765. Unlike the

---

[*] Excerpted from CRS Report RL31263, dated January 31, 2002.

Senate bill, however, H.R. 3448 includes provisions to protect community drinking water supplies from bioterrorism and it places more emphasis on upgrading facilities at the Centers for Disease Control and Prevention (CDC).

While lawmakers work towards final passage of new authorizing legislation, Congress has appropriated $3 billion to the Dept. of Health and Human Services (HHS) for FY2002 to increase bioterrorism preparedness at the federal, state, and local levels. HHS anti-bioterrorism funding was included in the FY2002 Labor-HHS-Education appropriations bill (P.L. 107-116, H.R. 3061) and in the $20 billion emergency spending package (P.L. 107-117, H.R. 3338). HHS is dispersing the funds according to existing authorities and the broad spending parameters set out in the appropriations bills.

INTRODUCTION

The September 11, 2001 terrorist attacks and the subsequent deliberate release of anthrax spores in the mail have focused policymakers' attention on the preparedness and response capability of the U.S. public health system. Though small in scale compared to the scenarios envisioned by bioterrorism experts and played out in recent government exercises, the recent anthrax attacks strained the public health system and exposed weaknesses at the federal, state, and local levels. Many bioterrorism experts believe that had those responsible for the anthrax attacks employed a more sophisticated delivery mechanism or released a deadly communicable biological agent such as smallpox, the health care system may have been overwhelmed.

Bioterrorism poses a unique challenge to the medical care and public health systems. Unlike an explosion or chemical attack, which results in immediate and visible casualties, the public health impact of a biological attack can unfold gradually over time. Until a sufficient number of people arrive at emergency rooms and doctors' offices complaining of similar illnesses, there may be no sign that an attack has taken place. The speed and accuracy with which doctors and laboratories reach the correct diagnoses and report their findings to public health authorities has a direct impact on the number of people who become ill and the number that die. The nation's ability to respond to a bioterrorist attack, therefore, depends crucially on the state of preparedness of its medical care systems and public health infrastructure.

Public health experts have for years complained about the deterioration of the public health system through neglect and lack of funding. They warn that the nation is ill-equipped and insufficiently prepared to respond to a bioterrorist attack. For example, they point out that there are too few medical personnel trained to spot biological attacks, a shortage of sophisticated laboratories to identify the agents, and inadequate supplies of drugs and vaccines to counteract the threat. They also contend that inadequate plans exist for setting up quarantines and emergency facilities to handle the sick and infectious victims. Improving public health preparedness and response capacity offers protection not only from bioterrorist attacks, but also from naturally occurring public health emergencies. Public health officials are increasingly concerned about our exposure and susceptibility to infectious disease and food-borne illness because of global travel, ubiquitous food imports, and the evolution of antibiotic-resistant pathogens.

In December 2001, the House and Senate each passed comprehensive bioterrorism preparedness legislation (H.R. 3448, S. 1765) with broad bipartisan support. This report summarizes H.R. 3448 and S. 1765 and provides a side-by-side comparison of the provisions in each bill and in current law. Lawmakers also appropriated $3 billion to the Dept. of Health and Human Services (HHS) for FY2002 to improve bioterrorism preparedness. Anti-bioterrorism funding was provided in the FY2002 Labor-HHS-Education appropriations bill (P.L. 107-116, H.R. 3061) and in the anti-terrorism emergency supplemental appropriations bill (P.L. 107-117, H.R. 3338). Details of HHS's bioterrorism funding, including the Administration's FY2003 budget request, are provided in Appendix A. Appendix B provides information on the HHS grant programs to improve public health and hospital preparedness. Appendix C lists all the bioterrorism-related hearings in the 107th Congress. In most cases, hearing testimony is available on the committee Web sites. Finally, Appendix D provides a list of bioterrorism-related Web sites.

HOUSE AND SENATE BIOTERRORISM LEGISLATION

Bioterrorism Preparedness Act (S. 1765)

Senators Frist and Kennedy introduced the Bioterrorism Preparedness Act (S. 1715) on November 15, 2001. In a procedural move aimed at bypassing committee consideration and allowing prompt floor consideration, the legislation's sponsors reintroduced the bill (S. 1765) with 74 cosponsors on December 4, 2001. On December 20,2001, the Senate took up the House bioterrorism bill (H.R. 3448, see below), substituted the text of S. 1765, and passed H.R. 3448, as amended.

The Bioterrorism Preparedness Act builds on the programs and authorities established in Title III of the Public Health Service (PHS) Act by the Public Health Threats and Emergencies Act of 2000 (P.L. 106-505, Title I). S. 1765 incorporates ideas and objectives from a number of other Senate bioterrorism bills introduced in the wake of the anthrax attacks.[1] It is intended to improve the health system's capacity to respond to bioterrorism, protect the nation's food supply from bioterrorist attacks, speed the development and production of new drug treatments and vaccines, improve coordination of federal anti-bioterrorism activities, and increase investment in state and local preparedness. S. 1765 is a 5-year authorization bill, which calls for a total of $3.25 billion in funding for FY2002 and such sums as may be necessary for the remaining years. Key provisions of the bill are summarized in the text box below, including the authorized appropriations for FY2002 (in parentheses).

---

[1] Senate bioterrorism preparedness bills introduced in response to the September 11 attacks and the anthrax incidents include: the Biological and Chemical Weapons Preparedness Act of 2001 (S. 1486) introduced by Senator Edwards on Oct. 3, 2001; the Biological and Chemical Attack Preparedness Act (S. 1508) introduced by Senator Corzine on Oct. 4, 2001; the State Bioterrorism Preparedness Act (S. 1520) introduced by Senator Bayh on Oct. 9, 2001; the Protecting America's Children Against Terrorism Act (S. 1539) introduced by Senator Clinton on Oct. 11,2001; the Bioterrorism Awareness Act (S. 1548) introduced by Senator Carnahan on Oct. 15,2001; the Protecting the Food Supply from Bioterrorism Act (S. 1551) introduced by Senator Clinton on Oct. 15, 2001; the Agricultural Bioterrorism Countermeasures Act of 2001 (S. 1563) introduced by Senator Hutchison on Oct. 17,2001; the Public Health Emergency Planning and Information Act of 2001 (S. 1574) introduced by Senator Rockefeller on Oct. 25,2001; the Pathogen Research, Emergency Preparedness and Response Efforts (PREPARE) Act of 2001 (S. 1635) introduced by Senator Hutchinson on Nov. 6,2001; and the Deadly Biological Agent Control Act of 2001 (S. 1661) introduced by Senator Feinstein on Nov. 8, 2001.

Bioterrorism Preparedness Act of 2001 (S. 1765)

I.   Federal Bioterrorism Preparedness and Response Capability:

- Expand the National Pharmaceutical Stockpile ($640 million).

- Upgrade CDC's bioterrorism response capability ($60 million).

- Improve public health laboratories ($59.5 million).

- Tighten controls on the possession and use of biological agents and toxins.

II.   State and Local Bioterrorism Preparedness and Response Capability:

- Authorize block grants to states ($667 million).

- Expand existing discretionary grant programs ($420 million).

- Authorize grants to improve hospital response capability ($370 million).

III.   Anti-Bioterrorism Drugs and Vaccines:

- Purchase smallpox vaccine ($509 million).

- Authorize long-term contracts for vaccine and drug development and provide limited exemption from federal antitrust laws.

IV.   Food Supply and Agriculture ($525.5 million):

- Strengthen FDA regulation of domestic and imported food.

- Expand and upgrade the safety and security of the nation's food supply, livestock, and crops.

Public Health Security and Bioterrorism Response Act (H.R. 3448)

Representatives Tauzin (R-LA) and Dingell (D-MI) introduced the Public Health Security and Bioterrorism Response Act (H.R. 3448) on December 11,2001. The bill was immediately considered under suspension of the rules and passed by the House the following day on a vote of 418–2 In many respects, H.R. 3448, which authorizes $3 billion in FY2002 to improve bioterrorism preparedness and response capacity, resembles the Senate-passed bill. Both bills would authorize funds to expand the National Pharmaceutical Stockpile, purchase smallpox vaccine, develop and produce anthrax vaccine, and provide grants to state and local governments and public health departments. However, there are a number of key differences between the House and Senate bills that are being addressed in conference.

S. 1765 contains several provisions aimed at combating agricultural terrorism, including one that would authorize the creation of a surveillance and response system to detect biological threats to animals and plants. Another provision would authorize the Secretary of Agriculture to award grants to universities to conduct research on improving the security of facilities at which hazardous biological agents and toxins are stored for agricultural research purposes. H.R. 3448 does not include any agricultural provisions. The Senate bill also provides a limited exemption from federal antitrust law that would enable drug companies to collaborate to develop vaccines. The House version has no such provision.

H.R. 3448 includes a set of provisions aimed at protecting the nation's drinking water supply, which are not included in S. 1765. The House bill would authorize a total of $170 million in FY2002 to assess the vulnerability of community drinking water systems, help communities develop emergency response plans, and take other steps to protect the water supply from acts of terrorism. H.R. 3448 also contains language that would strengthen FDA regulation of imported drugs, which is not present in S. 1765, and it places more emphasis on upgrading CDC's facilities and capacities. Key provisions of the House bill are summarized in the text box below, including the authorized appropriations for FY2002 (in parentheses).

Public Health Security and Bioterrorism Response Act of 2001 (H.R. 3448)

I.   Federal Bioterrorism Preparedness and Response Capacity:

- Expand the National Pharmaceutical Stockpile ($646 million).

- Upgrade CDC's bioterrorism response capacity ($450 million).

- Tighten controls on the possession and use of biological agents and toxins.

II.   State and Local Bioterrorism Preparedness and Response Capacity:

- Expand existing discretionary grant programs ($910 million).

- Relieve shortages of critical health care professionals ($40 million).

III.   Anti-Bioterrorism Drugs and Vaccines:

- Purchase smallpox vaccine ($509 million).

- Stockpile potassium iodide near nuclear power plants.

IV.   Food and Drug Supply:

- Strengthen FDA regulation of domestic and imported food ($100 million).

- Strengthen FDA regulation of imported drugs.

V.   Drinking Water:

- Upgrade safety and security of drinking water supplies ($170 million).

Table 1 below provides a side-by-side comparison of H.R. 3448, S. 1765, and, where applicable, current law. All the PHS Act Title III provisions relating to public health emergencies that were established by P.L. 106-505 (i.e., Sections 319, 319A–319G) are included in the table, regardless of whether they are amended by S. 1765 or H.R. 3448.

Table 1. Side-by-Side Comparison of Legislation on Public Health Preparedness for Bioterrorism

Topic	Current Law	S. 1765 Frist/Kennedy	H.R. 3448 Tauzin/Dingell
Establishing National Goals and Public Health Capacities, Assessing Public Health Needs			
Establishing National Goals, Reports to Congress	No statutory provisions.	Adds a new Title XXVIII to the Public Health Service (PHS) Act setting out the following national goals for bioterrorism preparedness: (i) provide federal assistance to states and localities in the event of an attack; (ii) improve public health preparedness and response; (iii) develop new vaccines and therapies; (iv) protect the food supply and agriculture. [Section 101] Adds a new Section 2811 to the PHS Act to require the Secretary to report to Congress within 1 year, and biennially thereafter, on progress made toward meeting the objectives of the Act, including recommendations for new legislative authority needed to protect public health. Requires the Secretary to report to Congress within 1 year on the vulnerability of rural communities to bioterrorism and recommend any new legislative authority needed to strengthen the preparedness of such communities. [Section 201]	Adds a new Title XXVIII to the Public Health Service (PHS) Act that requires the Secretary, building on existing authority in PHS Act Section 319A, to develop and implement a bioterrorism preparedness and response plan, in consultation with other federal agencies. The plan would coordinate the activities of state and local governments and meet the preparedness goals in the bill (e.g., effective assistance to state and local governments, laboratory readiness, effective communications networks, training, and surveillance). Requires the Secretary to evaluate the feasibility of utilizing the Dept. of Veterans Affairs' research capabilities. Similar reporting requirements to those in S. 1765. [Section 101]

Table 1. Side-by-Side Comparison of Legislation on Public Health Preparedness for Bioterrorism (Continued)

Topic	Current Law	S. 1765 Frist/Kennedy	H.R. 3448 Tauzin/Dingell
Establishing Public Health Capacities	Public Health Service (PHS) Act Section 319A requires the Secretary, together with state and local health officials, to establish what capacities are needed for national, state, and local public health systems to be able to detect, diagnose, and contain outbreaks of infectious disease, drug-resistant pathogens, or acts of bioterrorism. Authorizes $4 million for FY2001 and such sums as may be necessary for FY2002–FY2006.	No provisions.	No provisions.
Assessing Public Health Needs	PHS Act Section 319B authorizes grants to states and local public health departments to evaluate the extent to which they can achieve the capacities identified pursuant to Section 319A. Requires the Secretary to develop a national framework for the evaluations. Authorizes $45 million for FY2001, and such sums as may be necessary for FY2002–FY2003.	No provisions.	No provisions.
Federal (HHS) Preparedness and Response Capacity			
Assistant Secretary for Emergency Preparedness	No statutory provisions.	Adds a new Section 2813 to the PHS Act authorizing the appointment of an Assistant Secretary for Emergency Preparedness to head the Office of Emergency Preparedness and coordinate all HHS bioterrorism activities. [Section 211]	Adds a new Section 2811 to the PHS Act authorizing the appointment of an Assistant Secretary for Emergency Preparedness to coordinate all HHS bioterrorism-related activities under the Act and interface with other federal agencies. [Section 102]

Table 1. Side-by-Side Comparison of Legislation on Public Health Preparedness for Bioterrorism (Continued)

Topic	Current Law	S. 1765 Frist/Kennedy	H.R. 3448 Tauzin/Dingell
Public Health Emergencies	PHS Act Section 319 authorizes the Secretary to respond to public health emergencies, including diseases, disorders, or bioterrorist attacks, by supporting grants, contracts, and investigations. Establishes the Public Health Emergency Fund and authorizes such sums as may be necessary. Requires an annual report to Congress on expenditures from the Fund.	Amends PHS Act Section 319 to require the Secretary to notify Congress within 48 hours of declaring a public health emergency. Allows such a declaration to remain in effect for 180 days and permits the Secretary to extend that period, provided Congress is notified within 48 hours of the extension. Allows the Secretary, as a result of public health emergencies, to waive deadlines for the submission of data and reports by individuals or public or private entities pursuant to any law administered by the Secretary. [Section 212]	Amends PHS Act Section 319 as follows: (i) permits the Secretary during a public health emergency to transfer funds between appropriations accounts administered under this Act, without lengthy waiting periods, and requires the Secretary to notify Congress of the intent to make such a transfer; and (ii) provides that public health emergencies expire by announcement of the Secretary or after 90 days, whichever comes first, and permits the Secretary to renew emergency declarations. Similar waiver authority to S. 1765. [Section 131, 134]
Quarantine and Inspection	PHS Act Section 361 authorizes the Surgeon General, in consultation with the Secretary, to develop quarantine, inspection, fumigation, sanitation, and pest extermination regulations to prevent the introduction, transmission, or spread of communicable diseases. Section 363 authorizes the development of regulations for the apprehension and examination of infected individuals in times of war.	No provisions.	Amends PHS Act Secs. 361 and 363 by eliminating the prerequisite for a National Advisory Health Council recommendation before issuing a quarantine rule or a rule providing for the apprehension of individuals during wartime. Permits federal regulations under Secs. 361 & 363, as amended, to preempt state laws that conflict with the exercise of federal authority. [Section 132]

Table 1. Side-by-Side Comparison of Legislation on Public Health Preparedness for Bioterrorism (Continued)

Topic	Current Law	S. 1765 Frist/Kennedy	H.R. 3448 Tauzin/Dingell
Federal Working Groups and Advisory Committees	PHS Act Section 319F requires the Secretary to: (i) establish, with the Secretary of Defense, an interagency working group on bioterrorism preparedness, and (ii) establish, in collaboration with the Director of FEMA, the Attorney General, and the Secretary of Agriculture, an interagency working group to address the public health and medical consequences of a bioterrorist attack.	Amends PHS Act Section 319F by eliminating the two existing working groups and replacing them with a single interagency working group on the prevention, preparedness, and response to bioterrorism, to be established by the Secretary in coordination with the Director of FEMA, the Attorney General, and the Secretaries of Agriculture, Defense, Labor, and Veterans Affairs (VA), and with other federal officials as appropriate. Creates two advisory committees to the Secretary: (i) the National Task Force on Children and Terrorism; and (ii) the Emergency Public Information and Communications Task Force. Both Task Forces sunset after 1 year. [Section 213]	Amends PHS Act Section 319F by expanding the composition and responsibilities of the two existing interagency working groups. Requires the Secretary to establish the preparedness working group in coordination with the Director of FEMA, the Attorney General, the Secretaries of Agriculture, Defense, Energy, and the VA, and the EPA Administrator. Requires the Secretary to establish the public health and medical working group in coordination with the Director of FEMA, the Attorney General, the Secretaries of Agriculture, Defense, Labor, and the VA, and the EPA Administrator. Creates two advisory committees to the Secretary: (i) the National Advisory Committee on Children and Terrorism; and (ii) the Emergency Public Information and Communications Advisory Committee. Both committees sunset after 1 year. Requires a coordinated strategy on public health communications during a bioterrorist attack. [Section 104,108]

Table 1. Side-by-Side Comparison of Legislation on Public Health Preparedness for Bioterrorism (Continued)

Topic	Current Law	S. 1765 Frist/Kennedy	H.R. 3448 Tauzin/Dingell
National Disaster Medical System (NDMS)	No statutory provisions. The NDMS was established in 1984 as a partnership of four federal agencies (HHS, FEMA, DOD, VA), state and local governments, and the private sector to provide medical assistance and hospitalization for mass casualties in the event of a natural or man-made disaster. It consists of more than 7,000 volunteer health professionals and support personnel. For more information, go to [http://ndms.dhhs.gov].	Adds a new Section 2814 to the PHS Act providing statutory authorization for the NDMS, to be coordinated by the Secretary in collaboration with FEMA, DOD, and the VA. Appoints activated NDMS volunteers as temporary federal employees and establishes employment and reemployment rights for NDMS volunteers. [Section 211]	Adds a new Section 2811 to the PHS Act containing similar provisions to S. 1765, but with the following additional requirements and authorizations: requires the Secretary to collaborate with states and other public and private entities, and, within 1 year and periodically thereafter, to conduct exercises to test the capability and timeliness of the NDMS. Requires the Secretary to establish education and training criteria for NDMS personnel. Authorizes such sums as may be necessary for FY2002–FY2006 for NDMS and to provide for the Assistant Secretary of Emergency Preparedness. [Section 102]
National Pharmaceutical Stockpile (NPS)	No statutory provisions. The NPS, which was established and is managed by the CDC, includes pharmaceuticals, vaccines, and medical supplies that can be deployed anywhere in the country in response to a public health emergency. For more information, go to [http://www.cdc.gov/nceh/nps/default.htm].	Adds a new Section 2812 to the PHS Act requiring the Secretary, in coordination with the VA Secretary, to maintain a National Pharmaceutical Stockpile of vaccines, drugs, medical devices and supplies to meet the nation's emergency public health needs. Authorizes $640 million for FY2002, and such sums as may be necessary for FY2003–2006. [Section 201]	Similar provisions to S. 1765, but with additional requirements for periodic review of the stockpile and the development of a distribution plan. Requires the Secretary to consult with the Director of FEMA, the Attorney General, the Secretaries of Agriculture, DOD, Energy, and the VA, the EPA Administrator, and state and local agencies. Authorizes $1.155 billion for FY2002, of which $509 million is for purchasing smallpox vaccine, and such sums as may be necessary for FY2003–2006. [Section 121, 151]

Table 1. Side-by-Side Comparison of Legislation on Public Health Preparedness for Bioterrorism (Continued)

Topic	Current Law	S. 1765 Frist/Kennedy	H.R. 3448 Tauzin/Dingell
Upgrading CDC	PHS Act Section 319D authorizes funds for the construction and renovation of CDC facilities, and to support the agency's activities to combat threats to public health. Authorizes $180 million for FY2001, and such sums as may be necessary for FY2002–FY2010.	Amends PHS Act Section 319D to clarify CDC's role in responding to bioterrorism. Authorizes $60 million for FY2002, and such sum as may be necessary for FY2003–FY2006, to upgrade CDC's facilities and capacities. [Section 202]	Amends PHS Act Section 319D to clarify CDC's role in responding to bioterrorism. Requires the Secretary to upgrade CDC's facilities and capacities. Provides authorization and multi-year contracting authority for renovation, development, and security at CDC facilities. Authorizes $450 million for FY2002, of which $300 million is for upgrading facilities, $300 million for FY2003 to upgrade facilities, and such sums as may be necessary for FY2004–FY2006. [Section 103,151]
Public Health Laboratories Network, National Public Health Communications and Surveillance Network	No statutory provisions. Over the past 3 years, CDC has awarded grants to all 50 states and some metropolitan health departments to enhance state and local laboratory capacity and to help build an national electronic communications network connecting all the components of the public health community. For more information, go to [http://www.bt.cdc.gov].	Amends PHS Act Section 319D to provide grants to establish a coordinated network of public health labs. Authorizes $59.5 million for FY2002, and such sums as may be necessary for FY2003–FY2006. [Section 202]	Amends PHS Act Section 319D to provide grants to establish a coordinated network of public health labs and to develop a national public health communications and surveillance network. Authorizes such sums as may be necessary for FY2002–FY2006. [Section 103] Requires that all the FY2003 and FY2004 infrastructure grants provided by the National Telecommunications and Information Administration be awarded to health providers to facilitate participation in the national public health communications and surveillance network. [Section 139]

Table 1. Side-by-Side Comparison of Legislation on Public Health Preparedness for Bioterrorism (Continued)

Topic	Current Law	S. 1765 Frist/Kennedy	H.R. 3448 Tauzin/Dingell
Education and Training of Health Care Personnel: Children and Other Vulnerable Populations	PHS Act 319F requires the Secretary to develop programs to educate health professionals in recognizing and caring for victims of bioterrorist attacks and programs to train laboratory personnel in identifying bioweapons.	Amends PHS Act Section 319F to require the interagency working group on the public health and medical consequences of bioterrorism, in collaboration with professional organizations, to develop education programs that recognize the special needs of children and other vulnerable populations during public health emergencies. [Section 313; Note: The interagency working group to which this subsection of the Act refers would be replaced by two advisory committees under S. 1765, see above.]	Amends PHS Act Section 319F by requiring the Secretary, in collaboration with the interagency working group and professional organizations, to award grants for the development of education materials to teach health officials and other emergency personnel to identify potential bioweapons and care for victims, recognizing the special needs of children and other vulnerable populations during public health emergencies. [Section 105]
GAO Report	PHS Act 319F requires a GAO report to Congress, within 6 months, on federal bioterrorism-related activities, including research, preparedness, and response. [This report, GAO-01-915, was issued by GAO on September 28, 2001.]	Amends PHS Act Section 319F to require a new GAO report to Congress on federal bioterrorism-related activities, including the development of public health lab capacity. [Section 314]	No provisions.
Occupational Safety and Health	Section 22 of the Occupational Safety and Health Act of 1970 (29 U.S.C. 671) created the National Institute for Occupational Safety and Health (NIOSH) as the federal agency responsible for conducting research and making recommendations for the prevention of work-related disease and injury. NIOSH is part of the CDC.	Amends OSH Act Section 22 to expand NIOSH research on bioterrorism threats and attacks in the workplace. [Section 315]	Requires the Secretary, acting through the Director of NIOSH, to expand research on bioterrorism threats and attacks in the workplace. [Section 138]

Table 1. Side-by-Side Comparison of Legislation on Public Health Preparedness for Bioterrorism (Continued)

Topic	Current Law	S. 1765 Frist/Kennedy	H.R. 3448 Tauzin/Dingell
Agency for Toxic Substances and Disease Registry (ATSDR)	ATSDR, an agency within HHS, was created by the Superfund legislation to investigate and reduce the harmful effects of exposure to hazardous substances on human health.	No provisions.	Requires the Secretary to integrate ATSDR into plans for bioterrorism preparedness and response. Authorizes such sums as necessary for FY2002–FY2006. for ATSDR's bioterrorism-related activities. [Section 137]
Federal Bioterrorism Web Site	No statutory provisions.	Recommends establishing a federal Web site on bioterrorism with links to state and local government sites. [Section 214]	No provisions.
Miscellaneous Provisions	No applicable provisions.	No provisions.	Requires the Secretary, in consultation with other federal agencies, to conduct a study of the ability of local public health entities to maintain communications during a public health emergency. [Section 111] Adds a new Section 319J to the PHS Act allowing the Secretary to provide supplies, equipment, or services instead of, or in conjunction with, grants awarded under Sections 319 through 319I, or Section 319K. [Section 112] Requires the Secretary to conduct a study of best practices in local emergency response and report to Congress within 180 days. [Section 114]

Table 1. Side-by-Side Comparison of Legislation on Public Health Preparedness for Bioterrorism (Continued)

Topic	Current Law	S. 1765 Frist/Kennedy	H.R. 3448 Tauzin/Dingell
Medicare, Medicaid, and the State Children's Health Insurance Program (SCHIP)			
Emergency Waivers	Medicare covers medically necessary acute care and follow-up services (hospital, short-term nursing home care, physician services, home health and a variety of outpatient services) for all persons age 65 and over, as well as certain disabled persons. Medicare covers acute and long-term care services for low-income persons who are aged, blind, disabled, members of families with dependent children, and certain other pregnant women and children. The State Children's Health Insurance Program (SCHIP) covers uninsured children living in families with income above applicable Medicaid standards, typically up to or above 200% of the federal poverty level. In all three programs, providers must meet certain standards in order to participate and receive reimbursement for services rendered to program beneficiaries. For example, hospitals and other facilities must meet established conditions of participation, and laboratories must be certified under the Clinical Laboratories Improvement Act (CLIA). Physicians must be licensed to provide medical services in the state where medical care is rendered, and must follow established rules for obtaining prior approval to deliver certain types of services. Also, physicians must not refer patients to medical entities with which they have a financial relationship. Other statutory provisions require hospitals to fully stabilize patients receiving emergency care prior to transfer to another medical facility.	No provisions.	Authorizes the Secretary to temporarily waive conditions of participation and other certification requirements for any entity that furnishes health care items or services to Medicare, Medicaid, or SCHIP beneficiaries in an emergency area during a declared disaster or public health emergency. In addition, during such an emergency, authorizes the Secretary to waive: (i) participation, state licensing (as long as equivalent licensure from another state is held), and pre-approval requirements for physicians and other practitioners; (ii) sanctions for failing to meet requirements for emergency transfers between hospitals; and (iii) sanctions for physician self-referral. Requires the Secretary to provide Congress with a detailed written notice at least 2 days prior to exercising this waiver authority. Provides for the waiver authority to continue for 90 days. Permits the Secretary to extend the waiver period. Requires the Secretary, within 1 year after the end of the emergency, to provide Congress with an evaluation of the success of this approach and recommendations for improvements under this waiver authority. [Section 133]

Table 1. Side-by-Side Comparison of Legislation on Public Health Preparedness for Bioterrorism (Continued)

Topic	Current Law	S. 1765 Frist/Kennedy	H.R. 3448 Tauzin/Dingell
Regulation of Biological Agents and Toxins			
Use and Possession of Select Agents	The 1996 Antiterrorism and Effective Death Penalty Act (P.L. 104-132, Section 511) required the Secretary to establish a list of biological agents that could pose a severe threat to public health and safety, and establish safety procedures for transferring listed agents and toxins so as to protect public safety and prevent access by terrorists (see 42 C.F.R. 72).	Codifies and expands provisions of P.L. 104-132 in the PHS Act under a new Section 351A. Requires the Secretary to: (i) establish and, at least biennially, review and, if necessary, revise a list of biological agents and toxins that could pose a severe threat to public health and safety; (ii) establish safety procedures for transferring listed agents and toxins so as to protect public safety and prevent access by terrorists; (iii) establish standards and procedures for the possession and use of listed agents and toxins so as to protect public health and safety; and (iv) require registration for the possession, use, and transfer of listed agents and toxins and maintain a national database of the location of such agents and toxins. Requires the Secretary to establish security requirements for persons possessing, using, or transferring listed agents or toxins, as a condition of registration. Authorizes the Secretary to conduct compliance inspections. Authorizes the Secretary to establish exemptions from the requirements outlined in (ii) and (iii) above that are consistent with protecting public health and safety, including exemptions for the use of attenuated or inactive agents or toxins in research or for medical purposes. Exempts clinical labs presented with a listed agent or toxin for diagnosis, verification, or proficiency testing. Establishes civil penalties of up to $500,000 and criminal penalties of up to 5 years in prison for those in violation of the above requirements for the possession, use, and transfer of listed agents and toxins. Protects information collected under these regulations from mandatory disclosure under the Freedom of Information Act. Mandates a report to Congress within 1 year. Repeals current law. [Section 216]	Similar provisions to S. 1765, but with added security provisions: (i) requires the Secretary to consult with the Attorney General in establishing security requirements for persons possessing, using, or transferring listed agents or toxins; and (ii) requires the Secretary, in consultation with the Attorney General and other federal agencies, to establish a screening protocol to ensure that access to such agents and toxins is not permitted by certain specified types of individuals (e.g., those with criminal records, suspected terrorists, etc.). Requires the Secretary to coordinate regulations promulgated under these provisions with Dept. of Agriculture regulations governing use of biological agents in developing animal vaccines and treatments. Clarifies that the Secretary's new authorities do not limit existing authorities of the Secretary of Agriculture. Authorizes such sums as may be necessary for FY2002, and each subsequent fiscal year, to upgrade security at HHS facilities that contain listed agents and toxins. [Section 201]

Table 1. Side-by-Side Comparison of Legislation on Public Health Preparedness for Bioterrorism (Continued)

Topic	Current Law	S. 1765 Frist/Kennedy	H.R. 3448 Tauzin/Dingell
State and Local Preparedness and Response Capacity			
Bioterrorism Preparedness Grants to States and Local Public Health Agencies, and Health Care Facilities	PHS Act Section 319F(c) authorizes grants to states, localities, and health care facilities to increase their capacity to detect, diagnose, and respond to bioterrorist attacks, including training of personnel. [Note: For all activities under Section 319F, authorizes $215 million for FY2001, and such sums as may be necessary for FY2002–FY2006.]	Amends PHS Act Section 319F(c) by replacing the existing grant program with block grants to states based on population, but with each state guaranteed a minimum level of funding. Requires states to develop a detailed bioterrorism preparedness plan to be eligible for funding. Authorizes $667 million for FY2002, and such sums as may be necessary for FY2003. [Section 301]	Amends PHS Act Section 319F(c) by expanding the existing grant authorization to permit the use of funds for community-wide planning activities, training, and purchasing or upgrading equipment, supplies, pharmaceuticals, and other countermeasures. Authorizes $455 million for FY2002, and such sums as may be necessary for FY2003–FY2006. [Section 108, 151]
Core Capacity Grants to State and Local Public Health Agencies	PHS Act Section 319C authorizes grants to states and local governments, after they have completed a Section 319B evaluation, to address core public health capacity needs. Requires the Secretary to report to Congress on activities carried out under Sections 319A, 319B, and 319C by January 1, 2005. Authorizes $50 million for FY2001, and such sums as may be necessary for FY2002–FY2006.	Amends PHS Act Section 319C by authorizing $420 million for FY2002, and such sums as may be necessary for FY2003–FY2006. [Section 215]	Amends PHS Act Section 319C by expanding the existing grant authorization to permit the use of funds for purchasing or upgrading equipment, supplies, pharmaceuticals, and other countermeasures. Authorizes $455 million for FY2002, and such sums as may be necessary for FY2003–FY2006. [Section 109, 151]

Table 1. Side-by-Side Comparison of Legislation on Public Health Preparedness for Bioterrorism (Continued)

Topic	Current Law	S. 1765 Frist/Kennedy	H.R. 3448 Tauzin/Dingell
Demonstration Grants	PHS Act Section 319G authorizes up to three demonstration grants for up to 5 years to states, localities, or non-profit organizations to carry out programs to improve biopathogen detection, develop plans for responding to bioterrorist attacks, and train response personnel. Requires a GAO report to Congress at the conclusion of the demonstration programs describing the capabilities of the grantees. Authorizes $6 million for FY2001, and such sums as may be necessary for FY2002–FY2006.	No provisions.	No provisions.
Grants to Hospitals	No applicable provisions.	Amends PHS Act Section 319F by establishing a grant program for hospitals and other medical centers to improve bioterrorism preparedness and response capacity. To be eligible, a hospital must form a consortium with a public health agency and a local government, and its grant proposal must be consistent with the state's bioterrorism preparedness plan. Requires the Secretary to develop and publish technical guidelines relating to equipment, training, treatment, capacity, and personnel. Authorizes $370 million for FY2002, and such sums as may be necessary for FY2003–FY2006. [Section 301, 311]	No provisions.

Table 1. Side-by-Side Comparison of Legislation on Public Health Preparedness for Bioterrorism (Continued)

Topic	Current Law	S. 1765 Frist/Kennedy	H.R. 3448 Tauzin/Dingell
Grants to Address National Shortages of Specific Types of Health Professionals	No applicable provisions, although PHS Act Titles VII (Health Professionals Education) and VIII (Nursing Workforce Development) authorize federal support for training of health professionals for specific purposes.	No provisions.	Adds a new Section 319H to the PHS Act establishing a grant program to provide financial assistance for the education and training of individuals in any category of the health professions where there is a shortage that the Secretary determines should be alleviated to improve emergency readiness. Authorizes $40 million for FY2002, and such sums as may be necessary for FY2003–FY2006. [Section 106, 151]
Health Professional Volunteers	No applicable provisions.	No provisions.	Adds a new Section 3191 to the PHS Act requiring the Secretary to establish a national system to help verify the licenses, credentials, and hospital privileges of health professionals who volunteer to respond during public health emergencies. Authorizes $2 million for FY2002, and such sums as may be necessary for FY2003–FY2006. [Section 107]
State Public Health Emergency Announcements	The Stafford Act (42 U.S.C. 5121 et seq.) authorizes federal assistance when the President determines that a natural or man-made disaster has overwhelmed state and local resources. Stafford assistance is administered by the Federal Emergency Management Agency (FEMA).	Amends Section 613(b) of the Stafford Act by requiring states to include a plan for providing a coordinated public communications response in their submission for federal funds to help pay for state emergency preparedness personnel and administrative expenses. [Section 312]	Same provisions as S. 1765. [Section 135]

Table 1. Side-by-Side Comparison of Legislation on Public Health Preparedness for Bioterrorism (Continued)

Topic	Current Law	S. 1765 Frist/Kennedy	H.R. 3448 Tauzin/Dingell
Countermeasures (Research, Development, and Production of New Vaccines, Drugs, and Technologies)			
Antitrust Exemption	The Clayton Act (15 U.S.C. 12 et seq.) is one of the federal antitrust laws that seek to promote fair competition and protect consumers and businesses from anticompetitive business practices. It enumerates specific practices that are anti-competitive and therefore forbidden.	Amends Section 2 of the Clayton Act to exempt from antitrust law meetings between the Secretary and parties involved in the development, manufacture, distribution, purchase and sale of new priority countermeasures against bioterrorism. Permits the Attorney General, in consultation with the Chairman of the Federal Trade Commission, to grant a limited antitrust exemption to agreements reached at such meetings. Limited exemptions expire after 3 years, but may be renewed. Terminates the Attorney General's authority to grant limited antitrust exemptions after 6 years. [Section 401]	No provisions.
Smallpox Vaccine	No statutory provisions. In November 2001, HHS awarded a $428 million contact to Acambis, Inc. and Baxter International Inc. to produce 155 million doses of smallpox vaccine by the end of 2002. This is in addition to an earlier contract with Acambis to produce 54 million doses of the vaccine.	Adds new Section 2841 to the PHS Act requiring the Secretary to ensure adequate supplies of smallpox and other vaccines in the National Pharmaceutical Stockpile. Authorizes $509 million for FY2002, and such sums as may be necessary for FY2003–FY2006, to purchase smallpox vaccine. Adds a new Section 2842 to the PHS Act authorizing the Secretary to enter into long-term contracts with companies to purchase specific quantities of priority countermeasures at an agreed price. [Section 402]	Authorizes $509 million for FY2002, and such sums as may be necessary for FY2003–FY2006, to purchase smallpox vaccine. [Section 151]

Table 1. Side-by-Side Comparison of Legislation on Public Health Preparedness for Bioterrorism (Continued)

Topic	Current Law	S. 1765 Frist/Kennedy	H.R. 3448 Tauzin/Dingell
Research and Development	PHS Act Section 319F requires the Secretary, in consultation with the interagency working group, to conduct research on the epidemiology and pathogenesis of biopathogens, diagnostic tests for biopathogens, and vaccines and other therapeutics.	Amends PHS Act Section 319F to: (i) make the genetic sequencing of biopathogens a priority at NIH; and (ii) expand research on the epidemiology and detection of biological agents and toxins, and the development of new vaccines and therapies. [Section 403, 404]	Amends PHS Act Section 319F to expand research on countermeasures, including the epidemiology and detection of biological agents and toxins, and the development of new vaccines and therapies. Defines a priority countermeasure as any drug, device, biologic, or diagnostic test to treat, identify, or prevent infection by a listed biological agent or toxin, or prevent harm from any other agent that may cause a pubic health emergency. Directs the Secretary to consider research collaboration with the VA. [Section 125]
FDA Approval of Drugs and Biologics	Under the Federal Food, Drug, and Cosmetic Act (FFDCA; 21 U.S.C. 301 et seq.), manufacturers of drugs and biologics (e.g., vaccines) must provide clinical trial data to demonstrate that their product is safe and effective, in order to obtain FDA marketing approval. The FFDCA provides for the designation of products as fast track to expedite the approval process.	Authorizes the Secretary to designate a priority countermeasure (i.e., drug or device) as a fast-track product for accelerated approval by the FDA. Permits a drug seeking FDA approval on the basis of animal data to be designated a fast-track product. Requires the FDA, within 30 days, to issue as a final rule the October 5, 1999 proposed rule permitting the use of animal data for approving new drugs and vaccines, when ethical issues preclude conducting clinical trials. [Section 405, 406]	Authorizes the Secretary to designate a priority countermeasure (i.e., drug or biologic) as a fast-track product for accelerated approval by the FDA but does not permit a drug seeking FDA approval on the basis of animal data to be designated a fast-track product. Requires the FDA, within 180 days, to issue as a final rule the October 5, 1999 proposed rule permitting the use of animal data for approving new drugs and vaccines, when ethical issues preclude conducting clinical trials. [Section 122, 123]

Table 1. Side-by-Side Comparison of Legislation on Public Health Preparedness for Bioterrorism (Continued)

Topic	Current Law	S. 1765 Frist/Kennedy	H.R. 3448 Tauzin/Dingell
Security at Research and Production Facilities	No applicable provisions.	Adds a new Section 2843 to the PHS Act authorizing the Secretary, in consultation with the Secretary of Defense and the Attorney General, to provide technical or other assistance to enhance security at research and production facilities. Requires the Secretary to develop guidelines and best practices. [Section 402]	Adds a new Section 319K to the PHS Act authorizing the Secretary, in consultation with the Secretary of Defense and the Attorney General, to provide technical or other assistance to enhance security at research and production facilities. [Section 124]
Detection, Identification, Diagnosis, and Surveillance Technologies	No applicable provisions.	No provisions.	Requires the Secretary to evaluate and prioritize new and emerging technologies for responding to a bioterrorism attack or other public health emergency. Requires the Secretary to report to Congress within 180 days on those technologies whose development should be accelerated. [Section 126] Requires the Secretary of Energy and the Administrator of the National Nuclear Safety Administration, in coordination with the interagency working group, to expand research on the rapid detection and identification of biopathogens. Authorizes such sums as may be necessary for FY2002–FY2006. [Section 136]

Table 1. Side-by-Side Comparison of Legislation on Public Health Preparedness for Bioterrorism (Continued)

Topic	Current Law	S. 1765 Frist/Kennedy	H.R. 3448 Tauzin/Dingell
Potassium Iodide	No applicable provisions.	No provisions.	Requires the Secretary to make potassium iodide available from the national pharmaceutical stockpile to states and local governments that submit a plan for local stockpile and distribution to the population within 20 miles of a nuclear power plant. Requires the Secretary, within 6 months, to provide Congress with a progress report. [Section 127]
Antimicrobial Resistance			
Combating Antimicrobial Resistance	PHS Act 319E requires the Secretary to establish an Antimicrobial Resistance Task Force to coordinate federal programs on antimicrobial resistance and to work on surveillance plans and information systems for detection and control of drug-resistant pathogens. Authorizes research and development initiatives for new antimicrobial drugs and diagnostics. Directs the Secretary to conduct a nationwide campaign to educate the public and health care professionals about the appropriate use of antibiotics. Authorizes grants for public health agencies to combat antimicrobial resistance. Authorizes demonstration grants for hospitals, clinics, and other entities to promote the judicious use of antibiotics and to control the spread of resistant infections. Authorizes $40 million for FY2001, and such sums as may be necessary for FY2002–FY2006.	No provisions.	Amends PHS Act Section 319E to authorize additional research on priority pathogens. Authorizes $25 million for FY2002 and for FY2003, and such sums as may be necessary for FY2004–FY2006. [Section 110, 151]

Table 1. Side-by-Side Comparison of Legislation on Public Health Preparedness for Bioterrorism (Continued)

Topic	Current Law	S. 1765 Frist/Kennedy	H.R. 3448 Tauzin/Dingell
Drug and Device Supply Safety and Security			
Drug and Device Importation	FFDCA Section 510(i) requires foreign drug and device manufacturers that import into the United States to register with the Secretary their name, place of business, and the name of their U.S. agent. Section 801 governs the import and export of food, drugs, devices, and other items, and specifies the circumstances under which imported articles are inspected, detained, or refused entry into the United States.	No provisions.	Amends Section 510(i) of the FFDCA by mandating annual registration of foreign manufacturers engaged in the import of drugs and devices into the United States. Requires registration to include the name of each importer and carrier used by the manufacturer. Amends Section 801 so that an imported drug or device may be refused entry if the importer fails to give the Secretary a statement identifying each foreign establishment that, under the law, must also be registered. [Section 311]
Import Components Intended for Export	FFDCA Section 301 is the prohibited acts and penalties section of the statute. Section 801 governs the import and export of food, drugs, devices, and other items, and specifies the circumstances under which imported articles are inspected, detained, or refused entry into the United States.	No provisions.	Amends Section 801 of the FFDCA mandating a chain-of-possession identification and a customs bond for firms seeking to import components of drugs, devices, food additives, color additives, or dietary supplements for further processing and export. Requires certificates of analysis for components containing any chemical or biological substance intended for export. Permits the Secretary to exclude from importation any article for which there is credible evidence or information indicating that the article presents a serious health threat or death to humans or animals. Amends Section 301 making it illegal to knowingly submit false statements, certificates, records, or reports required under Section 801, as amended. [Section 312]

Table 1. Side-by-Side Comparison of Legislation on Public Health Preparedness for Bioterrorism (Continued)

Topic	Current Law	S. 1765 Frist/Kennedy	H.R. 3448 Tauzin/Dingell
Food Supply Safety and Security			
Strategic Plan for Food Safety and Security	Executive Order 13100 created the President's Council on Food Safety, headed by the Secretaries of Agriculture and Health and Human Services, the Administrator of the Environmental Protection Agency, and the Assistant to the President for Science and Technology. On January 18, 2001, the Council published a strategic plan for food safety that contained recommendations on making statutory changes to unify federal food safety regulations.	Requires the Council, along with the Secretaries of Commerce and Transportation, and in consultation with states, the food industry, and consumer and producer groups, to develop a crisis communications and education strategy for bioterrorist threats to the food supply that includes threat assessments, response and notification procedures, and public risk communication plans. Authorizes $500,000 for FY2002, and such sums as may be necessary in each subsequent fiscal year, to implement the strategy. [Section 511]	No provisions.
U.S. Department of Agriculture (USDA) Activities	USDA's Food Safety and Inspection Service (FSIS) inspects meat, poultry, and processed egg products sold for human consumption for safety, wholesomeness, and proper labeling. The Animal and Plant Inspection Service (APHIS) inspects cargo and passengers at U.S. ports for animal and plant pests, quarantines some of these products, and responds to animal disease outbreaks. The Agricultural Research Service (ARS) conducts research on animal diseases and food safety to support other USDA regulatory responsibilities.	Authorizes $15 million for enhanced FSIS inspections domestically and internationally and collaboration with other federal agencies; $30 million for APHIS for increased inspections, cooperative agreements with state and private veterinarians, and an automated, integrated, interagency emergency warning, response, and record-keeping system; and $180 million for upgrading biosecurity at ARS labs in New York and Iowa. Authorizes the Secretary of Agriculture to use $20 million in FY2002 to award up to $45,000 each to land grant universities to establish security at facilities, inventory hazardous toxins, develop a screening protocol for access to facilities, and develop industry-on-farm education program. Authorizes a total of $245 million for FY2002 for USDA biosecurity efforts and such sums as necessary for each fiscal year thereafter. [Section 512, 513, 515, 527]	No provisions.

Table 1. Side-by-Side Comparison of Legislation on Public Health Preparedness for Bioterrorism (Continued)

Topic	Current Law	S. 1765 Frist/Kennedy	H.R. 3448 Tauzin/Dingell
HHS and FDA Biosecurity	FFDCA Chapter IV prohibits the entry into interstate commerce of adulterated or misbranded foods. FDA monitors through inspections whether food manufacturers adhere to their legal responsibility to produce food that is not defective, unsafe, filthy, or produced under unsanitary conditions.	Requires the Secretary of HHS to secure existing facilities where potential animal or plant pathogens are housed and researched. Authorizes $59 million to expand FDA's inspections and collaboration with other federal, state, and tribal agencies. Authorizes $500,000 for the Secretary to develop best practices for biosecurity for use by food manufacturers, processors, and distributors. Authorizes a total of $59.5 million for FY2002 for HHS agencies and such sums as may be necessary for each fiscal year thereafter. [Section 514,516,518]	Authorizes a total of $100 million for the Secretary of HHS to increase inspections for the detection of intentional adulteration of imported food; to give high priority to improving FDA's information management systems; to develop tests and sampling methods to rapidly detect intentionally adulterated food; and to complete an assessment of threats to food posed by intentional adulteration and report its findings on these protective activities to Congress. [Section 301]
Food Detention	FFDCA Section 304 allows for the seizure of food in interstate commerce under restricted circumstances.	Amends FFDCA Section 304 to authorize the detention of food for 20 days, and if needed for 30 days, if an officer or qualified employee of FDA has credible evidence (and the Secretary approves) showing the food violates the FFDCA and presents a threat of serious adverse health consequences or death to humans or animals. The detained food must be secured, and the responsible person can file an appeal within 15 days with expedited procedures for perishable foods. Adds a new definition to FFDCA Section 310 prohibiting removal of product or mark or label from the detained product. [Section 531]	Similar to provisions in S. 1765, except that it limits detention approval authority to the Secretary or the Secretary's designee. It also does not set a time limit on the appeal, but does require that FDA make a final decision within 72 hours on the appeal. Authorizes the Secretary to request the Treasury Secretary to temporarily hold imported food at a port for 24 hours, if FDA has credible evidence indicating that the food presents a threat, to allow FDA to determine whether to detain it. Requires that the Secretary notify the state in which the involved port is located. [Section 302]

Table 1. Side-by-Side Comparison of Legislation on Public Health Preparedness for Bioterrorism (Continued)

Topic	Current Law	S. 1765 Frist/Kennedy	H.R. 3448 Tauzin/Dingell
Debarment for Food Imports	FFDCA Section 306 gives the Secretary of HHS authority to debar, temporarily deny approval, or suspend the rights of individuals who have been convicted of a felony to submit an application for approval of a drug.	Amends FFDCA Section 306 to debar from importing foods any person who is convicted of a felony related to the importation of food or who repeatedly imports, or knows, or should have known, that the imported food that was adulterated or misbranded. Amends FFDCA Section 402 to include in the definition of "adulterated food" any food imported by debarred persons. [Section 532]	Similar provisions. [Section 303]
Maintenance and Inspection of Records	FFDCA Section 704 authorizes FDA to conduct factory inspections. Currently, FDA inspectors have access to company records but can only request access to copy, and verify records for restricted medical devices, prescription drugs, not for foods. Inspectors may not require that records be kept nor do officials have authority to copy records found during inspections.	Add a new Section 414 to the FFDCA allowing the Secretary, if a food is believed to be adulterated or misbranded and presents a threat of serious adverse health consequences or death to humans or animals, to have access to and to copy all records related to the food. Excludes restaurants and farms, and has reduced requirements for small businesses (less than 50 employees.) Requires records to be kept for 2 years so food can be investigated. Excludes records on USDA-regulated foods (meat, poultry, and egg products), and on trade secrets and/or confidential information on recipes, and financial, pricing, personnel, research, and sales data. Amends FFDCA Section 704 to add a clause to allow the inspection of all records and other information described in the new Section 414. Requires final rules to be issued on record keeping within 18 months. [Section 533]	Similar provisions to S. 1765, but includes language that requires the Secretary to put into effect procedures to prevent unauthorized disclosure of any trade secrets or confidential information. Also provides authority to the Secretary to take into account the size of the business when imposing any record keeping requirements. Does not impose a time limit for promulgation of rules. [Section 304]

Table 1. Side-by-Side Comparison of Legislation on Public Health Preparedness for Bioterrorism (Continued)

Topic	Current Law	S. 1765 Frist/Kennedy	H.R. 3448 Tauzin/Dingell
Registration of Food Facilities	Currently, only States have records of food processing, packing and holding facilities. The federal government must ask the states for this information.	Creates a new Section 415 in the FFDCA requiring all facilities, domestic and foreign, that manufacture, process, and handle food to register with the Secretary all the identities (brand names) under which business is conducted, addresses of the facilities, and general food categories. Foreign registrations must name a U.S. agent. Requires the Secretary to give each facility a number and keep the list of registered facilities up to date. Exempts certain retail stores and farms from registration requirements. Registration does not imply a license. Requirements for registration would take effect 180 days after enactment. Amends Section 403 to prohibit interstate commerce of food from unregistered facilities. [Section 534]	Similar provisions to S. 1765, but applies requirements to facilities that manufacture, process, pack or hold food (excludes farms.) Adds that the Secretary may provide for and encourage the use of electronic submissions to register as long as there are authorization protocols used to identify the registrant and validate the data. Adds that the Secretary must within 60 days identify facilities required to register, and, as S. 1765, enforce the registration within 180 days of the Act's enactment. Exempts only retail establishments from registration requirements. Specifies that registration requirements would not apply to food products regulated by USDA. [Section 305]
Prior Notice of Imported Food Shipments	Under FFDCA Section 801, a food that (i) is found to be manufactured, processed, or packed under unsanitary conditions, (ii) is forbidden or restricted in the producing country or from where it was exported, or (iii) is adulterated or misbranded at the border, can have its admission deferred while the food is reconditioned, relabeled or destroyed.	Amends FFDCA Section 801 to require a producer, manufacturer, or shipper of imported food, at least 4 hours before it is imported, to document its identity, country of origin, and quantity imported to FDA and the U.S. Customs or the import can be refused entry. Exempts all USDA-regulated foods (meat, poultry, and egg products.) Prohibits knowingly making a false statement in the import documentation. [Section 535]	Similar provisions to S. 1765, except the advance period for submission of documentation is to be not less than 24 hours nor more than 72 hours before importation of the food. The required information includes a description of the food, the identity of the manufacturer and shipper, if possible the grower, the country of origin of the food, the country from which the article is shipped, and the anticipated U.S. port of entry. Without a notice, the food will be refused admission or held until the required information is provided and a determination that the food is not a serious health threat to humans or animals. The Secretary can ask for more information. This provision excludes USDA regulated products. [Section 306]

Table 1. Side-by-Side Comparison of Legislation on Public Health Preparedness for Bioterrorism (Continued)

Topic	Current Law	S. 1765 Frist/Kennedy	H.R. 3448 Tauzin/Dingell
Mark Articles Refused Admission	The FFDCA Section 403 defines misbranded foods as food whose labeling or advertising is false or misleading. Section 801(a) gives the Secretary the general authority to refuse imports deemed adulterated or misbranded.	Amends both Sections 403 and 801(a) definitions of misbranded food to include food that has been refused admission to the United States and not destroyed and which presents a threat of serious adverse health consequences or death, unless the packaging is clearly and conspicuously labeled: *United States: Refused Entry* at the expense of the food's owner until the food is brought into compliance. [Section 536]	Similar provisions to S. 1765. [Section 307]
Authority to Commission Other Federal Officials to Conduct Inspections	The FFDCA Section 702 states that the Secretary is authorized to conduct food inspections (examinations and investigations) through officers and employees of HHS, or any health, food, or drug officer of a state that has been duly commissioned by the Secretary as an officer of the Department.	Amends FFDCA Section 702 to provide the authority to commission qualified federal officials from other departments or agencies to conduct inspections. This can only happen if there are no current laws restricting the use of a department or agency officers, employees, or funds. [Section 537]	No provisions.
Prohibition against Port Shopping	The FFDCA Section 402 defines "adulterated" food as any food that bears or contains any poisonous or deleterious substance that may render it injurious to health.	Amends FFDCA Section 402 to require that an importer offering food that has been refused admission prove at his own expense that the food is in compliance with the applicable requirements of the Act. [Section 538]	Similar provisions to S. 1765 except that importer, at his own expense, must prove that the article is not adulterated, as determined by the Secretary. [Section 308]

Table 1. Side-by-Side Comparison of Legislation on Public Health Preparedness for Bioterrorism (Continued)

Topic	Current Law	S. 1765 Frist/Kennedy	H.R. 3448 Tauzin/Dingell
Grants to States for Inspections	The FFDCA Section 702 states that the Secretary is authorized to conduct food inspections (examinations and investigations) through officers and employees of HHS, or any health, food, or drug officer of a state that has been duly commissioned by the Secretary as an officer of the Department.	Creates a new Section 910 in the FFDCA authorizing $10 million for FY2002, and such sums as may be necessary for subsequent fiscal years, to provide grants to states to increase food safety examinations, inspections and investigations under FFDCA Section 702. [Section 539]	Creates a new Section 909 in the FFDCA authorizing grants to states and territories to conduct food safety examinations, inspections, and investigations under Section 702, like S. 1765, but does not specify an amount. Also, allows grants to states to assist in costs when responding to adulterated food that might injure public health. [Section 310]
Notices to States Regarding Imported Food	No provisions.	No provisions.	Requires that the Secretary notify the state that holds the food when there is credible evidence that it presents a threat of serious adverse health consequences or death to humans or animals. [Section 309]
Rule of Construction	USDA regulates meat under the Federal Meat Inspection Act (21 U.S.C. 601 et seq.), poultry under the Poultry Products Inspection Act (21 U.S.C. 451 et seq.), and processed egg products under the Egg Products Inspection Act (21 U.S.C. 1031 et seq.)	Prohibits FDA from regulating any food under USDA's jurisdiction. [Section 540]	No provisions.
Food Safety Grants	FoodNet, established in 1995 by USDA and FDA, tracks the incidence of illnesses caused by nine pathogens in nine geographic areas across the United States. PulseNet compares genetic patterns of bacteria isolated from patients with foodborne illness and/or contaminated food.	Amends PHS Act Title III to authorize $19.5 million for FY2002 in grants to states to expand the number participating in FoodNet and PulseNet and other surveillance networks and to maintain technical and laboratory capacity. [Section 541]	No provisions.

Table 1. Side-by-Side Comparison of Legislation on Public Health Preparedness for Bioterrorism (Continued)

Topic	Current Law	S. 1765 Frist/Kennedy	H.R. 3448 Tauzin/Dingell
Surveillance of Animal and Human Health	CDC has more than 20 surveillance programs that monitor outbreaks of food borne illness caused by specific pathogens.	Amends PHS Act Title III to authorize FDA, CDC, and USDA to develop and implement a plan for coordinating surveillance for zoonotic and human diseases. [Section 541]	No provisions.
Agricultural Bioterrorism Research and Development	Current research programs are in place in the Agricultural Research Service (ARS) and the Cooperative Research Service Education and Extension Service (CSREES).	Expands, with an authorization of $190 million for FY2002 and such sums as may be necessary for subsequent fiscal years, the programs of USDA's agencies ARS and CSREES to protect the food supply and expand links with the intelligence community and international organizations. [Section 542]	No provisions.
Drinking Water Security and Safety			
Vulnerability Assessments and Emergency Response Plans	PHS Act Title XIV, the Safe Drinking Water Act (SDWA), authorizes federal regulation of public water systems (including community water systems), particularly through a program that regulates contaminants in public water supplies. The Act defines a community water system as a public water system that serves at least 15 service connections served by year-round residents or that regularly serves at least 25 year-round residents. The SDWA is administered and enforced by the Environmental Protection Agency (EPA).	No provisions.	Adds a new Section 1433 to the SDWA to require each community water system serving more than 3,300 individuals to conduct a vulnerability assessment. Requires EPA, not later than March 1, 2002, to provide information to community water systems concerning probable threats. Establishes deadlines for systems to certify to EPA that they have conducted vulnerability assessments. Requires each community water system serving more than 3,300 individuals to prepare or revise an emergency response plan incorporating the results of the vulnerability assessment. Systems must certify to EPA, no later than 6 months after completing an assessment, that they have completed response plans. Directs EPA to provide guidance to community water systems serving fewer than 3,300 individuals on conducting vulnerability assessments, preparing emergency response plans, and addressing threats from terrorist attacks or other actions intended to disrupt the provision of safe drinking water. Authorizes $120 million for FY2002, and such sums as may be necessary for FY2003 and FY2004, to provide financial assistance to community water systems to conduct assessments and prepare response plans, and for expenses and contracts to address basic security enhancements and significant threats. [Section 401(1)]

Table 1. Side-by-Side Comparison of Legislation on Public Health Preparedness for Bioterrorism (Continued)

Topic	Current Law	S. 1765 Frist/Kennedy	H.R. 3448 Tauzin/Dingell
Review of Methods to Prevent, Detect, and Respond to the Intentional Introduction of Contaminants into Community Water Supplies	No statutory provisions.	No provisions.	Adds new SDWA Section 1434 directing the EPA Administrator, in consultation with CDC, and after consultation with other federal departments and state and local governments, to review current and future methods to prevent, detect and respond to the intentional introduction of chemical, biological or radiological contaminants into community water systems and their source waters. Provides that funding is authorized under Section 1435. [Section 401(1)]
Supply Disruption: Prevention, Detection and Response	No statutory provisions.	No provisions.	Adds new SDWA Section 1435 directing the EPA Administrator, in coordination with appropriate federal departments and agencies, to review methods and means by which terrorists or others could disrupt the supply of safe drinking water or take actions that render water unsafe, including methods and means by which water systems could be destroyed, impaired, or made subject to cross-contamination. EPA must also review methods and means by which systems could be reasonably protected from attacks, and by which alternative drinking water supplies could be provided if a water system was destroyed, impaired or contaminated. Authorizes $15 million for FY2002, and such sums as may be necessary for FY2003 and FY2004 to carry out Sections 1434 and 1435. [Section 401(1)]
Enforceable Requirements	SDWA Section 1414(i)(1) identifies the sections of SDWA for which the Act's enforcement authorities apply.	No provisions.	Amends SDWA Section 1414(i)(1) to include new Section 1433, requiring community water systems to conduct vulnerability assessments and to prepare emergency response plans, as an applicable and enforceable requirement under the Act. [Section 401(2)]

Table 1. Side-by-Side Comparison of Legislation on Public Health Preparedness for Bioterrorism (Continued)

Topic	Current Law	S. 1765 Frist/Kennedy	H.R. 3448 Tauzin/Dingell
Emergency Powers	SDWA Section 1431 grants the EPA Administrator emergency powers to take such actions as deemed necessary to protect persons served by a public water system upon receipt of information that a contaminant which is present in or is likely to enter a public water system or groundwater source may present an imminent and substantial endangerment to health of those persons.	No provisions.	Amends SDWA Section 1431 to specify that EPA's emergency powers include the authority to act when there is a threatened or potential terrorist attack or other intentional act to disrupt the provision of safe drinking water or to impact the safety of a community's drinking water supply. [Section 401(3)]
Penalties for Tampering with Public Water Systems	SDWA Section 1432 authorizes criminal and civil penalties for persons who tamper, attempt to tamper, or threaten to tamper with public water supplies.	No provisions.	Amends SDWA Section 1432 to increase criminal and civil penalties for tampering, attempting to tamper, or making threats to tamper with public water supplies. [Section 401(4)]
Technical Assistance	SDWA Section 1442(b) authorizes EPA to provide technical assistance and to make grants to states and public water systems to assist in responding to and alleviating emergency situations.	No provisions.	Amends SDWA Section 1442(d) to authorize appropriations to carry out Section 1442(b) of not more than $35 million for FY2002, and such sums as may be necessary for each fiscal year thereafter. [Section 401(5)]

APPENDIX A. HHS BIOTERRORISM FUNDING

FY1999–FY2001 Bioterrorism Initiative

HHS launched its bioterrorism initiative in FY1999. The initiative has six strategic goals: prevention of bioterrorism; infectious disease surveillance; medical and public health readiness for mass casualty events; the National Pharmaceutical Stockpile (NPS); research and development of new drugs and vaccines; and information technology infrastructure. Funding for these activities in the first 3 years (i.e., FY1999–FY2001) totaled about $730 million. CDC used the lion's share of those funds to begin the process of improving the bioterrorism preparedness and response capacity of state and local health departments. The agency awarded grants to state and major metropolitan health departments to support preparedness planning and readiness assessment; increase laboratory capacity for biological and chemical agents; and create the Health Alert Network, a nationwide, secure electronic communications network for state and local health departments. CDC has also used some of the funds to upgrade its own facilities and laboratory capacity and to establish and manage the NPS. In addition, HHS's Office of Emergency Preparedness (OEP) has expanded the National Disaster Medical System (see **Table 1**) and awarded grants to strengthen emergency medical response systems in metropolitan areas.

FY2002 FUNDING

For FY2002, Congress appropriated $3 billion to HHS to improve bioterrorism preparedness at the federal, state, and local levels. Bioterrorism funding was included in both the FY2002 Labor-HHS-Education appropriations bill and the anti-terrorism emergency spending package.

Labor-HHS-Education Appropriations

The FY2002 Labor-HHS-Education appropriations act (P.L. 107-116, H.R. 3061) included $243 million for the bioterrorism initiative: $182 million for CDC and $61 million for OEP.

Emergency Supplemental Appropriations

Congress passed a $40 billion emergency supplemental appropriations bill (P.L. 107-38, H.R. 2888) within days of the September 11 attacks to provide aid to the victims, repair damaged public facilities and transportation systems, expand law enforcement activities, and strengthen counter-terrorism capabilities. The first $10 billion was available immediately for allocation by the President. An additional $10 billion was available 15 days after the President notified Congress about how he would distribute the funds. In a series of notifications beginning on September 21, 2001, the Administration allocated all but $327 million of the first $20 billion before the 15-day prior notification period expired on November 25. Those allocations included $121 million for HHS to provide emergency assistance for health care and social services in the New York and Washington, DC, metropolitan areas.[2]

The second $20 billion was made subject to the appropriations process and was included as an amendment to the FY2002 Defense Department appropriations bill (P.L. 107-117, H.R. 3338). As enacted, H.R. 3338 provides HHS a total of $2.8 billion for bioterrorism-related activities. The appropriations act allocates that funding under several broad categories, including $593 million for the NPS, $512 million to purchase smallpox vaccine, $865 million for state and local health departments, $135 million to upgrade hospital capacity, $100 million to upgrade CDC's facilities and capacity, $155 for NIH research and lab construction, and $151 for FDA lab security, vaccine approval, and food safety. The act also provides $140 million to reimburse Medicare, Medicaid, and other health care providers for expenses or lost revenues attributable to the September 11 attacks.

While lawmakers work towards final passage of new bioterrorism authorizing legislation, CDC and the Health Resources and Services Administration (HRSA) have awarded a total of $1 billion in FY2002 funds to upgrade state and local health departments and improve hospital preparedness and response capacity. See Appendix B for more information on these grant programs.

FY2003 BUDGET REQUEST

The President's FY2003 budget would provide a total of $4.3 billion for HHS's bioterrorism preparedness programs and activities. The budget request includes funds for strengthening the federal medical and public health response capacity, upgrading CDC's facilities, improving state and local public health preparedness, developing vaccines and maintaining the National Pharmaceutical Stockpile, preparing the nation's hospitals, expanding FDA's regulatory oversight of drugs and biologics, and securing facilities to conduct critical scientific work. **Table 2** summarizes HHS's bioterrorism funding in FY2001, FY2002, and the FY2003 budget request.

Note that the table does not include the funding provided for recovery and relief efforts in response to the September 11 attacks (e.g., $121 million in emergency assistance to New York and Washington, DC, and $140 million to reimburse health care providers).

---

[2] The funds were used to provide emergency grants to health care providers, community health centers, and mental health and substance abuse centers, and to provide services for the disabled, home-delivered meals, and transportation for senior citizens in affected areas.

Table 2. HHS Bioterrorism Funding ($ millions)

Agency and Program	FY2001 Actual	FY2002 Enacted	FY2003 Request
Centers for Disease Control and Prevention (CDC)			
State and local public health preparedness	67	940	940
CDC capacity	22	116	144
National Pharmaceutical Stockpile	51	645	300
Smallpox vaccine procurement	0	512	100
Physical security and facilities	3	46	120
Other[a]	39	39	33
Subtotal, CDC	*$181*	*$2,298*	*$1,637*
Health Resources and Services Admin. (HRSA)			
Hospital preparedness and infrastructure	0	135	518
Other[b]	0	0	100
Subtotal, HRSA	*$0*	*$135*	*$618*
Food and Drug Administration (FDA)			
Food safety	1	98	98
Vaccine and drug approval	6	47	54
Physical security	2	13	7
Subtotal, FDA	*$8*	*$158*	*$159*
National Institutes of Health (NIH)			
Research	53	183	977
Physical security and facilities	0	92	521
Anthrax vaccine procurement	0	0	250
Subtotal, NIH	*$53*	*$274*	*$1,748*
Office of the Secretary (OS)			
Office of Emergency Preparedness[c]	33	76	117
Office of Public Health Preparedness	30	41	33
Subtotal, OS	*$63*	*$117*	*$150*
Substance Abuse & Mental Health Services Admin.	0	0	10
TOTAL, HHS Bioterrorism	*$305*	*$2,982*	*$4,322*

[a] Includes funding for anthrax vaccine evaluation and research, and national planning.

[b] Includes funding for poison control centers, medical curricula, and addressing children's needs.

[c] Includes funding for the National Disaster Medical System (NDMS), the Metropolitan Medical Response Systems (MMRS) program, and HHS cybersecurity.

Note: Columns may not add due to rounding.

Source: Dept. Health and Human Services FY2003 Budget Request

APPENDIX B. CDC AND HRSA BIOTERRORISM PREPAREDNESS GRANT PROGRAMS

For FY2002, Congress provided $940 million to CDC to upgrade state and local public health departments and $135 million to HRSA to increase hospital preparedness (see Table 2).

State and Local Public Health Department Preparedness

CDC established a cooperative agreement program (pursuant to authority in PHS Act Sections 319B, 319C, and 319F) to improve the preparedness of state and local public health departments to respond to bioterrorism, infectious disease outbreaks, and other public health threats and emergencies. On February 19, 2002, using a population-based allocation formula, CDC awarded $918 million in grants to the health departments of all 50 states, Washington DC, the five territories, and the nation's three largest cities (New York, Chicago, and Los Angeles County). While 20% of the award is available for immediate use, the remaining 80% is contingent on the approval of a state work plan to be submitted to CDC no later than April 15, 2002. According to the agency's guidance documents, work plans must describe the activities to be undertaken to develop and expand critical capacities in the following areas: preparedness planning and readiness assessment; surveillance and epidemiology; laboratory capacity; communications and information technology; and education and training. For more information on CDC's grant program, go to [http://www.bt.cdc.gov/Planning/Coop AgreementAward/index.asp].

Hospital Preparedness

HRSA's cooperative agreement program provides grants to improve the capacity of hospitals and other health care facilities to care for the victims of bioterrorism, natural infectious disease outbreaks, and other public health emergencies. The agency has awarded $125 million to the same entities that received CDC funding, using a similar population-based allocation formula. As with the CDC grants, the funds are being released in two phases. Phase one funding (20% of the total award) is subject to an application filed no later than Feb. 25, 2002. Phase two funding (80% of the total award) is contingent on an approved work plan due no later than April 15, 2002. Grantees are required to provide at least 80% of the phase two funds to hospitals. For more information on HRSA's hospital preparedness grant program, go to [http://www.hrsa.gov/bioterrorism.htm].

Coordination and Review of State Work Plans

DHHS has encouraged states to develop their public health and hospital preparedness plans in tandem. In an effort to ensure that the CDC and HRSA funds are used in a coordinated manner, grantees are required to submit both work plans to their governor (or mayor in the case of the municipalities) for approval. The governor (or mayor) is then required to transmit a letter of endorsement to the department. To date, HRSA has received 47 state work plans and granted extensions to three states. Montana and Utah have each received a one-month extension (until May 15), and Texas has been granted an extension until July 1. CDC has received 48 state work plans and granted one-month extensions to Montana and Utah. All four municipalities (i.e., Washington DC, New York City, Chicago, and Los Angeles County) have submitted their work plans to CDC and HRSA. The department's goal is to release all the grant funds to each state and municipality within 30 days of receipt of both work plans and the letter of endorsement from the governor (or mayor). For a table showing the amount of CDC and HRSA funding each state, territory, and municipality has received, go to [http://www.hhs.gov/news/press/2002pres/states.html].

APPENDIX C. BIOTERRORISM-RELATED HEARINGS (107TH CONGRESS)

Senate Appropriations Subcommittee on Labor, HHS, and Education

- October 3, 2001 Bioterrorism: Public health preparedness and response
- October 23, 2001 Public health response to anthrax attack
- November 2, 2001 Smallpox: Public health preparedness and response
- November 29, 2001 Funding for bioterrorism preparedness

Senate Appropriations Subcommittee on VA-HUD and Independent Agencies

- November 28, 2001 Anthrax decontamination

Senate Armed Services Subcommittee on Emerging Threats and Capabilities

- October 25, 2001 Bioterrorism and the Dark Winter exercise

Senate Commerce, Science and Transportation Committee

- February 5, 2002 Bioterrorism: Countermeasures R&D (Subcommittee on Science, Technology, and Space)

Senate Environment and Public Works Committee

- December 4, 2001 Anthrax decontamination

Senate Foreign Relations Committee

- September 5, 2001 Bioterrorism threat and the spread of infectious diseases

Senate Governmental Affairs Committee

- July 23, 2001 Bioterrorism: FEMA's role and public health preparedness (Subcommittee on National Security, Proliferation and Federal Services)
- October 17, 2001 Bioterrorism: Federal agency preparedness
- October 30-31, 2001 Anthrax in the mail: Protecting postal workers and the public
- April 18, 2002 Public health preparedness

Senate Health, Education, Labor, and Pensions Committee

- September 26, 2001 Psychological trauma of terrorism
- October 9, 2001 Bioterrorism: Public health preparedness and response
- November 2, 2001 Kids and terrorism (Subcommittee on Children and Families)

Senate Judiciary Committee

- November 6, 2001 Law enforcement and the domestic bioterrorism threat (Subcommittee on Technology, Terrorism and Government Information)

House Appropriations Subcommittee on Labor, HHS, and Education

- May 1, 2002 HHS bioterrorism preparedness

House Energy and Commerce Committee

- October 10, 2001 Bioterrorism preparedness and response (Subcommittee on Oversight and Investigations)
- November 1, 2001 Public health early-warning surveillance systems (Subcommittee on Oversight and Investigations)
- November 7, 2001 Physical security and NIH and CDC facilities (Subcommittee on Oversight and Investigations)
- November 15, 2001 Bioterrorism: Public health preparedness and response

House Government Reform Committee

- May 1, 2001 Management of medical stockpiles (Subcommittee on National Security, Veterans Affairs and International Relations)
- July 23, 2001 Federal response to a bioterrorism attack: Dark Winter (Subcommittee on National Security, Veterans Affairs and International Relations)
- October 5, 2001 Bioterrorism: Federal, state, and local preparedness (Subcommittee on Government Efficiency, Financial Management and Intergovernmental Relations)
- October 12, 2001 Assessing the threat of bioterrorism (Subcommittee on National Security, Veterans Affairs and International Relations)
- October 23, 2001 Vaccine research and development (Subcommittee on National Security, Veterans Affairs and International Relations)
- October 30, 2001 Anthrax and postal worker safety
- November 7, 2001 DOD medical readiness for chemical and biological warfare (Subcommittee on National Security, Veterans Affairs and International Relations)
- November 14, 2001 Medical care for bioterrorism victims
- November 29, 2001 Risk communication: National security and public health (Subcommittee on National Security, Veterans Affairs and International Relations)
- December 14, 2001 Bioterrorism response: Information sharing between local, state, and federal governments (Subcommittee on Technology and Procurement Policy)
- February 28, 2002 Anthrax antitoxin research
- March 1, 2002 Federal, state, and local response to biological and chemical attack (Subcommittee on Government Efficiency, Financial Management and Intergovernmental Relations)
- March 21, 2002 Combating terrorism (Subcommittee on National Security, Veterans Affairs and International Relations)

House International Relations Committee

- December 5, 2001 Bioterrorism and potential sources of anthrax

House Science Committee

- November 8, 2001 Anthrax decontamination
- December 5, 2001 Bioterrorism: Federal preparedness and response

House Veterans' Affairs Committee

- April 10, 2002 Bioterrorism legislation (H.R. 3253, H.R. 3254)

APPENDIX D. BIOTERRORISM-RELATED WEB SITES

Department of Health and Human Services

- Information on public health preparedness [http://www.hhs.gov/hottopics/healing]
- DHHS Office of Emergency Preparedness [http://www.oep.dhhs.gov]
- DHHS Office of Public Health Preparedness [http://www.hhs.gov/ophp]
- Metropolitan Medical Response Systems [http://www.mmrs.hhs.gov]
- National Pharmaceutical Stockpile Program [http://www.cdc.gov/nceh/nps]
- Centers for Disease Control and Prevention [http://www.bt.cdc.gov]
- Health Resources and Services Admin. [http://www.hrsa.gov/bioterrorism.htm]
- Food and Drug Administration [http://www.fda.gov/oc/opacom/hottopics/bio terrorism.html]
- National Institutes of Health [http://www.niaid.nih.gov/publications/bio terrorism.htm]
- National Library of Medicine [http://www.nlm.nih.gov/medlineplus/biologicaland chemicalweapons.html]

Department of Defense

- U.S. Army Medical Research Institute of Infectious Diseases [http://www.usa mriid.army.mil]
- DOD Anthrax Vaccine Immunization Program [http://www.anthrax.osd.mil]
- Nuclear, Biological, Chemical Medical Reference Site [http://www.nbc-med.org/others]

State and Local Health Departments

Many health departments have included information on bioterrorism and public health preparedness on their Web sites. For links to state and local health departments, go to [http://www.apha.org/public_health/state.htm].

Professional Associations

- American College of Emergency Physicians [http://www.acep.org/1,4634,0.html]
- American College of Physicians [http://www.acponline.org/bioterro]
- American Hospital Association [http://www.aha.org/Emergency/EmIndex.asp]
- American Medical Association [http://www.ama-assn.org/ama/pub/category/6671.html]
- American Society for Microbiology [http://www.asm.org/pcsrc/bioprep.htm]

- Association for Professionals in Infection Control and Epidemiology [http://www.apic.org/bioterror]
- Association of State and Territorial Health Officials [http://www.astho.org/infectious/emerging.html]
- Council of State and Territorial Epidemiologists [http://www.cste.org]
- Federation of American Scientists, Chemical & Biological Arms Control Program [http://fas.org/bwc]
- Nat. Assoc. of County & City Health Officials [http://www.naccho.org/files/documents/responds_to_bioterrorism.html]

Academic Resources

- Johns Hopkins Center for Civilian Biodefense Studies [http://www.hopkins-biodefense.org]
- The Henry L. Stimson Center [http://www.stimson.org/cbw]
- Monterey Institute of International Studies [http://www.cns.miis.edu]
- Chemical and Biological Arms Control Institute [http://www.cbaci.org]
- UCLA Center for Public Health and Disaster Relief [http://www.ph.ucla.edu/cphdr]
- University of Minnesota Center for Infectious Disease Research and Policy [http://www1.umn.edu/cidrap]
- St. Louis University Center for the Study of Bioterrorism and Emerging Infections [http://bioterrorism.slu.edu]

In: Bioterrorism: Prevention, Preparedness and Protection   ISBN 1-60021-180-1
Editor: J. V. Borrelli, pp. 43-81   © 2007 Nova Science Publishers, Inc.

Chapter 2

RESEARCH ON AMERICANS' RESPONSE TO BIOTERRORIST THREATS AND EMERGING EPIDEMICS

Robert J. Blendon,[1] John M. Benson, Catherine M. DesRoches,
Kathleen J. Weldon, Kalahn Taylor-Clark
and Channtal Fleischfresser
Harvard School of Public Health, Boston, USA

ABSTRACT

The purpose of this chapter is to aid public officials in communicating more effectively during a biological security emergency. Experience suggests that officials need to find out in real time what Americans know and believe, whom they trust, and what actions they are taking in response to the crisis. Using examples from four years of research by the Project on the Public and Biological Security at the Harvard School of Public Health (HSPH), the chapter examines the role surveys of the general public can play during a biological security crisis.

The HSPH project has conducted twenty surveys of the general public for the purpose of advising the Centers for Disease Control and Prevention (CDC), national security officials, and state and local health officials on how to improve communications with the public in the event of a bioterrorist attack or a widespread attack of a newly emerging infectious disease. These surveys have been used to assess public knowledge, attitudes, and behavior in response to threats of bioterrorism, such as smallpox and anthrax, and emerging infectious diseases, such as SARS, and in response to the shortage of influenza vaccine in 2004.

Our results suggest some overarching conclusions for those planning to respond to such events. Different publics will trust different information sources. In addition, the

[1] Robert J. Blendon, ScD, Department of Health Policy and Management, Harvard School of Public Health, 677 Huntington Ave., Boston, MA 02115. Tel: 617-432-4502. Email: rblendon@hsph.harvard.edu.

public's response to attacks and their need for information is likely to differ according to the type of attack in question. It is important to know whom these different groups trust as a reliable source of information. Because of the high level of public trust of physicians, it is important for public health authorities to develop ongoing communications with primary care and emergency room physicians.

It is also necessary to know and address the public's specific beliefs about a biological threat. In the face of a threat, the public will make decisions based on what they believe to be true, whether or not these beliefs are true. Many times, they may be acting based on incorrect information. Likewise, it is imperative that the behavior of public leaders be consistent with their advice to the public concerning the threat and what the facts suggest should be done.

GENERAL BACKGROUND

This chapter presents an extensive summary of four years of research by the Project on the Public and Biological Security at the Harvard School of Public Health (HSPH). This effort began following the anthrax attacks that occurred in September 2001. Since that time, the HSPH Project has conducted twenty surveys of the general public for the purpose of advising the Centers for Disease Control and Prevention (CDC),[2] national security officials, and state and local health officials on how to improve communications with the public in the event of either a bioterrorist attack or a widespread outbreak of a newly emerging infectious disease.[3] These surveys have been used to assess public knowledge, attitudes, and behavior in response to threats of bioterrorism, such as smallpox and anthrax, and emerging infectious diseases, such as SARS, and in response to the shortage of influenza vaccine in 2004.

While there are inherent differences between epidemics caused by bioterrorism and those that occur naturally, the HSPH Project uses the results of surveys on newly emerging infectious diseases to inform potential communication efforts in the event of an outbreak of disease due to bioterrorism. Because the United States has experienced only one bioterrorist attack, we must rely on information about public reactions to naturally emerging epidemics in order to predict how the public would react in the event on an actual attack.

The HSPH Project's research has been unique in that its surveys have been conducted relatively rapidly after the onset of these biological threats. The surveys are carried out quickly because health officials need to find out as soon as possible what Americans know and believe, whom they trust, and what actions people are taking in response to the crisis in order to communicate effectively with the public. Short-duration surveys can provide vital information to guide public officials in their emergency responses and communication efforts.

---

[2]   The Harvard School of Public Health Project on the Public and Biological Security is funded by the Centers for Disease Control and Prevention through a grant to the Association of State and Territorial Health Officials (ASTHO). HSPH provides ASTHO and the CDC with technical assistance for public health communication by monitoring the response of the general public to public health threats.

[3]   Except for one survey conducted in Toronto, the telephone interviews for each of these surveys were done for the HSPH Project by ICR/International Communications Research.

Prior research has shown that such surveys, when statistically re-weighted, can offer timely results without unacceptable risk of bias.[4]

Reviewing results from surveys we conducted during periods of various biological threats, this chapter examines the role such surveys can play during a public health crisis and what conclusions can be drawn from this research for public health officials facing a bioterrorism emergency.

The studies reported here differ in the specific biological threat in question, but they include a similar set of research questions important to public officials. These include: 1) Americans' level of concern with the threat, 2) How they are responding to government alerts, 3) How the public believes the disease or agent is transmitted, 4) Whether or not the public is familiar with, or carrying out, any recommended precautions, 5) How many people the public believes have contracted the disease and how many have died, 6) Whether or not the public believes there is a vaccine or an effective treatment, 7) Whether or not the public knows where to go for information and care, 8) Whether or not the public believes certain groups are discriminated against in treatment, 9) Whom the public trusts as a spokesperson, and 10) Whether or not the public supports specific policy measures (e.g., quarantine or vaccination policy).

The chapter is organized to focus on major biological threats that have emerged in recent years. Two of these, anthrax and the threat of a smallpox attack, are possible bioterrorist threats. The others—SARS, the threat of Mad Cow disease, and the 2004 flu vaccine shortage—were not themselves bioterrorist threats, but involved elements similar to circumstances that might occur if there were a bioterrorist attack.. The chapter will also examine the public's response to the Department of Homeland Security's Readiness Campaign in March 2003, as well as CDC proposals to improve communications with air travelers who may have been exposed to a contagious disease while traveling. From these results, the authors draw some important lessons for public health officials dealing with these types of situations.

ANTHRAX

The first bioterrorism-related surveys by the HSPH Project were conducted in October-December 2001, following the beginning of the multi-city anthrax attacks in the U.S. These attacks began on September 18 when letters containing anthrax were sent to several media outlets. Such letters were also later discovered in the offices of Senators Thomas Daschle (D-SD) and Patrick Leahy (D-VT). Post offices were found to be contaminated and five Americans died from anthrax inhalation as a result of contact with contaminated mail. The

---

[4] R.J. Blendon, J. M. Benson, C. M. DesRoches, and K.J. Weldon, "Using Opinion Surveys to Track the Public's Response to a Bioterrorist Attack." Journal of Health Communications, Vol. 8 (Fall 2003), pp. 83-92; S. Keeter, C. Miller, A. Kohut, R.M. Groves, and S. Presser, "Consequences of Reducing Nonresponse in a National Telephone Survey." Public Opinion Quarterly, Vol. 64 (Summer 2000), pp. 125-48; R. Curtin, S. Presser, and E. Singer, "The Effect of Response Rate Changes on the Index of Consumer Sentiment." Public Opinion Quarterly, Vol. 64 (Winter 2000), pp. 413-28; Pew Research Center for the People and the Press. "Polls Face Resistance, But Still Representative: Survey Experiment Shows." April 20, 2004, http://people-press.org/reports/display.php3?ReportID=211 (accessed November 28, 2005).

HSPH Project and the Robert Wood Johnson Foundation carried out four surveys, one conducted nationwide, the other three in areas affected by the anthrax incidents.[5]

At that time, there was a great deal of media attention surrounding these incidents. However, our survey showed that despite all this coverage, most Americans thought they and their families had a relatively low risk of contracting anthrax. Far more Americans believed they or someone else in their immediate family might get the flu (73 percent very or somewhat likely) or be injured in a fall (50 percent) or automobile accident (41 percent) during the next 12 months than that they would contract anthrax (14 percent).

Although most Americans were not overly concerned about anthrax, most had started taking some sensible precautions. Many were being more careful with their mail and gathering emergency supplies of food, water or clothing, a common measure when preparing for an emergency. A majority (57 percent) had taken one or more precautions in response to reports of bioterrorism. Substantial numbers reported taking precautions when opening the mail (37 percent) and maintaining emergency supplies of food, water, or clothing (25 percent). However, 43 percent reported taking none of the 12 precautions, and only 13 percent reported taking three or more. This was an indication that most Americans were not panicking. [Figure 1]

Inhalational anthrax, if diagnosed in the early stage of the disease, is treatable with antibiotics, as is the cutaneous form of the disease. At the time, most Americans appeared to be aware that the disease is treatable and were optimistic about their chances of survival, should they contract the disease. The majority believed they would be very or somewhat likely to survive with appropriate medical treatment were they to contract the skin or inhaled form on anthrax. They were slightly more likely to believe they would survive the skin form (91 percent) of the disease than the inhaled form (78 percent). This belief about survivability may have accounted for the relatively low percentage of Americans who reported that they were taking multiple precautions against the disease.

The survey found that the majority of the public did not trust any one national political figure as a source of reliable information during the outbreak. Americans were more likely to trust public health officials and physicians than administrators who did not share such medical or public health backgrounds. More Americans reported a great deal or quite a lot of trust in nationally-recognized medical experts, such as the Director of the CDC (48 percent), the U.S. Surgeon General (44 percent), and the President of the AMA (42 percent), than in senior appointees without medical backgrounds, such as the Secretaries of Health and Human Services (37 percent) and Homeland Security (34 percent), and the Director of the FBI (33 percent).

On the local level, a majority expressed a great deal or quite a lot of trust in the directors of the local fire department (61 percent), the state or local police department (53 percent), and the state or local health department (52 percent) as sources of reliable information in the event of an outbreak in local communities. The fire department leadership on the local level was rated the highest. Three-fourths (77 percent) of Americans had a great deal or quite a lot of trust in their own doctor, a finding that highlights the importance of educating physicians about bioterrorist threats. [Figure 2]

---

[5]   Some of these results were reported in R.J. Blendon, J.M. Benson, C.M. DesRoches, W.E. Pollard, C. Parvanta, M.J. Herrmann, "The Impact of Anthrax Attacks on the American Public," Medscape General Medicine, Vol. 4, No. 2 (April 17, 2002), http://www.medscape.com/viewpublication/122_toc?vol=4&iss=2&templateid=2 (accessed November 28, 2005; subscription required).

Precautions Americans Have Taken Against Possible Bioterrorism

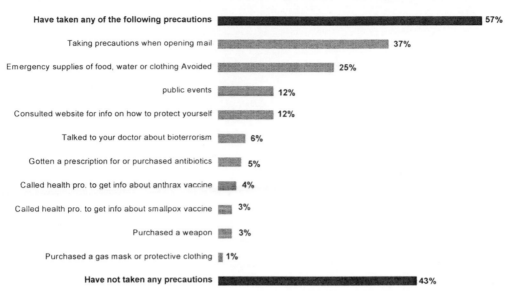

Source: Harvard School of Public Health Project on the Public and Biological Security/Robert Wood
Johnson Foundation, October 2001.

Figure 1.

Whom Americans Trust as a Source of Reliable Information
in case of outbreak of disease caused by bioterrorism in your own community

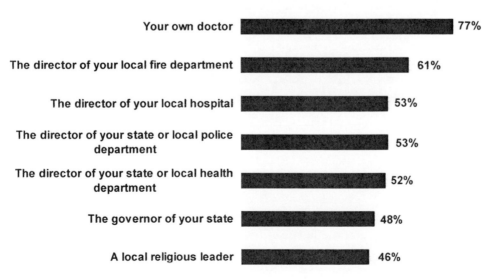

Source: Harvard School of Public Health Project on the Public and Biological Security/Robert Wood
Johnson Foundation, October 2001.

Figure 2.

The second set of studies focused on three cities where anthrax incidents were reported: the Boca Raton (FL), Washington (DC), and Trenton/Princeton (NJ) metropolitan areas. Residents of New York City, the other major area where cases of anthrax had been reported, were not interviewed because the events of September 11 made it difficult to isolate the effects of the anthrax incidents on behavior and views.

The surveys found that a large proportion of people had been affected directly or indirectly in three of the metropolitan areas where cases of anthrax had occurred. About one in five residents of the Washington, DC (21 percent) and Trenton/Princeton (19 percent) areas reported that they, a friend, or a family member had been exposed to or tested for anthrax, or had had their workplace closed because of anthrax or suspected anthrax. Nine percent of respondents in the Boca Raton area had been affected, compared with 4 percent of adults nationwide. [Figure 3] Results for the "affected" group in the Boca Raton-area are not reported here as the sample was too small for analysis.

Impact of Anthrax, Nationally and in Three Metropolitan Areas

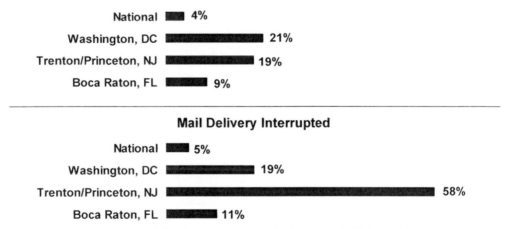

Affected
You, a friend or a family member exposed to or tested for anthrax, or had workplace closed because of anthrax or suspected anthrax

National **4%**
Washington, DC **21%**
Trenton/Princeton, NJ **19%**
Boca Raton, FL **9%**

Mail Delivery Interrupted
National **5%**
Washington, DC **19%**
Trenton/Princeton, NJ **58%**
Boca Raton, FL **11%**

Source: Harvard School of Public Health Project on the Public and Biological Security/Robert Wood Johnson Foundation, October 2001.

Figure 3.

Among the "affected" group in the Washington metropolitan area, 43 percent were very or somewhat worried that they could contract anthrax from opening their mail at work or at home (compared with 30 percent of area residents who were not affected and 24 percent of all adults nationally). Almost half (47 percent) of those "affected" were currently taking precautions when opening their mail, including washing their hands after opening mail, wearing gloves, or completely avoiding opening their mail (compared with 34 percent of those not affected and 32 percent of all adults nationally). [Figure 4]

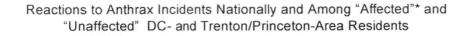

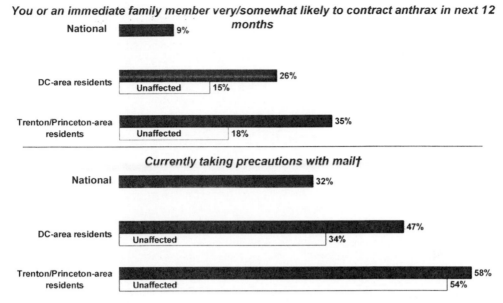

Reactions to Anthrax Incidents Nationally and Among "Affected"* and "Unaffected" DC- and Trenton/Princeton-Area Residents

*Affected = You, a friend or a family member exposed to or tested for anthrax, or had workplace closed because of anthrax or suspected anthrax.
†Wearing gloves, completely avoiding opening mail or washing hands after opening mail.

Source: Harvard School of Public Health Project on the Public and Biological Security/Robert Wood Johnson Foundation, November - December 2001.

Figure 4.

One-fourth (26 percent) of the "affected" DC-area residents thought they or an immediate family member was likely to contract anthrax during the next 12 months (compared with 15 percent of those not affected and 9 percent of all adults nationally). Twelve percent of the "affected" said that they or someone in their household had gotten a prescription for or purchased antibiotics because of reports of bioterrorism (compared with 3 percent of those not affected and 4 percent of all adults nationally).

The results showed that most Americans remained relatively untouched by the anthrax incidents, but the people who experienced these incidents either directly or indirectly through friends or family members were worried about the future.

Half (51 percent) of the "affected" group in Trenton/Princeton was worried about contracting anthrax by opening mail (compared with 37 percent of those not affected). More than half (58 percent) of "affected" Trenton/Princeton-area residents were taking precautions opening their mail. A similar proportion (54 percent) of the unaffected group was taking such precautions, probably because so many Trenton/Princeton-area residents had had their mail delivery interrupted due to fears of anthrax contamination. Fifty-eight percent of Trenton/Princeton-area residents reported interruptions of mail delivery for some period of time, compared with 19 percent in the Washington area, 11 percent in the Boca Raton, and 5 percent of adults nationwide.

One-third (35 percent) of the "affected" Trenton/Princeton-area residents thought they or an immediate family member were likely to contract anthrax during the next 12 months (compared with 18 percent of those not affected). Ten percent of the "affected" said that they or someone in their household had gotten a prescription for or purchased antibiotics because of reports of bioterrorism (compared with 2 percent of those not affected).

Circumstances in the Washington area, including both the September 11 attack on the Pentagon and the recent anthrax incidents, seem to have made those affected by the latter more wary of other possible attacks. More than one-third (36 percent) of "affected" Washington-area residents thought they or an immediate family member were likely to get injured by some other type of terrorist act besides anthrax or smallpox during the next 12 months (compared with 20 percent of those not affected and 18 percent of adults nationally).

"Affected" people in the Washington and Trenton/Princeton areas were no more likely than other residents of those areas to say that they or someone in their household has taken such precautions against bioterrorism as avoiding public events or maintaining emergency supplies of food, water, or clothing.

Nationally, the vast majority of Americans continued to believe that they or members of their immediate families were unlikely to contract anthrax during the next 12 months. More Americans thought they or a family member were likely to get injured by some other terrorist act (18 percent) than by either anthrax (9 percent) or smallpox (8 percent).

Implications of these Research Findings for Public Health Officials

Because the public trusts some types of leaders more than others when it comes to advice on how to protect themselves and their families, it is important for public health officials to identify trusted spokespeople within different communities. When these people are identified, public officials should provide training opportunities for them and ensure that they are adequately prepared should there be an emergency situation.

In a public health crisis, Americans look to their own physicians for information and advice. In such situations, it is critically important for public health officials to have direct communication with practicing physicians in order to keep them informed of any new developments. This should be the equivalent of an emergency broadcast system, only used in the case of a national emergency. Public health officials should explore multiple methods of contacting physicians in preparation for a national emergency.

During the anthrax incidents, the news media repeatedly showed images of Americans buying guns and gas masks. However, our data indicate that while most Americans were taking sensible precautions, such as washing their hands after opening the mail, very few were purchasing gas masks and guns. This underscores the importance of up-to-date information for public health professionals. This information could provide them with a clear picture of the public's response to an attack, while relying on the news media for information on what the public is doing is likely to provide a skewed picture of public actions in response to the crisis.

In general, it would be helpful for public health officials to track the percentage of Americans who are concerned when there is a new disease or a new epidemic. Our data suggest that people do not begin to take precautions until they are concerned. Tracking this number would give the public health officials information regarding the public's willingness to take precautions.

SMALLPOX

The threat of a national smallpox outbreak emerged at the outset of the Iraq War in March 2002, when government intelligence reports warned of the possibility of bioterrorist attacks involving smallpox. This possibility, coupled with the military action against Iraq, which was thought to have biological weapons, raised the question of what national precautions should be taken in the event of a smallpox attack. The debate, which was covered extensively in the media and professional journals, centered on three issues: whether front line health care workers should be vaccinated in the absence of any cases of smallpox, whether it would be appropriate to make smallpox vaccination available to the general public, and whether states should be given additional emergency powers to respond to bioterrorist attacks.

In order to assess how the American public would respond to this potential biological threat, the Harvard School of Public Health Project and the Robert Wood Johnson Foundation conducted a survey of adults nationwide in May 2002. At the time, not a single case of smallpox had been reported in the United States. Yet three in five Americans (59 percent) said they would get vaccinated as a precaution against a bioterrorist attack using smallpox if a vaccine were made available to them, even though they were told that the vaccination could produce serious side effects in a small number of cases. [Figure 5]

More than three-fourths (81 percent) of Americans said that, if cases of smallpox were reported in their own community, they would get vaccinated. This includes the 59 percent who had already said they wanted to get vaccinated in the near future, even without cases having been reported, as well as an additional 22 percent who became interested in vaccination once local cases were mentioned. One in ten (9 percent) would not get vaccinated even if an outbreak of smallpox occurred in their community.

The survey found that the substantial public interest at the time in receiving a smallpox vaccination grew in part from continuing fears about a future bioterrorist attack. Nine months after the September 11th attacks, more than four in ten (43 percent) reported being worried about a future attack using smallpox. About half (49 percent) of women, compared with 36 percent of men, were worried about such an attack. The interest in vaccination may also have reflected Americans' familiarity with the smallpox vaccine. Nearly three in five Americans (56 percent) reported having been vaccinated earlier in their lives.

As of May 2002, the public saw little risk that they or a family member would get smallpox. Only one in twelve Americans (8 percent) believed that they or someone in their immediate family was likely to contract smallpox during the next 12 months. This compares with 20 percent who believed they or a family member were likely to be injured in some other type of terrorist attack.

Americans Who Would Get Smallpox Vaccination as Precaution Against Terrorist Attack
Vaccine may produce serious side effects in a small number of cases
If vaccine made available
59%
33%
If cases of smallpox reported in community
81%
9%
Would get vaccinated
Would not get vaccinated

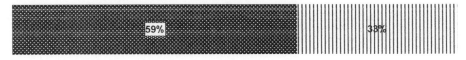

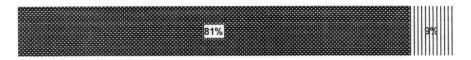

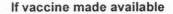

Source: Harvard School of Public Health Project on the Public and Biological Security/Robert Wood Johnson Foundation, May 2002.

Figure 5

Most Americans (74 percent) were at least moderately optimistic that they would survive if they contracted smallpox and received immediate medical care. Forty-four percent saw it as *very* likely that they would survive, while 30 percent thought it *somewhat* likely.

The survey also found reasonably high levels of confidence in the health system to respond to this threat. [Figure 6] The public was somewhat optimistic that adequate planning, preparation, and professional education had taken place in their community in regards to a possible smallpox attack. Most Americans (84 percent) reported confidence that their own doctor could recognize the symptoms of smallpox. Almost half of respondents (45 percent) were *very* confident in their doctors' abilities.

About two-thirds of Americans (70 percent) believed that their local hospital emergency room was prepared to diagnose and treat people with smallpox. However, only 23 percent thought their local ER was *very* prepared. Similarly, two-thirds (66 percent) were confident that their local health department was prepared to prevent smallpox from spreading if there were an outbreak of the disease, but only 19 percent thought the local health department was *very* prepared.

If they showed symptoms of what they thought might be smallpox, most Americans would seek help from their usual source of health care. The most common place to turn for diagnosis or treatment would be their own doctor or medical clinic (83 percent), followed by a hospital emergency room (62 percent) or outpatient department (52 percent). Very few Americans (27 percent) would seek assistance from a public health department clinic.

Public Confidence in the Health System in Case of Smallpox Attack

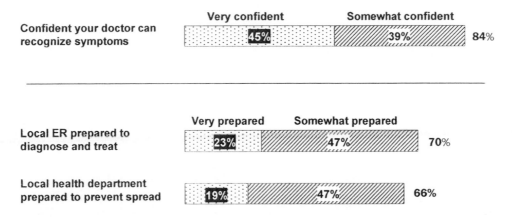

Confident your doctor can recognize symptoms

Very confident 45%   Somewhat confident 39%   84%

Local ER prepared to diagnose and treat

Very prepared 23%   Somewhat prepared 47%   70%

Local health department prepared to prevent spread

19%   47%   66%

Source: Harvard School of Public Health Project on the Public and Biological Security/Robert Wood Johnson Foundation, May 2002.

Figure 6.

The survey found no single public official whom the public most trusts on the issue of smallpox. When asked, in the event of an outbreak of disease caused by bioterrorism, which of six public officials they trusted most to provide correct information about how to protect themselves and their families from the disease, 43 percent said that they would trust a senior scientist from the Centers for Disease Control and Prevention (CDC). No other official was chosen by more than 16 percent. The other choices were the heads of the Department of Health and Human Services, Office of Homeland Security, and FBI, the U.S. Surgeon General, and the city or state health commissioner.

Asked whom they trusted most to provide correct information about *where to go* if they were exposed to a disease caused by bioterrorism, Americans were nearly evenly split between the CDC (28 percent) and their city or state health commissioner (26 percent). Nineteen percent chose the head of the Department of Health and Human Services.

The survey probed the question of public concerns about discrimination should there be a smallpox outbreak. A minority of Americans believed there would be some episodes of discrimination if there were an outbreak of smallpox. About three in ten (28 percent) believed that if they had smallpox, their local hospital was likely to refuse them treatment because they might infect other people at the hospital.

In addition, one in six Americans (17 percent) believed health professionals would discriminate against elderly people. Americans aged 65 and over were no more likely than others to think the elderly would face discrimination.

Only one in eight of the total American population (12 percent) thought African-Americans would face discrimination from health professionals in these circumstances. However, nearly three in ten African-Americans (28 percent) believed such discrimination would occur.

The Harvard School of Public Health Project and Robert Wood Johnson Foundation conducted a second smallpox survey from October to December 2002, following up their earlier results.[6] The survey investigated the circumstances under which the public would want the smallpox vaccine made widely available. Nearly two-thirds (65 percent) of Americans supported a policy of making the smallpox vaccine available to the general public on a voluntary basis. Three in five Americans (61 percent) said they would take the smallpox vaccine or be re-vaccinated as a precaution against a bioterrorist attack involving smallpox if the vaccine were made available to them.

The survey also showed that the actions of physicians significantly influenced the decision to be vaccinated. If people were told that their own physician and most other physicians were getting the smallpox vaccine, the proportion of the public willing to be vaccinated increased to 73 percent. However, if they heard that their own physician and many other physicians were refusing to take the vaccine, only 21 percent said they would be willing to get vaccinated. [Figures 7-8]

Deaths resulting from smallpox vaccination were also likely to have a significant effect on Americans' decisions. Hearing that "some people" died from the smallpox vaccine decreased the proportion willing to be vaccinated to one in three (33 percent).

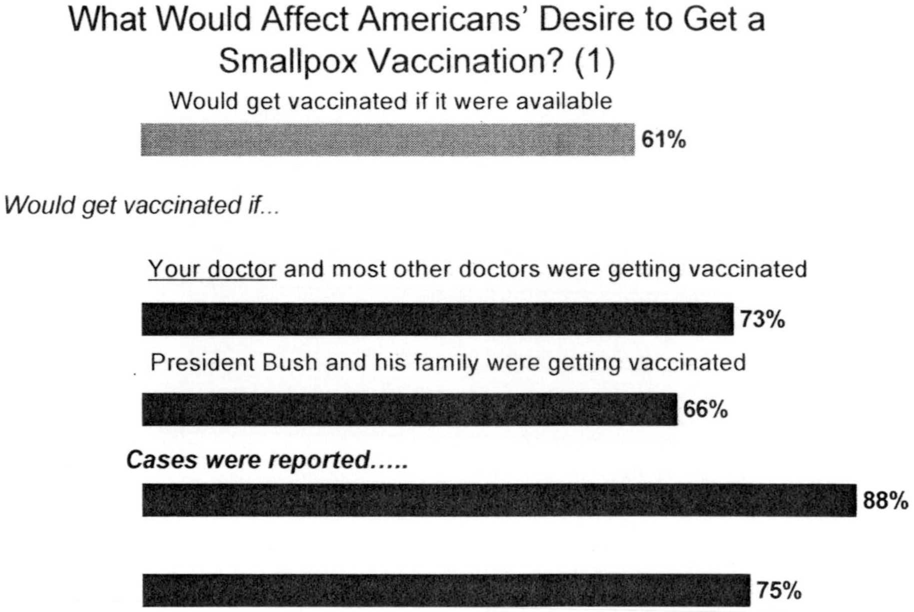

What Would Affect Americans' Desire to Get a Smallpox Vaccination? (1)

Would get vaccinated if it were available

61%

Would get vaccinated if...

Your doctor and most other doctors were getting vaccinated

73%

President Bush and his family were getting vaccinated

66%

Cases were reported.....

88%

75%

Source: Harvard School of Public Health Project on the Public and Biological Security/Robert Wood
    Johnson Foundation, October-December 2002, as published in New England Journal of Medicine,
    January 30, 2003.

Figure 7.

---

[6] Some of these results were reported in R.J. Blendon, C.M. DesRoches, J.M. Benson, M.J. Herrmann, K. Taylor-
    Clark, and K.J. Weldon, "The Public and the Smallpox Threat," New England Journal of Medicine, Vol. 348
    (January 30, 2003), pp. 426-32.

What Would Affect Americans' Desire to Get a Smallpox Vaccination? (2)

Would get vaccinated if it were available

 **61%**

Would still get vaccinated even if...

<u>Your doctor</u> and many other doctors refuse to get vaccinated

 **21%**

You heard that some people died from the vaccine

 **33%**

Source: Harvard School of Public Health Project on the Public and Biological Security/Robert Wood Johnson Foundation, October-December 2002, as published in New England Journal of Medicine, January 30, 2003.

Figure 8.

In addition, the survey found low levels of trust in government statements about the adequacy of vaccine supply. At the time, government sources said that there were enough doses of the vaccine for everyone in the U.S. Only 16 percent of Americans believed that this was the case.

Knowledge and Beliefs about Smallpox

The two surveys showed that Americans' knowledge about smallpox was mixed. More than three-fourths (85 percent) knew that smallpox is contagious. Nine in ten (90 percent) knew that if someone has contracted smallpox and shows symptoms, they should be kept isolated from uninfected people.

But the study also found that public knowledge and beliefs about smallpox and the smallpox vaccine were often incorrect, leading to the possibility of poor public judgment as a threat increased. Many Americans hold a number of mistaken beliefs about smallpox and the smallpox vaccine, according to information provided by the CDC. These misconceptions could have led some people to make inappropriate choices about how they would respond to the threat of smallpox.

Survey results emphasized the fact that it had been a long time since Americans had had experience with smallpox, and they had limited knowledge about the disease. The last case of smallpox was reported in the U.S. in 1949 and in the world in 1977. However, three in ten Americans (30 percent) believed there had been smallpox cases in the U.S. during the past five years, and 63 percent thought there have been cases somewhere in the world during that time. [Figure 9]

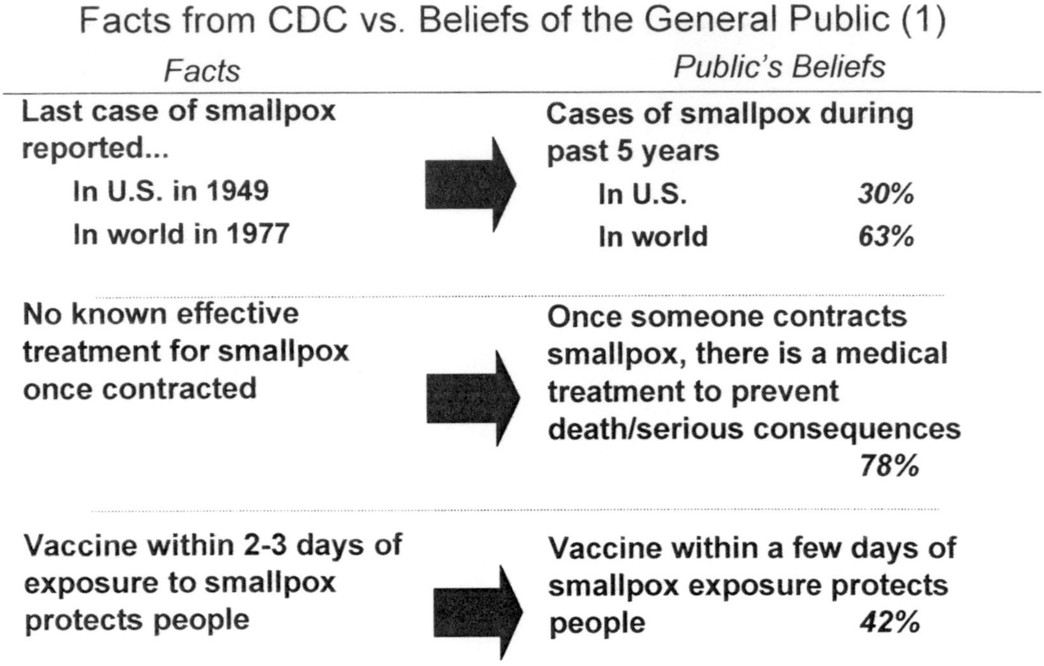

Facts from CDC vs. Beliefs of the General Public (1)

Facts	*Public's Beliefs*
Last case of smallpox reported... **In U.S. in 1949** **In world in 1977**	**Cases of smallpox during past 5 years** **In U.S.** **30%** **In world** **63%**
No known effective treatment for smallpox once contracted	**Once someone contracts smallpox, there is a medical treatment to prevent death/serious consequences** **78%**
Vaccine within 2-3 days of exposure to smallpox protects people	**Vaccine within a few days of smallpox exposure protects people** **42%**

Source: Facts: CDC; Harvard School of Public Health Project on the Public and Biological Security/Robert Wood Johnson Foundation, October-December 2002, as published in New England Journal of Medicine, January 30, 2003.

Figure 9.

There is no known effective treatment for smallpox once a person has contracted the disease. However, three-fourths of Americans (78 percent) believed that if someone came down with the disease, there was a medical treatment that would prevent them from dying or experiencing serious consequences. Similarly, only 42 percent of the public knew that a vaccine given within two or three days of exposure to smallpox would protect people against the virus.

Prior research had shown that serious adverse reactions to the vaccine were expected to be relatively rare in patients without health conditions contraindicative to a vaccination. But many Americans thought it was likely that they would suffer serious side effects from the vaccine. One-fourth thought they were very (6 percent) or somewhat likely (19 percent) to die and four in ten thought they were very (11 percent) or somewhat likely (30 percent) to suffer serious illness from the smallpox vaccine. [Figure 10]

The results also suggest that this lack of knowledge is a central issue for public health education. Americans need to know that according to experts, if people are exposed to smallpox but do not yet have symptoms, an immediate vaccination would help protect them against the disease. The message must emphasize that people should not wait until they get sick to take preventative measures. If they have been exposed, they should get vaccinated right away, because after the onset of symptoms, there is no treatment to stop the course of the disease.

Facts from CDC vs. Beliefs of the General Public (2)
Facts   *Public's Beliefs*

Serious adverse reactions to smallpox vaccination relatively rare, except for those with health conditions that contraindicate vaccination	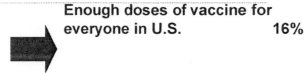	As result of smallpox vaccination

As result of smallpox vaccination

Death	
Very likely	6%
Somewhat likely	19%
Serious illness	
Very likely	11%
Somewhat likely	30%

Government sources say enough doses of smallpox vaccine for everyone in U.S.	Enough doses of vaccine for everyone in U.S. 16%

Source -Reactions: CDC; Doses: New York Times, October 12, 2002; Public's Beliefs: Harvard School of Public Health Project on the Public and Biological Security/Robert Wood Johnson Foundation, October-December 2002, as published in New England Journal of Medicine, January 30, 2003.

Figure 10.

Implications of these Research Findings for Public Health Officials

Our findings are taken from surveys conducted at the onset of the Iraq war when there was substantial public concern about a smallpox outbreak. Many of the implications of our work related to that specific time period, but some of our conclusions can also be applied to the future. Should the federal government suggest that mass smallpox vaccination become necessary, our data suggest that physicians would play a central role in providing advice and care related to smallpox vaccination and treatment. The majority of the public reported that they would go to their own doctor, rather than an emergency room or a public health department, if they thought they had smallpox. Thus, primary care physicians will be on the frontlines in helping their patients decide about vaccination and in the event of a smallpox outbreak.

If the threat of a smallpox attack were to increase, Americans' individual decisions about vaccination would be strongly influenced by what practicing physicians chose to do. If physicians were reluctant to be vaccinated, large numbers of Americans would be unwilling to do it voluntarily.

The survey findings suggest the need for mass public education about smallpox, since many Americans have beliefs about the disease that are incorrect according to scientific knowledge. Although many of the aspects of the disease remain unclear, there is general agreement that some important areas of public education need reinforcement, including: the eradication of the disease worldwide, the lack of effective treatment, the lack of immunity from a prior vaccine, the effectiveness of vaccination after exposure to the disease, the availability of sufficient doses of the vaccine, and the likelihood of serious complications among those with no contraindications for smallpox vaccination.

Our results suggest that at that time, the view held by many public health officials and leaders of the medical community – that the smallpox vaccine should not be widely available to the general public – was at odds with the public's desire for access to the vaccine. If the threat of smallpox attack persisted, public health officials needed to clarify to the public the basis for their decision to limit access to the vaccine.

The "ER" Smallpox Episode: A Natural Experiment

In addition to these findings, our research group was offered the opportunity to evaluate a natural experiment. As mentioned previously, Americans had very little experience with smallpox. How would they respond if more media attention were paid to this issue? On May 16, 2002, the viewers of "ER" saw a segment about possible smallpox infection in a patient in a busy urban emergency room. At the time that the survey was taken, the show "ER" is one of the five most watched television shows, with a large national audience.

In the episode, two children whose parents worked for the Foreign Service came to the emergency room with pox-like lesions. Smallpox was suspected and tissue samples were sent to the Centers for Disease Control and Prevention. By episode's end, smallpox had not been confirmed, and bioterrorism was not considered as a likely cause. According to the Nielsen ratings, 27.5 million Americans watched the episode.

The Harvard School of Public Health Project and Robert Wood Johnson Foundation conducted surveys before and after the "ER" episode. Of the 261 regular "ER" viewers interviewed during the week before the episode, 71 percent said they would go to a hospital emergency room if they had symptoms of what they thought was smallpox. A separate HSPH/RWJF survey conducted after the episode found that a significantly smaller proportion (59 percent) of the 146 regular "ER" viewers who had seen the episode, or had heard, read, or talked about it, would go to an emergency in this circumstance. This difference may reflect the pandemonium that broke out in the fictional emergency room when the suspected smallpox cases were first seen.

Regular "ER" viewers who saw or knew about the smallpox episode were also less likely (19 percent as compared to 30 percent) than regular "ER" viewers interviewed before the show to believe that their local hospital emergency room was *very* prepared to diagnose and treat smallpox.

The biggest difference before and after the show involved the level of knowledge about smallpox vaccination. A key message for public education about smallpox is that if a person has been exposed to the disease, he or she should get vaccinated right away rather than waiting until symptoms emerge, because at that point there is no treatment to stop the course of the disease. A majority (57 percent) of regular "ER" viewers who saw or knew about the smallpox episode knew that if a person has been exposed to smallpox but does not have symptoms, getting a smallpox vaccination will prevent the person from coming down with the disease. Only 39 percent of regular "ER" viewers interviewed before the show knew this key fact.

The post-episode survey group was also more likely to know that a person who has contracted smallpox and has symptoms should be kept isolated from uninfected people, although the level of knowledge was high (98 percent and 91 percent, respectively) among both post- and pre-episode survey groups.

However, the show had other limited effects. The "ER" episode did not lead most regular "ER" viewers who watched or knew about the show to talk about smallpox with other people. Interviewed during the five days after the show, more than three-fourths (80 percent) of that group reported that they had not talked with anyone else about smallpox during the past week.

The analysis was confined to regular "ER" viewers in order to reduce the chance that differences between the pre- and post-episode groups might be caused by pre-existing differences between regular "ER" viewers and non-viewers. It is still possible that a greater proportion of certain types of regular "ER" viewers–for instance, those more interested in or worried about smallpox–watched this particular episode. However, it is unlikely that differences in the make-up of the pre- and post-episode groups of "ER" viewers account for the differences in their responses. The two groups were similar demographically, with no statistically significant differences in their gender, racial, age, or educational composition. In addition, on one measure of interest – being worried about the possibility that terrorists may use smallpox in future attacks – the groups' responses did not differ significantly.

The research found no significant difference on 18 other survey questions about smallpox and related issues. For instance, the two groups did not differ in their level of confidence in their own doctor to recognize smallpox symptoms or in their local health department's preparedness to prevent smallpox from spreading.

In spite of efforts to create comparable before and after groups, however, changes in attitudes and levels of knowledge cannot necessarily be attributed to watching or knowing about the show.

Other researchers have suggested that coverage of an issue on popular television programs has a substantial influence on public knowledge and beliefs about that issue.[7] However, our study about the "ER" smallpox episode suggests that one individual program does not have such a broad impact.

SARS

SARS is an example of an emerging epidemic that is similar in potential impact on public beliefs and behavior to what might happen in a bioterrorist attack. On March 12, 2003, the World Health Organization issued a global alert about an outbreak of an acute respiratory syndrome. At the time of the announcement China had reported 305 cases of an acute respiratory syndrome (SARS) of unknown etiology in six provinces. Cases in Hong Kong and

---

[7] N. Tomes, "The Making of a Germ Panic, Then and Now," American Journal of Public Health, Vol. 90, No. 2 (2000), pp. 191-98; D. McQuail, "The Influence and Effects of Mass Media," in D.A. Graber, ed. Media Power in Politics (Washington, DC: CQ Press, 1994), pp. 7-24; W.C. Adams, D.J. Smith, A. Salzman, R. Crossen, S. Hiebert, T. Naccarato, W. Vantine, and N. Weisbroth, "Before and After 'The Day After': The Unexpected Results of a Television Drama," in Graber, ed., Media Power in Politics, pp. 54-65.

Vietnam were traced back to this outbreak in China. By March 19, 2003, cases of SARS were reported in 11 countries, including Singapore, Canada, Taiwan, and the United States.

SARS was an infectious, contagious viral disease with no vaccine and no effective treatment. Measures that were available to public health authorities to control the epidemic could be categorized by a number of different policies: protecting people who had not been exposed to the disease (e.g., encouraging citizens to wear masks in public to prevent the spread of illness, canceling public events, or closing schools), isolating cases and quarantining contacts, monitoring and enforcing compliance, and screening for illness. In the case of SARS, temperature screenings were required before people were allowed to enter public places in some countries. Those with a high temperature were suspected of having the disease and were excluded from entry. In many countries, public health officials had the authority to make these measures compulsory in order to prevent a small number of exposed individuals who chose not to comply with restrictions on their movement from spreading the disease. Those who did not comply could face fines or arrest.

Thousands of people were quarantined worldwide due to potential exposure to the SARS virus. These people included travelers from SARS-affected regions, health care workers, family members, friends and co-workers of SARS patients. How were Americans responding to this threat at a time when neighboring Canada was reporting a growing number of cases? The Harvard School of Public Health surveyed the American public about this question in April 2003.[8]

The survey results showed that, although there were few cases of SARS in the United States, many Americans were avoiding international air travel and Asian retailers due to the threat of SARS. The survey found that 17 percent of Americans who had traveled outside of the United States in the past year had avoided international air travel recently due to reports about SARS. Sixteen percent of the public reported avoiding people they thought may have recently traveled to Asia. In addition, 14 percent of Americans said they were avoiding Asian restaurants and/or stores. [Figure 11]

In response to reports of SARS, the public also reported using a disinfectant at home or at work (21 percent), avoiding public events (10 percent), carrying something to clean objects that may have been in contact with someone who had SARS (9 percent) and consulting a web site for information about how to protect themselves from SARS (9 percent). Despite the widely televised images of people in Asia wearing face masks, very few Americans said they bought a face mask (3 percent) or talked to a doctor about health issues related to SARS (5 percent).

Eighty-three percent of Americans believed that SARS is a disease that requires quarantine in order to keep it from spreading, and 41 percent knew that people were being quarantined for SARS in the U.S. at the time of the survey. Fully 94 percent of the public reported that they would agree to be isolated for two or three weeks in a health care facility if they had SARS. A similar percentage (92 percent) would agree to be quarantined for up to 10 days in their home if they were exposed to someone who had SARS but did not know if they themselves had the disease. [Figure 12] Only 13 percent of Americans thought that President

---

[8] Some of these results were reported in R.J. Blendon, J.M. Benson, C.M. DesRoches, E. Raleigh, and K. Taylor-Clark, "The Public's Response to Severe Acute Respiratory Syndrome in Toronto and the United States," Clinical Infectious Diseases, Vol. 38 (April 1, 2004), pp. 925-31.

Bush's recent executive order adding SARS to the list of diseases for which people can be quarantined was a threat to their personal rights and freedoms.

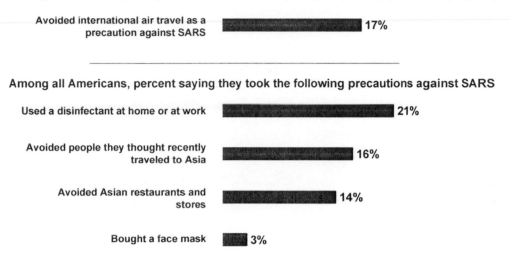

Precautions

Among Americans reporting international travel in past year (n=179), percent saying they

Avoided international air travel as a precaution against SARS — 17%

Among all Americans, percent saying they took the following precautions against SARS

Used a disinfectant at home or at work — 21%

Avoided people they thought recently traveled to Asia — 16%

Avoided Asian restaurants and stores — 14%

Bought a face mask — 3%

Source: Harvard School of Public Health Project on the Public and Biological Security, April 2003.

Figure 11.

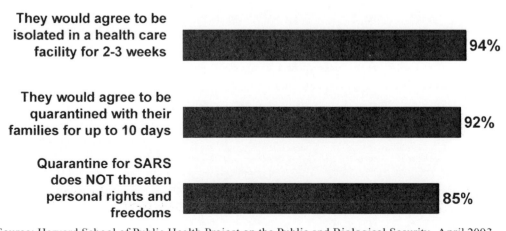

Quarantine and Isolation

Percent of Americans reporting...

They would agree to be isolated in a health care facility for 2-3 weeks — 94%

They would agree to be quarantined with their families for up to 10 days — 92%

Quarantine for SARS does NOT threaten personal rights and freedoms — 85%

Source: Harvard School of Public Health Project on the Public and Biological Security, April 2003.

Figure 12.

Beliefs about transmission

Percent saying that is possible to contract SARS through...

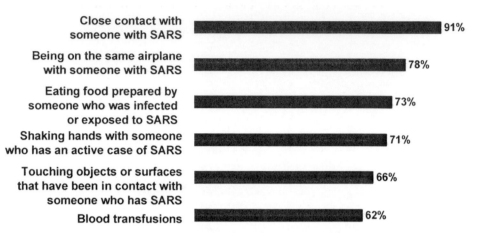

Source: Harvard School of Public Health Project on the Public and Biological Security. April 2003.

Figure 13.

At that time, one in four Americans thought it was likely (5 percent very, 20 percent somewhat) that they or someone in their immediate family would contract SARS in the next 12 months. Americans were more likely to believe that they would contract SARS than to believe they would contract anthrax (3 percent very, 9 percent somewhat) or smallpox (3 percent very, 9 percent somewhat). In addition, 32 percent of the public reported being concerned about contracting SARS.

The majority of Americans (92 percent) knew that SARS is contagious and 82 percent believed that it spread easily (46 percent very, 35 percent somewhat). The majority of the public thought that it was possible to get SARS from being in close contact with someone who has SARS (91 percent), being on the same airplane with someone who has SARS (78 percent), eating food that had been prepared by someone who was infected with or exposed to SARS (73 percent), shaking hands with someone with an active case of the disease (71 percent), touching objects or surfaces that someone who had SARS had been in contact with (66 percent), and blood transfusions (62 percent). [Figure 13]

The survey showed that if SARS spread more widely in the US, public concern would be likely to escalate due to a number of factors: eighty-four percent of the public knew that there was no vaccine for SARS and one-half (51 percent) knew there was no effective treatment. In addition, a substantial number of Americans believed that SARS was more deadly than it actually was. Four in ten Americans said that one-quarter or more of people with SARS died from the disease. The actual death rate was between six and 10 percent. Moreover, as the majority of the population believed, and the CDC reported, the disease spread easily through multiple routes of transmission.

As part of our research effort to track public attitudes and response to the threat of SARS in the U.S., the Harvard School of Public Health conducted a second survey in May 2003. With only a few reported cases in the U.S., the proportion of Americans who thought it was very or somewhat likely that they or an immediate family member would contract SARS in the next 12 months decreased from 25 percent in April 2003 to 17 percent in May 2003. However, about one-third of Americans (35 percent) believed that SARS had made it unsafe to travel to Canada. Canadian economists estimated that the SARS crisis produced a net loss of up to $1.5 billion dollars as a result of lost tourism and business-related travel. The World Health Organization lifted its travel advisory for Toronto on May 14, after the survey was completed.

Between April 2003 and May 2003, the proportion of the public who said they were avoiding Asian restaurants and stores due to worries about SARS fell from 14 percent to 9 percent. Likewise, the percentage of Americans avoiding people who they thought had recently traveled to Asia fell from 16 percent in April 2003 to 11 percent in May 2003. In May, other actions taken in response to reports of SARS included using a disinfectant at home or work (16 percent), consulting a website (8 percent), avoiding public events (7 percent), talking with a physician about health issues related to SARS (6 percent), carrying something to clean objects that may have been in contact with someone who had SARS (6 percent), and purchasing a face mask (3 percent). Among those who had traveled internationally in the past 12 months, 9 percent reported avoiding international air travel due to concerns about SARS. [Figure 14]

Precautions Against SARS

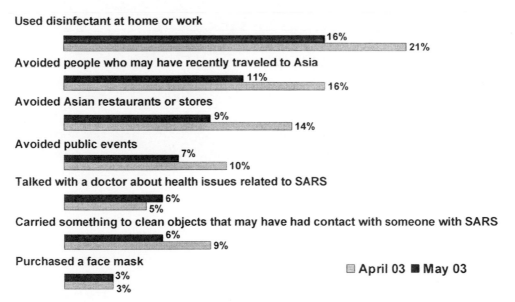

Used disinfectant at home or work
16%
21%

Avoided people who may have recently traveled to Asia
11%
16%

Avoided Asian restaurants or stores
9%
14%

Avoided public events
7%
10%

Talked with a doctor about health issues related to SARS
6%
5%

Carried something to clean objects that may have had contact with someone with SARS
6%
9%

Purchased a face mask   ▨ April 03 ■ May 03
3%
3%

Source: Harvard School of Public Health Project on the Public and Biological Security, April 2003, May 2003.

Figure 14.

Seventy-one percent of the public said that showing a video on international flights that describes SARS and what to do in the event of exposure to the disease would be helpful. Only 26 percent thought it would needlessly alarm people.

The survey also asked about the use of face masks during air travel as a precaution against SARS. Sixty-one percent of Americans said they would want to use a face mask on a domestic flight if another passenger were coughing a lot and the airline made these masks available. Seventy-three percent would want a face mask on an international flight if there were someone coughing on the plane. This suggested that if cases of SARS continued to grow internationally, many Americans were going to want airlines to show that they were taking precautions to protect travelers.

Eight-four percent of Americans knew that SARS was a disease that required people to be quarantined in order to prevent further spread. The vast majority said they would agree to isolation if diagnosed with the disease (95 percent) or quarantine (93 percent) if health officials determined it was necessary. Again, this showed positive public support for public health measures to contain the spread of the epidemic.

The Harvard School of Public Health conducted a third SARS survey in June 2003. The intent was to compare the impact of SARS on the U.S. public to that of the public in the Toronto, Canada, metropolitan area. The purpose was to learn how this emerging infectious disease might have affected the U.S. if more cases had occurred. The study, developed by the Harvard School of Public Health and Health Canada (the federal department of health in Canada), compared the impact of SARS in Toronto to the United States and found that 42 percent of residents of Toronto were concerned that they or someone in their immediate family might get sick from SARS during the next 12 months. This compared to 26 percent of Americans being concerned about SARS and 17 percent believing they or a family member were likely to contract the disease.

The Greater Toronto area had 5.1 million residents[9] and was the largest metropolitan area outside of Asia to have been impacted by SARS. Toronto had the largest number of confirmed cases of SARS in Canada.[10] As of mid-June 2003, there were 243 cases and 32 deaths nationwide in Canada, and 15,000 residents had been quarantined,[11] Most of the Canadian SARS cases had been related to in-hospital exposure to the virus.

At that time, Toronto-area residents were taking a number of precautions against SARS, such as using disinfectant at home or at work (47 percent), consulting a web site for information about protecting against SARS (27 percent), carrying something to clean objects that may have come into contact with someone who had SARS (22 percent), avoiding people who they thought may have recently traveled to Asia (17 percent), talking with their doctor about health issues related to SARS (19 percent), and buying a face mask (14 percent). [Figure 15]

In addition, a number of Toronto-area residents were taking precautions that could have a negative impact on the region's economy. About one in five (19 percent) reported avoiding Asian restaurants and stores, and 16 percent said they were avoiding public places because of SARS. About one in 10 Toronto residents who had traveled outside the country in the past 12 months reported avoiding international air travel. [Figure 16] Tourism is also likely to have

9   Ontario Ministry of Finance, "2001 Census: Population Growth in Ontario's CMAs and the GTA," http://www.fin.gov.on.ca/english/demographics/dtr0204e.pdf (accessed November 28, 2005).

10   William Foreman, "Taiwan Points SARS Finger at Toronto," The Toronto Star, June 11, 2003.

11   Public Health Agency of Canada, "Summary of Severe Acute Respiratory Syndrome (SARS) Cases: Canada and International. June 13, 2005, http://www.phac-aspc.gc.ca/sars-sras/eu-ae/sars20030613_e.html (accessed November 28, 2005); Theresa Boyle, "Premier Agrees to SARS Inquiry," The Toronto Star, June 11, 2003.

been affected by the belief of about one-third (35 percent) of Americans that SARS had made it unsafe to travel to Canada.

Precautions

Percent reporting they took the following precautions against SARS

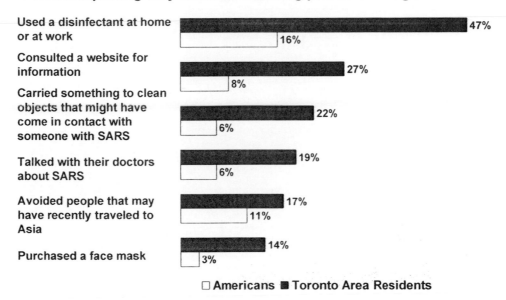

Source: Harvard School of Public Health Project on the Public and Biological Security/Health Canada, June 2003; Harvard School of Public Health Project on the Public and Biological Security, May 2003.

Figure 15.

In the U.S., where there were 71 cases of SARS and no deaths,[12] the public was less likely than residents of Toronto to report taking precautions against SARS. For example, 9 percent reported avoiding Asian restaurants or stores, and 7 percent said they were avoiding public events. Among those who had traveled outside the United States in the past 12 months, 9 percent reported avoiding international air travel recently.

The survey showed that Toronto residents knew that quarantine was necessary to keep SARS from spreading (96 percent) and said they would comply with a quarantine order if they were exposed to someone who had SARS (97 percent). Almost one-in-four residents of Toronto (22 percent) had a friend or a family member who was quarantined due to SARS exposure. Although the overwhelming majority supported quarantine, one-quarter of those who had either been quarantined themselves (2 percent) or had a friend or family member quarantined (22 percent) said that being quarantined was a major problem. When asked about specific problems relating to quarantine, the top two "major" problems were emotional difficulties relating to the confinement (11 percent) and not getting paid because they had to miss work (10 percent). [Figure 17]

---

[12] World Health Organization, "Cumulative Number of Reported Probable Cases [of SARS]," June 11, 2003, http://www.who.int/csr/sars/country/en/ (accessed November 28, 2005).

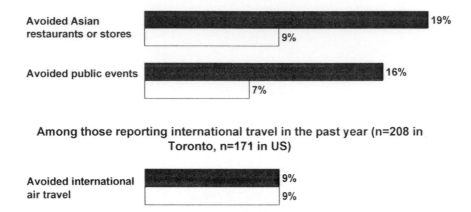

Economic Impact of SARS

Percent reporting they…

Avoided Asian restaurants or stores — 19% / 9%

Avoided public events — 16% / 7%

Among those reporting international travel in the past year (n=208 in Toronto, n=171 in US)

Avoided international air travel — 9% / 9%

☐ Americans ■ Toronto Area Residents

Source: Harvard School of Public Health Project on the Public and Biological Security/Health Canada, June 2003; Harvard School of Public Health Project on the Public and Biological Security, May 2003.

Figure 16.

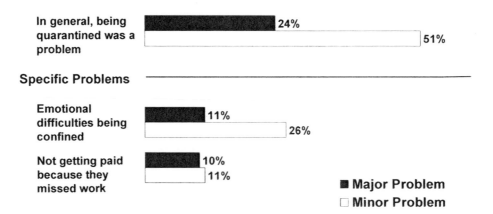

Percent experiencing problems while quarantined

BASE: Toronto area residents who had been quarantined or had a friend or family member who had been quarantined (n=111)

In general, being quarantined was a problem — 24% / 51%

Specific Problems

Emotional difficulties being confined — 11% / 26%

Not getting paid because they missed work — 10% / 11%

■ Major Problem
☐ Minor Problem

Source: Harvard School of Public Health Project on the Public and Biological Security/Health Canada, June 2003.

Figure 17.

The latter findings are of significance. It was a positive sign that three-quarters of Toronto residents who had experience with quarantine did not find it to be a major problem. The results also show that people in Toronto had become very knowledgeable about the disease, demonstrating the effectiveness of public health and media communication.

Implications of these Research Findings for Public Health Officials

A number of implications emerge from these surveys. The data suggests that the success of efforts to educate the public about the risk of SARS and about appropriate precautions against disease was mixed. Large majorities of the public knew that SARS was contagious and supported the principle of quarantine. Most said that they would comply with a quarantine order. In addition, the public was generally knowledgeable about how the disease spreads and that there was no vaccine for SARS. However, one-half of those surveyed did not know that there is no effective treatment for SARS, and many reported taking unnecessary precautions that could have a negative economic impact.

The results suggest if there were an epidemic of SARS in the U.S. that could not be contained quickly, it would have a significant economic impact on any major city where cases occurred. Also, Americans' general level of concern would tend to be higher than their assessment of their own personal risk. Studies in Toronto showed that as the number of cases of SARS increased, the proportion of people who were concerned grew substantially, even though many of those concerned knew that their risk of contracting the disease remained low.[13]

Should there be a bioterrorist attack in the US similar to an outbreak of SARS, communication efforts should focus on appropriate precautions, in order to minimize the economic effects of the disease. In addition, the findings suggest that media coverage of an outbreak of infectious disease can be a double edged sword. On the positive side, news media inform people about how the disease is spread, what precautions to take, and whether a vaccine is available. On the other hand, because of national and international news coverage of an outbreak, people who are distant from the site of the outbreak can become concerned and start taking precautions as if they were in the affected area. In an ideal world, news media would be more effective conveying the level of risk and the relative need for precautions in high-risk versus low-risk areas. One way to achieve this in the future would be to work with local broadcast journalists in advance of a threat to ensure that they know to whom they can turn for up-to-date and credible information.

An important warning for the future is that a SARS-like bioterrorist attack could result in the stigmatization of immigrant or specific ethnic groups in the US. In order to minimize this in the future, the CDC should describe the affected group in the least discriminatory way possible. Describing the affected group as recent immigrants from Taipei and China, or people who recently traveled to China may result in less discriminatory behavior by the general public than describing the group as Asians. In addition, when an epidemic is centered within an ethnic or racial group, using media that is tightly focused on that area, rather than

---

[13] Blendon et al., "The Public's Response to Severe Acute Respiratory Syndrome in Toronto and the United States."

general broadcast media, will lessen the stigma and ensure that communication messages are targeted to the high risk population.

MAD COW DISEASE

One important issue to consider is how the public might respond to bioterrorism involving the food supply. Although not caused by a bioterrorist attack, the scare about a possible outbreaks of Mad Cow Disease provides an insight into possible public reaction should there be an attack on the food supply.

In January 2004, the first recent case of Mad Cow Disease in livestock was reported in the U.S. This followed a much more widespread outbreak in the U.K. in 1996, which had seen a huge economic impact on the country and widespread public concern and anxiety.[14] This outbreak led many countries to ban the importation of British beef, a move which had a devastating effect on the beef industry in the U.K. In response to the British outbreak, media sources were filled with pictures of herds of cows being destroyed, as well as stories of the small number of human cases of the related Creutzfeld-Jacob disease, a fatal brain-wasting disease linked to the consumption of contaminated beef.

The Harvard School of Public Health conducted a national survey in January 2004 to examine the public's reaction to the possible spread of this food-borne disease. The survey found that most Americans were not concerned about getting Mad Cow Disease. Less than one in five (18 percent) were concerned that they or someone in their immediate family would be infected by the disease. Less than one in 10 (9 percent) thought they or a family member were likely to become infected by Mad Cow Disease in the next 12 months, compared to 70 percent who thought they or a family member were likely to get the flu.

However, one in six Americans (16 percent) said that they or someone in their family had stopped ordering beef at fast food restaurants because of reports about Mad Cow Disease. [Figure 18] Similarly, 14 percent say they or a family member had stopped buying beef at the grocery store. Among those who were concerned that they or a family member would become infected with the disease, four in 10 reported having stopped ordering beef at fast food restaurants (41 percent) and stopped buying beef at the grocery store (40 percent).

The results suggest that if there had been more cases and Americans had become more concerned about the threat of Mad Cow Disease, it could have had a substantial impact on the beef industry, even though the disease might only affect a small number of people.

At the time, one in four Americans (27 percent) mistakenly believed that Mad Cow Disease had been found in humans in the U.S. Only a single case of Mad Cow Disease was reported in cattle, and no humans were found to have contracted the disease in the U.S. This shows the ease with which mass misinformation can spread during an outbreak such as this.

---

[14] S. Jasanoff, "Civilization and Madness: The Great BSE Scare of 1996." Public Understanding of Science, Vol. 6, No. 3 (1997), pp. 221-32.

Americans' Response to Reports about Mad Cow Disease

% who say they or someone in their family has...

Stopped ordering beef at fast food restaurants

16%

Stopped buying beef at the grocery store

14%

Stopped ordering beef at other restaurants

13%

Stopped eating hamburger or ground beef

13%

Stopped eating beef completely

7%

Started buying and eating only organic or grassfed beef

4%

Sources: Harvard School of Public Health Project on the Public and Biological Security, January 2004.

Figure 18.

At the time of the survey, four in ten Americans (41 percent) said that they had only some (26 percent) or very little (15 percent) confidence in the meat inspection system to protect Americans from becoming infected by Mad Cow Disease. Among those who were concerned that they or a family member might become infected with the disease, six in ten (60 percent) did not have confidence in the inspection system. Again, public trust in government authorities to carry out their health protection was not found to be high.

Also, the survey found that there was no public consensus regarding what official should bear future responsibility for prevention of the spread of Mad Cow Disease in the U.S. Nearly the same proportions thought that cattle food producers (33 percent), the federal government (31 percent), and the American beef industry (29 percent) should be mainly responsible for preventing spread of the disease.

Implications of these Research Findings for Public Health Officials

The findings from this study of public reaction to a short-lived threat from Mad Cow Disease has a number of implications for dealing with a possible bioterrorist attack on the food supply. A case of Mad Cow Disease in a single cow in the US generated significant media coverage and reported changes in consumer behavior. Should a human case of Mad Cow Disease appear that cannot be traced back to another country of origin, the public alarm and outcry would be tremendous. One would expect that a human case of a food-borne disease caused by a bioterrorist attack would raise at least as much concern. Public health officials should be prepared for this by creating communication messages prior to the incident case. Responding quickly will help to calm public fears and possibly reduce the impact on the food industry involved.

Even with only one case reported, a significant proportion of the American public reported that they stopped eating at least some beef in response to reports about Mad Cow Disease. This could have serious implications for the beef industry should the disease become more widespread in the US. There are several strategies that public health professionals could pursue to help mitigate some of the impact.

First, they should try to learn from the British experience of 1996 – public health officials should review case studies of the British experience of dealing with Mad Cow Disease.

Second, other research indicates that the public will be influenced by the actions of those in leadership positions. It is essential that those in leadership positions are consistent in the information they are giving the public. During the crisis in the U.K., the secretary of state for the environment assured the public that British beef was safe to eat, while at the same time the government's chief scientific advisor for human mad cow disease said that his grandson was not allowed to eat beef. This led to a serious breakdown of public trust in government.

Finally, public health and agricultural officials may want to support more stringent screening and inspection of livestock and dairy products by the Department of Agriculture in the future. Specific information about how a new system would make the food supply safer would help reassure the public if other cases of emerge.

THE 2004 INFLUENZA VACCINE SHORTAGE

Major shortages of health services, pharmaceuticals, and vaccines occur relatively rarely in the United States. But during a bioterrorist attack one might expect a shortage of vaccines, particularly if the biological agent was one against which we were not well-prepared. Actual experience with a vaccine shortage occurred in a non-bioterrorist situation in October 2004, following the British government's decision to suspend operations of the Chiron Corporation plant in Liverpool, England, because of bacterial contamination. The plant is one of the two major influenza vaccine suppliers to the United States. This decision reduced the expected U.S. supply of vaccine by forty-eight million doses—nearly half the anticipated doses needed for the 2004–2005 influenza season. Because of this sharp reduction in supply, the Advisory Committee on Immunization Practices (ACIP), which advises the U.S. Centers for Disease Control and Prevention (CDC), recommended that the remaining vaccine supply should be reserved for certain groups of people at high risk for serious health problems from influenza, health care workers in direct contact with patients, and close contacts of children under age six months. Other members of the public were to be discouraged from seeking the vaccine in the 2004–05 flu season, a policy recommendation contrary to long-term CDC efforts to encourage widespread vaccination among the general population.

How did the American public respond to this major shortage of vaccine in 2004, and what are the implications for potential bioterrorist or major epidemic events in the future? Using results from a survey conducted by the Harvard School of Public Health in October-November 2004 and four other national opinion surveys conducted by media organizations, we examined five issues: (1) How concerned were the public about this major shortage of flu vaccine? (2)Who did they believe was responsible for the shortage? (3) In the future, who should be principally responsible for ensuring that there is an adequate supply of vaccine? (4) Who should decide how the vaccine should be allocated in a shortage, and was the current allocation system seen as fair and equitable? (5) What did the public believe about the safety of an imported vaccine? How might these perceptions affect demand for the vaccine?[15]

The surveys show that the public was aware of the shortage of influenza vaccine. The majority of respondents believed that their community was experiencing a shortage of influenza vaccine (66 percent), and six in ten of those were concerned about the shortage (31 percent very concerned, 31 percent somewhat concerned).

The public did not hold any one group responsible for the shortage of influenza vaccine. Thirty-nine percent blamed vaccine manufacturers and pharmaceutical companies, and 29 percent blamed federal government public health agencies. The public was much less likely to blame state and local governments, non-high risk vaccinees, health plans and insurers, or physician organizations. Similarly, other polling found that 37 percent of respondents thought that "the vaccine manufacturer that had problems with the safety of its facility" was most at fault, one-third thought that a federal health agency was most at fault, and 26 percent said that they did not know who was at fault. In a third survey, only one in three Americans said that the Bush administration was to blame.

Similarly, the public did not hold any one group responsible for ensuring an adequate supply of the flu vaccine in the future. When asked who should be primarily responsible for making sure that the country has an adequate supply of the flu vaccine, 45 percent of respondents cited federal public health agencies and 26 percent, vaccine manufacturers and pharmaceutical companies.

When it came to the allocation system for the vaccine then in short supply, there were some public concerns. The survey asked respondents' views about the CDC's vaccine allocation guidelines. Although the public was generally supportive of reserving the vaccine for those at the highest health risk, a sizable proportion believed that the responsibility for allocating the vaccine should not lie with the CDC. Respondents were far more likely to say that individual doctors and nurses should decide who receives it; many fewer thought that a government agency should have this responsibility. In addition, there was much skepticism among the public about how this allocation system would work in reality. Only 14 percent reported being very confident that "government agencies, together with the vaccine industry" would assure that the limited supply of vaccine would be distributed fairly. Two-thirds of respondents believed that wealthy or influential people would be able to get the vaccine even if they were not in a high-risk group. [Table 1]

Similarly, after being told that there were limited supplies of the influenza vaccine, respondents were asked what would be the best way to distribute the vaccine fairly. Slightly more than half said that the vaccine should be reserved for high-risk groups, one-third believed that doctors and nurses should decide who should get the vaccine, and 4 percent thought that the vaccine should be given to anyone who wants it until it is gone.

---

[15] Some of these results were reported in C.M. DesRoches, R.J. Blendon, and J.M. Benson, "Americans' Responses to the 2004 Influenza Vaccine Shortage," Health Affairs, Vol. 24, No. 3 (2004), pp. 822-31.

Table 1. Americans' Views of the Vaccine Allocation System

	Percent
Who should decide who gets the flu vaccine	
Individual doctors and nurses	56
The CDC	16
State health department	13
Local health department	11
Confidence that the vaccine will be distributed fairly	
Very confident	14
Somewhat confident	46
Not confident at all	15
Not very confident	23
Wealthy and influential people will be able to get the vaccine even if they are not in a high risk goup	66
Best way to distribute the vaccine fairly	
It should be reserved for high risk groups	54
Doctors and nurses should decide on a case by case basis	35
It should be distributed some other way	7
It should be given to anyone who wants it until it is gone	4
Which comes closer to your view?	
People who are not at a high risk for getting a serious case of the flu	
Should not be allowed to get the vaccine because there are people who need it more	62
Should be able to get the vaccine because they thmselves are the best judge of how much they need it	33
Don't know	4
Who should be responsible for ensuring that the vaccine is only given to people at high risk*	
The doctors who give the vaccines	58
Local health authorities	22
The CDC	10
The people themselves	9

* Base = those who said people who are not at a high risk for getting a serious case of the flu should not be allowed to get the vaccine because there are people who need it more.

Source: Harvard School of Public Health Project on the Public and Biological Security, November 2004.

The survey also gave respondents the following scenario: "Some people who are not at a high risk for getting a serious case of influenza as defined by the CDC have been trying to get the flu vaccine." Respondents were then asked which came closer to their view: "These people should not be allowed to get the vaccine because there are people who need it more than they do," or, "these people should be able to get the vaccine because they themselves are the best judge of how much they need it." About two-thirds responded that those who are not at high risk should not be allowed to get the vaccine. Among those, 58 percent believed that the doctors who give the vaccines should be responsible for ensuring this; one-fifth thought that local health authorities should have this responsibility, and approximately equal proportions said that the CDC (10 percent) or the American people themselves (9 percent) should be responsible.

In understanding the public's reaction to the flu vaccine shortage, it is important to examine beliefs about the seriousness of influenza and the safety and efficacy of the vaccine. The survey asked the public about their knowledge of influenza, the effectiveness of the vaccine and other preventive measures that they could take to avoid becoming ill with influenza, and worries about side effects from the vaccine.

The public underestimated the severity of influenza as an illness. When asked to estimate the number of Americans who die each year from influenza, 27 percent of respondents said less than 1,000; one-third said 1,000–19,999; only one-tenth said 20,000–39,999; and approximately one-quarter said that they did not know. The CDC estimates that influenza accounts for approximately 36,000 deaths each year.

When asked specifically about the 2004–05 flu vaccine, only 30 percent believed that it would be very effective in preventing people from getting influenza. Also, although the risk of serious side effects from the vaccine has been shown to be very low, a minority reported concerns about side effects. One-fifth said that it was very likely that a person who received the vaccine would experience at least one of the following side effects: fever or extreme tiredness, influenza or a serious illness, or death. There were no significant differences in concerns about side effects between Americans in high-risk groups and those who were not at high risk for serious complications from influenza.

To ease the vaccine shortage, the U.S. Department of Health and Human Services (HHS) announced that it would purchase up to four million doses of the vaccine from Germany. This vaccine, Fluarix (manufactured by GlaxoSmithKline), is fully approved for use in Germany; however, it is not approved for general use in the United States and is therefore considered investigational for legal purposes. After being informed of the vaccine's status, respondents were asked about their willingness to receive it if no other vaccine were available. More than half said that they would be willing to take it if no other vaccine were available. However, after respondents were told that they would have to sign a waiver stating that they were aware that the imported vaccine was considered investigational, their willingness to receive the vaccine decreased more than ten percentage points. Among African Americans, willingness to receive the imported vaccine decreased from 54 percent to 34 percent when they were told they would have to sign a waiver. Overall, 15 percent reported being very worried about either the safety or the efficacy of the imported vaccine. Similarly, a survey taken after HHS announced plans to import the influenza vaccine from Germany found that only 36 percent of Americans would feel safe receiving this vaccine.

Implications of these Research Findings for Public Health Officials

These findings suggest a number of implications for communicating with the public about future outbreaks of a major epidemic, including one caused by a bioterrorist attack. An article published shortly after the flu vaccine shortage argued that the 2004 flu vaccine shortage provided a successful experiment in health care rationing.[16] Our survey suggests that we may not be able to generalize these successful results to other situations. Even in the case of influenza, a disease perceived by most of the public as relatively benign, four in ten respondents did not believe that the vaccine should be reserved for high-risk groups. The willingness of many Americans to go along with the vaccine allocation system in 2004 may have been a result of a mild influenza season or of believing that influenza is not a serious illness, that the vaccine is not effective, or that there was a risk of serious side effects from the vaccine. However, the U.S. experience might be very different in the case of a disease that is perceived to be highly lethal and highly contagious, and for which the public believes there is an effective vaccine. Surveys taken immediately prior to the Iraq war found that the public would be willing to take the smallpox vaccine—even when they were told that there is a considerable risk of serious side effects—and that Americans wanted the vaccine to be available to the general public rather than being reserved for health care workers. This suggests that in these instances the demand for the vaccine might make it much more difficult for physicians and public health officials to ration a limited supply based on categories of health risk.

It is possible, as it was in the case of the flu vaccine, that a significant proportion of the public will overestimate the risk of receiving a vaccine in a bioterrorist threat. Many people may believe they can contract the disease from the vaccine or that the vaccine may have serious side effects. Public health officials need to work on effective public communication on this issue, because people who think they can be harmed by a vaccine are less likely to take it.

Also, again as we see in the case of the flu, a substantial proportion of the public may underestimate the fatality of certain bioterrorist threats. This has important implications for public health officials trying to ensure that everyone in a high-risk group receives the vaccination.

Lastly, it is important that the public believe the vaccine is effective. If the vaccine is only partially effective, public health officials should be candid about the level of benefit and recommend it only for the highest risk groups. Strongly recommending a vaccine that is only partially effective will serve to harm public health officials' credibility in the future.

PREPARING THE PUBLIC FOR A TERRORIST/BIOTERRORIST ATTACK

In 2003, the Department of Homeland Security launched its "Be Ready" campaign. This campaign provided guidelines to the general public for preparing for a terrorist or bioterrorist attack. The "Be Ready" website (www.ready.gov) offered advice for preparing an evacuation plan, sheltering in place, and how to protect against the effects of a conventional terrorist attack such as a bombing, a nuclear attack, or a chemical or biological attack. In March 2003 the Harvard School of Public Health surveyed the public to learn of its level of responsiveness to their campaign. The survey results showed few Americans making preparations in case of a terrorist attack despite Department of Homeland Security warnings and recommendations. The study found that although most Americans (73 percent) knew that

---

[16] T.H. Lee, "Rationing InfluenzaVaccine," New England Journal of Medicine, Vol. 348, No. 3 (2004), pp. 2365-66.

the nation was on a high level of alert (orange) against a terrorist attack, few developed evacuation plans or made arrangements for "sheltering in place" as recommended by government officials.

One in four (28 percent) Americans said they had given some thought to making an evacuation plan for themselves and their family. [Figure 19] However, only 12 percent actually made a plan. Very few Americans reported practicing their evacuation plan (4 percent). One of the reasons for this lack of planning may be that Americans are not sure what government officials mean when they talk about the need for an evacuation plan—only 55 percent said they thought they knew. When asked what they thought an evacuation plan included, 42 percent said this involved a plan for getting to a community shelter, and 35 percent said an evacuation plan included a plan for getting out of their community. In fact, both are recommended by the Department of Homeland Security.

Evacuation Plans

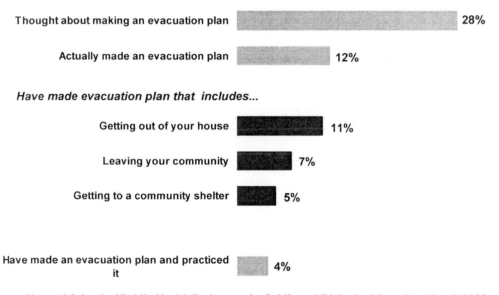

Source: Harvard School of Public Health Project on the Public and Biological Security, March 2003.

Figure 19.

Only 37 percent of the public reported having a windowless room in their home where they could shelter in place. While most Americans (75 percent) had duct tape that could be used to shelter in place, only a third (32 percent) reported having plastic sheeting and only 28 percent had both. Again, this lack of preparation could be due to confusion on the part of the public. Only one quarter of Americans (24 percent) reported that they had heard the term "shelter in place" and knew what it meant. [Figure 20]

Sheltering In Place

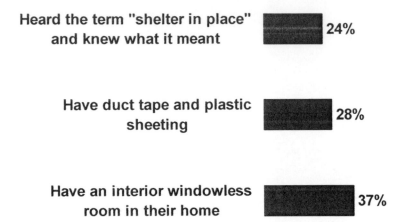

Source: Harvard School of Public Health Project on the Public and Biological Security, March 2003.

Figure 20.

Steps Americans Have Taken Because of Terrorist Threat

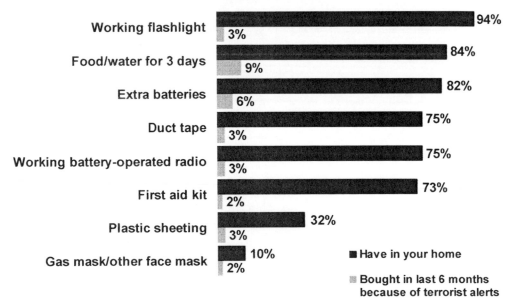

Source: Harvard School of Public Health Project on the Public and Biological Security, March 2003.

Figure 21.

The survey also found that the majority of Americans had many of the items that the government recommended buying as a precaution against a terrorist attack. The most commonly owned items were: a working flashlight (94 percent), adequate supplies of food and water for three days (84 percent), extra batteries (82 percent), duct tape (75 percent), a working battery operated radio (75 percent), and a first aid kit (73 percent). They did not report buying these items because of the heightened terror alert. In fact, only 3 percent of Americans said they bought duct tape or plastic sheeting after the heightened terror alerts. [Figure 21]

The public reported being concerned about the level of precautions being taken in the places where they work or go to school. Only 38 percent of those who worked or went to school, believed that the place where they worked or went to school had made adequate preparations for a terrorist attack. Further, only 27 percent of Americans reported that someone at work or school had discussed with them plans for evacuation of the building in the case of a terrorist attack.

Among parents with children in school or daycare, 50 percent reported that, to the best of their knowledge, the school or daycare had a plan in place in case of a terrorist attack. Seventy-six percent of parents who knew of the plan said the school or day care had done a good job in informing them of it. The majority of parents with children who attended school or daycare thought their children would be adequately cared for and safe if they had to remain at the school due to a terrorist attack for a day (85 percent), overnight (76 percent), or for three days (55 percent).

Most Americans have taken basic precautions, such as storing extra food and water. However, in the absence of a direct threat, the public does not pay very close attention to preparedness messages and does not take precautions that may be more difficult to implement. This suggests the need to take advantage of teachable moments by having materials prepared in advance of crisis. This advance preparation would allow the public health officials to communicate with the public quickly should an event occur that would heighten public awareness.

The terms "evacuation plan" and "shelter in place", both used frequently by professionals, are not commonly used by the public. Many Americans do not know what these terms mean. Communication messages using these terms should include concise, clear definitions. The survey showed that the public was confused about what they should do when government officials spoke about evacuation plans and sheltering in place. The results indicated a need for government officials to focus more on telling Americans what they should do in an emergency and spend less time talking about issues such as duct tape and extra batteries.

In addition to confusion over terms, many Americans reported being unable to shelter in place because they did not have an interior room in their home. This issue of feasibility could affect how the public views the recommendations for preparing for a terrorist attack. If some of the government recommendations are not possible to implement, it may lead people to ignore all of them. It could also lead many Americans to believe that the government is "out of touch" with their lives.

Implications of these Research Findings for Public Health Officials

When communicating with the public about evacuation plans, it is important to know what people know and believe about this already and what plans they already have to evacuate.

The data also suggest that the 24-hour news cycle does not always accurately reflect what the general public is doing. Following the release of the "Be Ready" campaign, the news media was filled with stories of Americans buying duct tape, while our survey suggests that for the majority of Americans, this was not the case. This underscores the importance of up-to-date information for public health professionals, so that they may relay this information on to the public. Relying on the news media for information on what the public will provide a skewed picture of public actions in response to the crisis.

Survey findings suggest that one of the most frequently cited reasons given for not complying with government advice in an emergency is concern about children and other family members. Only one-half of parents reported that their child's school or daycare had an emergency plan. Among those who knew about the plan, the majority were satisfied that their child would be well cared for. This suggests that the public health officials should work with schools and daycares to ensure that they 1) have an adequate plan in place and 2) have made parents aware of the plan.

AIR TRAVELERS AND BIOLOGICAL SECURITY EMERGENCIES

Contagion from a bioterrorist attack could spread easily through international travel. The worldwide SARS epidemic in 2003 highlighted how quickly infectious disease can travel the world. The virus was spread from Asia to the western hemisphere through airline travel. Tracing passengers who may have been exposed to the virus on an airplane proved difficult for public health officials, particularly after these passengers left the airport. This contact tracing is an essential public health tool, allowing officials to both quarantine those who may have been exposed to the virus and offer treatment to those who were infected. These experiences raised questions as to what could been done to make such contact tracing easier. Similar circumstances could be envisioned for air travelers exposed to bioterrorist agents or other serious contagious diseases while traveling.

A critical question is whether the general public would be willing to provide travel contact information prior to boarding an airplane to help health officials contact them in case of a biological security emergency. The Harvard School of Public Health conducted a national survey investigating this issue in June 2004. The study found that the vast majority (94 percent) of air travelers would want public health authorities to contact them if they might have been exposed to a serious contagious disease on an airplane. Large majorities of Americans who fly domestically or internationally are willing to provide information that would help public health officials contact them in such an event. [Figure 22]

Currently, international air travelers are required to provide emergency contact information, and a large majority of such travelers are willing to continue doing so. Nearly nine in ten Americans who travel internationally (89 percent) would be willing to give the airlines the name and telephone number of someone who could be contacted in case of an emergency. Similarly, about nine in ten (88 percent) of those international air travelers who take a cell phone, pager, or hand-held wireless email when they fly are willing to provide the phone or pager number or email address for these devices. Nearly three-fourths (73 percent) are willing to provide the addresses and telephone numbers of the places they are going. Overall, 89 percent of international fliers are willing to provide at least one type of contact information, 7 percent are unwilling to provide any, and 4 percent don't know.

Willingness of Air Traveler to Provide Emergency Information

If you had been on an airplane with someone who had a highly contagious disease...

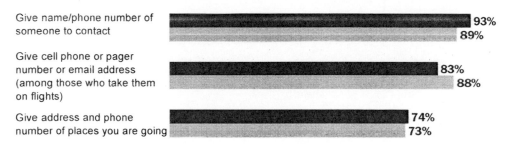

■ Domestic Fliers
▦ International Fliers

Would want public health officials to contact you, warn you of potential exposure — 94% / 94%

In order to help public health officials contact you as quickly as possible, willing to....

Give name/phone number of someone to contact — 93% / 89%

Give cell phone or pager number or email address (among those who take them on flights) — 83% / 88%

Give address and phone number of places you are going — 74% / 73%

Source: Harvard School of Public Health Project on the Public and Biological Security, June 2004.

Figure 22.

Domestic air travelers are not currently required to provide emergency contact information, but most of them are willing to. The proportion of domestic travelers willing to provide such information is nearly identical to that of international travelers. Overall, 93 percent are willing to provide at least one type of contact information, 5 percent are unwilling to provide any, and 2 percent don't know.

The survey results suggest that the combination of possible threats of bioterrorism carried out on airplanes and newly emerging infectious diseases has left most Americans willing to cooperate with public health authorities who need emergency contact information to curb the spread of dangerous diseases.

In addition, the survey found that about half of domestic (52 percent) and international air travelers (50 percent) believe that public health authorities today can quickly obtain air passengers' emergency contact information to warn them about possible exposure to a serious contagious disease.

There was an important caveat to air travelers' willingness to provide emergency contact information: most were not willing to wait very long to provide such information. More than three in five domestic (61 percent) and international fliers (66 percent) said they would either not be willing to give emergency information at all or would no longer be willing to do so if it added 10 minutes to the time it took to make a reservation or to check in.

In addition, about two-thirds of fliers said they were concerned that the privacy of their emergency information would not be protected. Nearly four in ten domestic (37 percent) and international fliers (38 percent) said they were very concerned.

These findings suggested support for airlines and public health officials working together to find some simple system where this information can be entered and retrieved easily while maintaining passengers' privacy.

About three in five domestic (60 percent) and international (63 percent) travelers who take a cell phone, pager, or hand-held wireless email with them when they fly said that the numbers or email addresses for these devices were the easiest form of emergency information for them to provide. A majority of those who do not take along such devices when they fly domestically (68 percent) and internationally (55 percent) said that it was easiest to provide the name and telephone number of someone who could be contacted in case of an emergency. Air travelers considered the least convenient type of emergency information to be providing the addresses and telephone numbers of the places they were going. For each of the types of emergency information air travelers were willing to provide, air travelers said that the easiest time to supply this information would be when they make their airline reservation.

Implications of these Research Findings for Public Health Officials

The research suggests a few important implications: though Americans are concerned with maintaining their privacy, they are willing to make some tradeoffs in order to be protected from the threats of a serious contagious disease. Secondly, the success of any system to provide contact information depends on its administrative simplicity for the air traveler.

CONCLUSIONS

Our research has been aimed at gaining insights into ways government health authorities can improve their communications with the public during a biological security crisis. One lesson from our work is that communicating with the public in an emergency situation is a two-way street. It is not simply a process where health authorities tell Americans what they need to do and how to respond to emergencies. To be effective in their communications, health officials need to know as the crisis is unfolding what Americans believe, what they know and understand, whom they trust and what actions they are taking in response to the crisis. This is the case both nationally and in areas most affected by an emergency. The communications resources of government money—the amount of time, and public attentiveness—can be scarce during a crisis. Such resources can be used most effectively if there are recent data about what the public needs to learn.

In addition, in an emergency situation, public health officials need to see a larger picture of events as they unfold than what is provided by television new stories, telephone calls, emails, letters, and demands from legislators. Timely polls can provide an important reality check for officials who may be overwhelmed with calls even when only a small proportion of the public is concerned or affected. They can also give public health officials information about where to send resources, such as doctors, nurses, and prescription drugs.

Our results suggest several overarching conclusions for those planning to respond to such events. Different publics will trust different information sources. In addition, the public's response to attacks and their need for information is likely to differ according to the type of attack in question. It is important to know whom these different groups trust as a reliable source of information. Because of the high level of public trust of physicians, it is important for public health authorities to develop ongoing communications with primary care and emergency room physicians.

It is also necessary to know and address the public's specific beliefs about a biological threat. In the face of a threat, the public will make decisions based on what they believe to be true, whether or not these beliefs are true. Many times, they may be acting based on incorrect information. Likewise, it is imperative that the behavior of public leaders be consistent with their advice to the public concerning the threat and what the facts suggest should be done.

In addition, our results suggest that in a crisis people will be concerned that the government will not treat everyone equitably regardless of income or ethnicity, and the public may suspect discrimination by government and health providers against certain groups. This is particularly true among minority Americans. It will be essential for public health officials to treat all affected groups equally. It is possible that some groups will be more affected by an outbreak than others. In this case, public health officials will need to clearly explain why certain groups are being differentially treated, in order to avoid the appearance of bias.

Likewise our results suggest that when implementing a controversial policy, public health officials need to delineate, in a way that is understandable to the public, the basis of these policy choices. The widespread distrust of government decision-makers found in our studies also suggests the importance of securing endorsements from major medical and scientific leaders for government policies before they are implemented.

In: Bioterrorism: Prevention, Preparedness and Protection   ISBN 1-60021-180-1
Editor: J. V. Borrelli, pp. 83-123   © 2007 Nova Science Publishers, Inc.

Chapter 3

NANOTECHNOLOGY FOR PROTECTION FROM CHEMICAL AND BIOLOGICAL WARFARE AGENTS: SEPARATION AND DECONTAMINATION ASPECTS

Barhate Rajendrakumar Suresh[1], Ramakrishnan Ramaseshan[2], Yingjun Liu[1], Subramanian Sundarrajan[2], Neeta L. Lala[2] and Seeram Ramakrishna[1, 2, 3,]*

[1] Department of Mechanical Engineering
[2] NUS Nanoscience and Nanotechnology Initiative
[3] Division of Bioengineering, Singapore

ABSTRACT

Future war/terrorist attacks may include invisible hazards such as a variety of deadly poisonous chemicals without prior warning. Materials responsible for chemical vapor/gas decontamination in existing respirators are activated carbon impregnated with metal oxides (such as copper, zinc, molybdenum and silver). For additional protection against blood agents, triethylenediamine (TEDA) can be incorporated. Biological weapons are characterized by low visibility, high potency, substantial accessibility, and relatively easy delivery. These can be eliminated only through simple filtration by virtue of their size. So far, there is no protection system, which is both breathable and highly efficient for biodefense. Recently, there has been an increasing attention of researchers throughout the world to improve the protection from chemical and biological warfare agents. Here, we have discussed how nanotechnology comes into potential use for protection from the various warfare agents. It is extremely essential to improve the protection spectrum and decontamination capacity of existing personnel protection devices without compromising on the user friendly traits. The importance of nanomaterials for effective performance has been highlighted. Various approaches for decontamination of the warfare agents through

* Corresponding Author: Prof. Seeram Ramakrishna; Phone: +65-65162142; E Mail: seeram@nus.edu.sg; Fax: +65-67730339

fabrication of catalytic nano-filters have been described. The major requirements for supportive material for catalyst are high specific surface area, high number of binding sites which are also selective and continuous porous structures to minimize the transport limitations and increase the user comfort. Nanofibers have intrinsically high specific surface areas namely surface-to-volume or surface-to-mass values. They can be easily produced at a large from various polymeric materials by the popular method of electrospinning. The different functional modifications (both chemical and biological) of the nanofibers are explained in detail in context with the detoxification mechanism. These techniques include both polymeric and non-polymeric nanomaterials fabricated by electrospinning. Two main strategies viz. pre-spinning and post-spinning functionalization are discussed and compared. With future advances in biotechnology and material science, we can expect these "smart materials" to play an integral role in personal protection with advanced sensing abilities.

I. INTRODUCTION

Chemical Warfare Agents

Chemical Warfare Agents (CWA) generally are stored and transported as liquids and deployed as either liquid aerosols or vapors. Victims usually are exposed to agents via one or more of 3 routes: skin (liquid and high vapor concentrations), eyes (liquid or vapor), and respiratory tract (vapor inhalation) [1]. These agents are characterized by two inversely related physical properties: volatility (i.e. tendency of liquids to vaporize, which directly increases with temperature) and persistence (i.e. tendency of liquids to remain in a liquid state). In general, volatile liquids pose the dual risk of dermal and inhalation exposure, while persistent liquids are more likely to be absorbed across the skin. The effects of vapors largely are influenced by ambient wind conditions; even a slight breeze can blow nerve agent vapor away from its intended target. [2] Effects of vapor are enhanced markedly when deployed within an enclosed space. These deleterious compounds and their chemical structure are comprehensively reported in the media [3].

Classes of Chemical Agents

Nerve Agents

Among lethal CW agents, the nerve agents have had an entirely dominant role since the Second World War. Nerve agents acquired their name because they affect the transmission of nerve impulses in the nervous system. All nerve agents belong to the group of organo-phosphorus compounds. They are stable and easily dispersed, highly toxic and have rapid effects both when absorbed through the skin and via respiration. Nerve agents can be manufactured by means of fairly simple chemical techniques. The raw materials are inexpensive and generally readily available.

The nerve agents include: Tabun (NATO military designation, GA), Sarin (NATO military designation, GB), Soman (NATO military designation, GD), GF (Cyclohexyl methyl phosphonofluoridate), VX (Methylphosphonothioic acid S-(2-(bis(1-methylethyl)amino) ethyl) O-ethyl ester), GE (Phosphonofluoridic acid, ethyl-, isopropyl ester), VE (Phosphonothioic acid, ethyl-, S-(2-(diethylamino)ethyl) O-ethyl ester), VG (Amiton), VM (Phosphonothioic acid, methyl-, S-(2-(diethylamino)ethyl) O-ethyl ester). The "G" agents tend to be non-persistent whereas the "V" agents are persistent. The agents which were discovered by Germans came to be known as G agents. Some "G" agents may be thickened with various substances in order to increase their persistence, and therefore the total amount penetrating intact skin. At room temperature, GB is a comparatively volatile liquid and therefore non-persistent. GD is also significantly volatile, as is GA though to a lesser extent. VX is a relatively non-volatile liquid and therefore persistent. It is regarded as presenting little vapor hazard to people exposed to it. In the pure state nerve agents are colorless and oily liquids. In an impure state nerve agents may be encountered as yellowish to brown viscous liquids. Some nerve agents have a faint fruity odour. GB and VX doses which are potentially life-threatening may be only slightly larger than those producing least effects. Death usually occurs within 15 minutes after absorption of a fatal VX dosage (2 mg).

Although only about half as toxic as GB by inhalation, GA in low concentrations is more irritating to the eyes than GB. Symptoms appear much more slowly from a skin dosage than from a respiratory dosage. Respiratory lethal dosages kill in 1 to 10 minutes, and liquid in the eye kills almost as rapidly [4]

Blister/Vesicant Agents

Blister or vesicant agents are likely to be used both to produce casualties and to force opposing troops to wear full protective equipment thus degrading fighting efficiency, rather than to kill, although exposure to such agents can be fatal. Blister agents can be thickened in order to contaminate terrain, ships, aircraft, vehicles or equipment with a persistent hazard. Blister agents include Lewisite (L), Mustard-Lewisite (HL), Nitrogen mustards (HN-1, HN-2 and HN-3), Phosgene oxime (CX), Sulfur mustards (H, HD, HT). Normal mustard agent, bis-(2-chloroethyl)sulfide, reacts with a large number of biological molecules. The effect of mustard agent is delayed and the first symptoms do not occur until 2-24 hours after exposure [5].

Blood Agents

During and immediately after exposure, there is likely to be coughing, choking, a feeling of tightness in the chest, nausea, and occasionally vomiting, headache and lachrymation. The presence or absence of these symptoms is of little value in immediate prognosis. Some patients with severe coughs fail to develop serious lung injury, while others with little sign of early respiratory tract irritation develop fatal pulmonary edema. A period follows during which abnormal chest signs are absent and the patient may be symptom-free. This interval commonly lasts 2 to 24 hours but may be shorter. It is terminated by the signs and symptoms of pulmonary edema. Casualties may very rapidly develop severe pulmonary edema. If casualties survive more than 48 hours they usually recover. These agents include: Cyanogen chloride (CK) and Hydrogen cyanide (AC) [6].

Pulmonary Agents

Inhalation of selected organohalides, oxides of nitrogen (NOx), and other compounds can result in varying degrees of pulmonary edema, usually after a symptom-free period that varies in duration with the amount inhaled. Chemically induced acute lung injury by these groups of agents involves a permeability defect in the blood-air-barrier (the alveolar-capillary membrane); however, the precise mechanisms of toxicity remain an enigma. Perfluoroisobutylene (PFIB) is a toxic pyrolysis product of tetrafluoroethylene polymers encountered in military materiel (e.g., Teflon7, found in the interior of many military vehicles). The oxides of nitrogen (NOxs) are components of blast weapons or may be toxic decomposition products [7].

Delivery and Physical Properties

Chemical agents can be released by artillery shells, rockets, bombs, grenades, mines, aircraft sprays, and missiles [8]. Additionally, they can be sprayed from air, land, and water vehicles or covertly used to contaminate food and water supplies. Common forms of chemical agents include:

Gases and Vapors

Gases and vapors are usually invisible. However, gas clouds may be visible for a short time after their release or in areas where there is little air movement to dissipate them. Their primary route of entry is through the respiratory tract, although some agents in heavy concentrations can penetrate the eyes and exposed skin. Gases and vapors may linger for up to several hours, with heaviest concentrations occurring in low-lying, dead air spaces such as buildings, caves, shell craters, ravines, and wooded areas.

Liquids

Liquid agents can be clear to dark in color and have the viscosity of fine machine oil; thickened agents may have the appearance of motor oil. Chemical agents used in liquid form can be extremely difficult to detect with the unaided eye. The most reliable method of both detecting and identifying liquid nerve and blister agents is M8 chemical detector paper. Finally, liquid agents also release toxic vapors that can be inhaled and can remain effective for many days.

Solids (Powders)

Some agents are released in powder form. They can enter the body through the skin or be inhaled. Agents in dust-like form are released in a variety of climatic conditions and can remain effective for many weeks. These "dusty" agents are difficult to detect unless wetted. Once detected, they may be decontaminated with a 5 percent chlorine bleach solution.

Biological Warfare Agents

Biological weapons include any organism or toxin found in nature that can be used to incapacitate, kill, or otherwise impede an adversary. Biological weapons are characterized by low visibility, high potency, substantial accessibility, and relatively easy delivery. The potential spectrum of bioterrorism ranges from hoaxes and use of non–mass casualty agents by individuals or small groups to state-sponsored terrorism that employs classic biological warfare (BW) agents and can produce mass casualties. Such scenarios would present serious challenges for patient treatment and for prophylaxis of exposed persons. Environmental contamination could pose continuing threats. The use of biological agents is not a new concept, and history is replete with examples of biological weapon use. Before the 20th century, biological warfare took on 3 main forms: (1) deliberate poisoning of food and water with infectious material, (2) use of microorganisms or toxins in some form of weapon system, and (3) use of biologically inoculated fabrics.

Classes of Biological Agents: [9]

- *Bacteria*: Bacteria are small free-living organisms, most of which may be grown on solid or liquid culture media. The organisms have a structure consisting of nuclear material, cytoplasm, and cell membrane. They reproduce by simple division. The diseases they produce often respond to specific therapy with antibiotics. The bacteria are spread widely in the form of spores. The spores are extremely resistant to heat and adverse climatic conditions thereby making it tuff to decompose them. E.g. anthrax bacterial spores.
- *Viruses*: Viruses are organisms which require living cells in which to replicate. They are therefore intimately dependent upon the cells of the host which they infect. They produce diseases which generally do not respond to antibiotics but which may be responsive to antiviral compounds, of which there are few available, and those that are available are of limited use.
- *Rickettsiae*: Rickettsiae are microorganisms which have characteristics common to both bacteria and viruses. Like bacteria, they possess metabolic enzymes and cell membranes, utilize oxygen, and are susceptible to broad-spectrum antibiotics. They resemble viruses in that they grow only within living cells.
- *Chlamydia*: Chlamydia are obligatory intracellular parasites incapable of generating their own energy source. Like bacteria, they are responsive to broad-spectrum antibiotics. Like viruses, they require living cells for multiplication.
- Fungi: Fungi are primitive plants which do not utilize photosynthesis, are capable of anaerobic growth, and draw nutrition from decaying vegetable matter. Most fungi form spores, and free-living forms are found in soil. The spore forms of fungi are operationally significant. Fungal diseases may respond to various antimicrobial.
- *Toxins*: Toxins are poisonous substances produced and derived from living plants, animals, or microorganisms; some toxins may also be produced or altered by chemical means. Toxins may be countered by specific antisera and selected pharmacologic agents.

Delivery and Physical Properties

Biological agents are easy to acquire, synthesize, and use. The small amount of agents that is necessary to kill hundreds of thousands of people in a metropolitan area make the concealment, transportation, and dissemination of biological agents relatively easy. In addition, BW agents are difficult to detect or protect against; they are invisible, odorless, and tasteless, and their dispersal can be performed silently [10].

Dissemination of BW agents may occur by aerosol sprays, explosives (artillery, missiles, detonated bombs), or food or water contamination. [11] Variables that can alter the effectiveness of a delivery system include particle size of the agent, stability of the agent under desiccating conditions, UV light, wind speed, wind direction, and atmospheric stability. The use of an explosive device to deliver and disseminate biological agents is not very effective, since such agents tend to be inactivated by the blast. Contamination of municipal water supplies requires an unrealistically large amount of agent and introduction into the water after it passes through a regional treatment facility. To be an effective biological weapon, airborne pathogens must be dispersed as fine particles less than 5 mm in size. Infection with an aerosolized agent usually requires deep inspiration of an infectious dose. Advanced weapons systems (e.g. warheads, missiles) are not required for the aerosolized delivery of biological agents. Low-technology aerosolization methods including agricultural crop-dusters; aerosol generators on small boats, trucks, or cars; backpack sprayers; and even purse-size perfume atomizers suffice. Aerosolized dispersal of biological agents is the mode most likely to be used by terrorists and military groups. [12]. Detection of biological agents involves either finding the agent in the environment or medical diagnosis of the agent's effect on human or animal victims. Early detection of a biological agent in the environment allows for early specific treatment and time during which prophylaxis would be effective. Unfortunately, currently no reliable detection systems exist for BW agents. The US Department of Defense has placed a high priority on research and development of a detector system. Methods are being developed and tested to detect a biological aerosol cloud using an airborne pulsed laser system [13] to scan the lower altitudes upwind from a possible target area. A detection system mounted on a vehicle also is being developed. This system will analyze air samples to provide a plot of particle sizes, detect and classify bacterial cells, and measure DNA content, ATP content, and identify agents using immunoassays.

II. CURRENT ART FOR RESPIRATORY PROTECTION FROM CHEMICAL AND BIOLOGICAL AGENTS

Respirators are being used by civilians, industry personals and soldiers throughout the world. Doney et al. [14] have presented the survey of respirator use within the private sector of US business establishment. Military respirators differ from the civilian and industrial respirators. Military respirators are designed to achieve protection from a wide range of threats like chemical/biological, radiological and nuclear threats; while the respirators for industrial usage are designed to protect from specific hazards. Respirators for industrial usage can be constructed either using the high efficiency particulate filter or adsorbing component/s (also called as gas filter) or combinations thereof, depending upon the kind of hazard. However, military respirators always contain particulate as well as gas filters due to the requirement of filtering out the unknown threats of warfare agents. Broadly respirators can be divided into two following categories.

- *Air-supplied Respirators:* Air-supplied respirators deliver breathable air from a supply source either by the means of a hose runs from an outside source such as compressor or large air cylinder or self-contained breathing apparatus (SCBA) etc.
- *Air-purifying Respirators:* Air-purifying respirators produce breathable air through mechanical/chemical/mechanical and chemical (combination) treatments. Air purifying respirators can be further subdivided into the following types.
- *Mechanical type (Particulate respirators):* The particulate respirators contain a mask and aerosol filter (high efficiency particulate filter); these respirators can be used to filter the particulate aerosolized matter (and not the gases/vapors).
- *Chemical type (Non-particulate respirators or gas/ vapor purifying respirators):* Non-particulate respirators contain a mask and gas filter (adsorbent); these respirators can be used only in the case of the hazards for which the gas filter (adsorbent) is rated.
- *Combination type (Particulate and non-particulate respirators):* Combination type respirators contain mask, aerosol filter and gas filter; these respirators can be used for both the situations and offer the protection from the aerosolized matter as well as the gas and vapor contaminants.

Respirator Details

A typical construction of *non-power air purifying respirator* is shown in Figure 1. The respirator consists of face mask and filtering device (it could be either canister or cartridge). The only difference between canister and cartridge is the amount of adsorbent they contain. When canister/cartridge is used with a face piece, the respirator is called a gas mask. The face mask may be made up of light weight and elastic materials such as Hycar rubber [15] or Chlorobutyl rubber [16]. The face mask contains voicemitter (provision for communication), nose cup and a pair of eye-piece. The canister/cartridge is the heart of a respirator, which essentially accommodates aerosol filter (also called as *particulate filter*) and adsorptive filter (also called as *gas filter*). The only difference between a cartridge and a canister is the amount of adsorbent they contain. Cartridges contain smaller amount of adsorbent when compared to canisters.

A typical construction of canister/cartridge is shown in Figure 2. The canister/cartridge is generally cylindrical in shape with a casing of nylon or plastic like materials [17], polyamide or all sheath black nylon [18]. The top side comprises of a central opening for the passage of contaminated air to stream in; while its bottom side has 40 mm diameter outlet with the male threading to couple the face mask. The *top portion* of canister/cartridge is coupled with *bottom portion* to form a *seam*, which is accomplished by friction wielding. Lying below the *top portion* is the *sealant deflector* to deflect the sealant when injected through the inlet during spinning process. The sealant is deflected to the sides of the canister by centrifugal force to produce rings of sealant. This sealant ring encapsulates, the edges of the pleated particulate filter from top to bottom portion thus ultimately achieves the leak proof joints [17]. The material and design of a particulate filter in the respirators varies from manufacture to manufacture. Typically, particulate filter in respirators is a *high efficiency filter layer* made of pleated glass fibers, HEPA filter or other inert fibers [19]. It is arranged in the pleated (folded) fashion, thus providing the large surface area which substantially reduces pressure drop across the particulate filter.

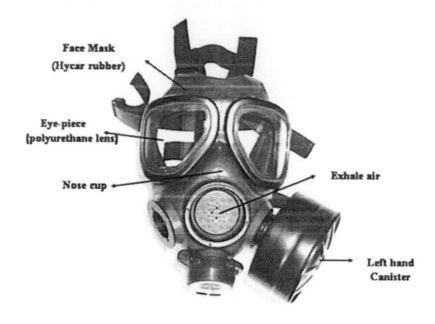

Figure 1. A Combination (Particulate & Non-Particulate Type) Respirator (Reprinted with permission from ILC Dover; www.ilcdover.com).

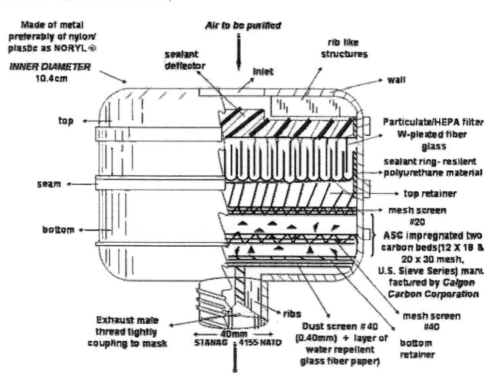

Figure 2. Typical Construction of a Canister/ Cartridge

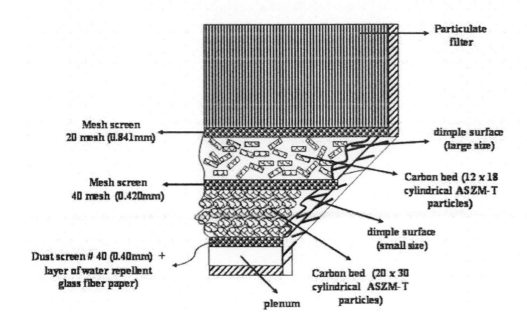

Figure 3. Cross section of a typical canister cartridge

Below the particulate filter lies the *absorbent layer/s as shown* Figure 3. The absorbent layer [20-22] is comprised of one, or two or more beds (different mesh size) of activated and impregnated charcoal material/s placed below the particulate filter. The *retainers* and *mesh screens* (top and bottom) help to keep the absorbent layer in its position. Additionally, the bottom mesh screen assists to filter off the dust from the activated charcoal. The size, shape, packing density and the extent of activation (physical treatment to increase the porosity and surface area) of adsorbents/s are noteworthy in controlling the adsorptive surface area of adsorbents. Charcoal can be impregnated with the metals like copper, silver [23], chromium, [24] tungsten and molybdenum, vanadium, etc; [25] and chelating agents like triethylenediamine (TEDA) [26] in suitable proportions. Military grade adsorbents are ASC-TEDA (copper-silver-chromium-triethylenediamine impregnated charcoal media) [21] and ASZM-TEDA (copper-silver-zinc-molybdenum-triethylenediamine impregnated charcoal media) [27, 28]. ASC-TEDA is no longer in use since chromium is suspected to be carcinogenic by NIOSH of U.S. [29]. Calgon Corporation Inc. USA, [30] is a major supplier of military grade adsorbent for the canister. The *mesh screens* not larger than #20 U.S. sieves (0.841mm) are used to separate the coarse and fine adsorbent layer adsorbent layer from the particulate filter. The carbon bed of sieve#12 x 18 (upstream side) and 20 x 30 (downstream side) cylindrical ASZM-T carbon particles are separated by the *mesh screen* not larger than #40 U.S.sieve (0.420mm). This mesh screen serves to separate the particles of two different sizes of the carbon bed. Mesh screens are made of high strength thermoplastic or aluminum or steel. The interior wall of the bottom portion has large and small sized *dimpled surfaces* which are formed by the rolling process serving to hold the different sized and packing density of adsorbent material. At the bottom lies the *dust screen* of the similar mesh size # 40 U.S. sieve being placed between the downstream side of the carbon bed and plenum with a layer of water repellant glass fiber. This water repellent filter layer prevents the entry of moisture from exhaled air into the adsorbent. Depending on the requirement of the user, many design and construction parameters are constantly being modified.

III. STANDARDS FOR AIR PURIFYING CBRN RESPIRATORS

Materials used for manufacturing of protective respirators (particularly filters) should meet various requirements like they should retain their integrity during the course of application i.e. they should not degrade during usage time. The canister used in respirators for protection from CBRN warfare agents should excellently resist permeation (molecular passage) and penetration (non molecular passage) of these warfare agents through it. Other important concerns while designing CBRN canister for non-powered air purifying negative pressure respirators are breathing (air flow) resistance and protection duration and efficiency.

Breathing Resistance

The pressure drop across a respiratory facemask (ΔP) indicates resistance for breathing while using that mask. The higher ΔP values, the more difficult is to breathe through mask. ΔP is required to move a given mass of air, which is flow rate dependent. In order to make a quantitative comparison between the different masks for breathing ability, it is necessary to specify air flow rate (more precisely, a face velocity of air if faced cross sectional area of filter in the canister varies) during the course of measurement of ΔP. For example, at 85 liters/min air flow rate, a pressure drop of about 800 Pa is observed in case of vintage mask, which was used in World War II. At the same flow rate, the pressure drop for the M17 and M40 masks are 450 Pa and 500 Pa, respectively [31]. By way of contrast, breathing at a rate of 85 L/min without a mask creates a pressure drop of 150 Pa [32].

The air flow rate used in US Testing protocols during dates back to the First World War for measuring breathing resistances was 42.5 liters/minute. The resistance values in Federal rules and regulations (1995) are reported at air flow rate of 85 ±2 Liters per minutes, this flow rate is recommended later for measurement of resistance [33]. Federal rules and regulations of US (1995) state that the inhalation and exhalation resistances for the particulate type of respirators should not exceed by 300 Pa and 200 Pa, respectively; while for non-particulate type of respirators (for gas/vapor removal) like chemical cartridge respirators, maximum initial inhalation resistance is 400 Pa. A small increase in maximum allowable breathing resistance for particulate respirators does not add substantially to physiologic burden for respirator users and often it compensates by offering increased protection. Industry standard for a face mask typically accepts pressure drop of 15 to 20 Pa across the filtration media and about 20 to 40 Pa across the complete face mask [34]. Japanese standard states that the inhalation resistance of gas mask without canister and cartridge should not exceed 70 Pa at 40 liters/min air flow rate for front or back mounted type gas masks, while for chin-style gas masks and cartridge respirators it should not exceed 50 Pa at 40 liters/min air flow rate [35]. The above Japanese standard also states the maximum acceptable inhalation resistance for various types of canisters/cartridges, which is given in the following table:

Table 1. Maximum Acceptable Inhalation Resistances

Category	Type of gas mask		Acceptable ΔP limit (max) across canister or cartridge at 40 L/min air flow rate (in Pa)		
			Front or back mounted type gas mask	Chin-style gas mask	Chemical-cartridge respirator
For carbon monoxide	With particulate filtration function	S1 &L1	310	-	-
		S2 &L2	320	-	-
		S3 &L3	400	-	-
	Without particulate filtration function		280	-	-
For gases other than carbon monoxide	With particulate filtration function	S1 &L1	310	280	280
		S2 &L2	320	290	290
		S3 &L3	400	370	370
	Without particulate filtration function		250	220	220

From the above table, it can be noted that when HEPA filter is combined with adsorptive filter (like carbon bed as in case of the particulate respirators), ΔP across canister or cartridge increases by 30 to 150 Pa depending upon the particles rejection efficiency of HEPA filter in the canister or cartridge. National Institute of Occupational Safety and Health (NIOSH) has a specification for the allowed pressure drop across a respirator filter, which manufactures must meet in order to get the NIOSH certification for that product.

A few standards define resistance across the facemask and filter media especially for military application [36-39]. The commercial military product, Avon NBC Filter Canister AMF12 (NATO Stock No. 4240-21-912-5397), shows pressure drop of 95, 170 and 300 Pa at 30, 50 and 85 liter/min airflow rate. The new National Institute for Occupational Safety and Health (NIOSH) CBRN standard for full-facepiece gas masks was issued on March 7, 2003. NIOSH respiratory standards development program defined the maximum allowable air resistance for the CBRN canister at inhalation airflow of 85 liters/minute, which should be less than or equal to 500 Pa [40]. This program also defined the maximum allowable air resistance for the face piece of air purifying CBRN (chemical, biological, radiological, and nuclear) respirator at air flow rate of 85 liters per minute, which is given in table2.

Table 2. Maximum Allowable Resistance for the Face-piece of CBRN Respirator

Parameter		Resistance (Pa)	
		Chin Style	Non Facepiece Mounted
Inhalation	Initial	650 Pa	700 Pa
	Final (at the end of service)	800 Pa	850 Pa
Exhalation		200 Pa	200 Pa

If an application requires strict filtration requirements, then user should select a HEPA filter with a labeled efficiency number of 100 [41]. Any HEPA filters certified under

NIOSH's current part 84 requirements are generally acceptable for negative pressure air purifying respirator for protection against all aerosols, mists, fumes, and dusts.

Particulate Filtration Efficiency

The new NIOSH 'part 84' regulation classified the particulate filters into the nine classes depending upon the oil resistance and efficiency of the particulate filter used in the respirators. Firstly, filters are graded into three categories depending on the oil degradation resistance namely N-series, R-series and P-series. N-series filters are not resistant to oil, while R-series filters are resistant to oil and P-series filters are oil-proof. Secondly, filters are graded further into three subcategories depending on their efficiency for (0.3 micron size) particulate retention namely moderate filtering efficiency (95%), high filtering efficiency (99%) and highest filtering efficiency (99.97%). So, the nine classes of particulate filters are named as follows: N95, N99, N100, R95, R99, R100, P95, P99 and P100. For CBRN respirator, filter should meet the requirements of P100 particulate filter as described in Federal rules and regulations, 42 CFR, Part 84 paragraphs 84.170, 84.179 and 84.181 [42]. The nuclear grade, high density, high efficiency, particulate air filter goes much further with retention efficiency of 99.999% for 0.12 um sized particles [43].

Federal rule recommends neutralized-dioctyl phthalate (DOP) or equivalent liquid aerosol for testing the particulate filtration efficiency of "P" series filters, at the following testing conditions: flow rate of air 84±4 liters/min, temperature 25±5°C, concentration of aerosol less than 200 mg/m^3 and particle size distribution with count median diameter between 0.185±0.02 micrometer and a standard geometric deviation not exceeding 1.60. According to Federal rules, 20 filters should qualify a criteria indicated in paragraph 84.181 of 42 CFR, Part 84 and 6 additional filters should be environmentally conditioned as specified in section 4.4.9 Environmental Conditioning before testing. The above rule also states that minimum efficiency of each tested filter is to be greater than or equal to 99.97% for P100. The particulate filtration efficiency of filter depends upon the size of particles and flow rate of air [44] and of course the filter morphology. Federal rules are more thorough and are still recommended by NIOSH for testing particulate filtration ability of filters.

Gas/Vapor Adsorption Efficiency

The air purifying respirator should resist the permeation and penetration of Distilled Sulfur Mustard (HD) and Sarin (GB) at least for 8 hours when tested by mounting on "smartman" and connecting to a breathing machine operating at an air flow rate of 40 liters per minute (L/min), 36 respirations per minute, 1.1 liters tidal volume. In order to qualify criteria for CBRN protection, respirator should resist the permeation and penetration of HD and GB vapor at least for 8 hour when tested at the test conditions (NIOSH CBRN Respirator Standards Development for Full face piece air purifying respirators indicated in Table 3 (APR) to protect emergency response workers against CBRN agents. [40]

Table 3. Vapor Challenge Test Conditions for CBRN Respirators

Vapor challenge	Challenge Concentration (mg/m^3)	Vapor Challenge duration (min)	Breathing Rate (L/min)	Maximum Peak Excursion (mg/m^3)	Max Breakthrough (conc integrated over minimum service life) $(mg\text{-}min/m^3)$	No. of Systems Tested	Minimum Service Life (hours)
HD	50	30	40	0.300	3.00	3	8
GB	210	30	40	0.044	1.05	4	8

Since sarin (GB) is the most weakly adsorbed among all the nerve agents and mustard agents, a stimulant dimethylmethylphosphonate (DMMP) performance is an adequate assessment of an activated carbon's ability to filter all nerve and mustard agents [45].

IV. Specifications and Performance of Canisters

Specification

The cartridge/canister may be cylindrical or elliptical convex in shape [17]. The cartridge/canister has standard 40 mm diameter outlet [29] and 1/8 inch the male threading [46] to couple with the face mask. Typically, cylindrical cartridge/canister has the inner diameter of 10 to 11 cm and a casing of nylon/plastic. Often, the diameter of canister is restricted below 11 cm due to wearer vision provision. The weight of canister varies from 250 to 300 grams depending upon the weight of adsorbent in the adsorptive filter layer. Most of the canisters contain 100 to 105 g of adsorbent packed in 1.7-1.8 cm thick layer [47]. The canisters/cartridges contain a pleated (folded) particulate air filter and an activated impregnated charcoal bed through which the canister absorbs toxic gases and removes particles of a size (0.15 to 5   m) that constitute a toxicological threat [48].

A HEPA grade P- series filter of Minimum Efficiency Reporting Value (MERV) from 17 to 20 is useful for the particulate filtration in protective mask. HEPA media used in military mask consist of a nonwoven sheet of glass fibers and polymeric fibers ranging in diameter from about 0.5 to 10 microns [49]. HEPA/ULPA filters in accordance with EN 1822 have thickness less than 1 mm [50]. Particulate filter media's thickness varies greatly from manufacture to manufacture, however it can be typically considered between 0.57 mm and 1 mm. HEPA filter offer a relatively high resistance (minimum final resistance of 350 Pa when tested as per the procedure of ASHRAE standard 52.2-1999) to air flow (ASHRAE Testing for HVAC Air Filtration: Standard 52.2-1999, The American Society of Heating, Refrigeration and Air Conditioning Engineers (ASHRAE)). Hollingsworth and Vose Company supplies particulate filters to US and Canadian military for preparation of M-4 gas masks [51]. The canisters contain a pleated P-100 filter to remove chemical/biological particulates, radio-nuclides and other solid particulates. It may be arranged in pleated, rosette or pad manner [52]. The pleated arrangement is generally preferred as it provides large surface area with a low pressure drop with increasing the filtration efficiency. Pleated arrangement of filter considerably reduces the pressure drop (air resistance) across the particulate air filter. The air flow resistance can be reduced by 35 to 50 % by pleating the particulate filter. The high efficiency particulate filter (HEPA) provides 99.97% filtration efficiency at 0.3μm particle size.

Coconut shell derived microstructure (pore size from 0.5 to 4 nm) activated charcoal having specific surface area above to 1000 m²/g and mesh size 12X18 to 20X50 is being used for the preparation of adsorbent for the canister. The mesh size of charcoal granule controls the absorptive surface area and its activity. Smaller granules are more effective due to large surface area. The size, shape, packing density and the extent of activation are critical in controlling the adsorptive surface area of adsorbents. In the adsorbent manufacturing process, these charcoal granules are impregnated with metals like copper, silver, zinc, chromium, tungsten, molybdenum, vanadium and complexing agents like triethylenediamine (TEDA) in suitable proportions to carry out catalytic degradation (decontamination) of chemical warfare agents on the adsorbent. Impregnation of these metal ions on the activated charcoal also enhances the ability of adsorbent to adsorb the chemical warfare agents. The Centers for Disease Control and Prevention and the National Institute for Occupation Safety and Health have identified hexavalent chromium (CrVI) as potential human carcinogen [53]. Therefore, presently respirator manufacturers prefer chromium free adsorbents. The impregnant loading on ASZM-TEDA carbon is copper as cupric carbonate (5 %), silver in elemental form (0.05 %), zinc as zinc carbonate (5%), molybdenum as ammonium dimolybdate (2%) and triethylenediamine (3%) [49]. The impregnant loading on adsorbent for decontamination of chemical warfare agents is 7.23 % Cu, 2.92 % Cr and 0.051 % Ag and 4.7 % TEDA [26]. The quantity of metal ions on the adsorbent determines the total adsorptive filtration capabilities; while the quantity of individual metal ions on the adsorbent determines its decontamination capability for a specific category of chemical warfare agents. Commercial military grade adsorbents are ASZM-TEDA, ASC and LC-HA; supplied by Calgon Carbon Corporation, USA (www.waterlink.com). The trade name "ASZM-TEDA" denotes its impregnation composition: Copper (A), Silver (S), Zinc (Z), Molybdenum (M) and triethylenediamine (TEDA) [30]. The adsorbent packing density varies from 85 to 115 % of a bulk density of the activated carbon as measured in accordance with ASTM Standard D 2854-96 (US Patent No. 6840986). The anterior wall of the canister is often dimpled to afford greater packing density of adsorbent [29].

Performance

The canister performs filtration operation at particulate (non-molecular) and non-particulate/gaseous (molecular) levels. The particulate filtration is achieved by HEPA filter; while non-particulate/gas filtration is achieved by efficient impregnated adsorbent layer. Particulate filtration media provides filtration efficiency at least 99.97 % for 0.3   m size particulate. The filtration efficiency of the HEPA media does not depend on the physical state (solid or liquid) of aerosol. The particulate filtration efficiency increases with the particulate loading on the media. This increase occurs because the spaces between fibers, which reduce as particles, accumulate over the filter media. However, accumulation of particle over filter media has a negative effect on the air flow resistance of filter. Factors which greatly contribute to the variability in the aerosol capacity are air flow velocity through the media (can be manipulated by pleating) and extents of accumulation of particulates over filter media. The nature of the particulate material also affects the air flow resistance. Particulates which are hygroscopic or water mist greatly build the airflow resistance on the filter media because of adhesion and clumping. NBC particulate filtration can remove low volatile liquids (tear gas and nerve agents) in addition to biological agents and radioactive particles [49].

The adsorptive filter (vapor filter) consists of efficient impregnated adsorbent, which can adsorb both the low and high volatile chemical warfare agents. Metals ions impregnated on adsorbent trigger the catalytic breakdown of toxic gases into non-toxic byproducts. The detailed mechanisms of degradation can be viewed from literature [54-56]. These metal ions of suitable valence help in decontamination of chemical warfare agents by physical adsorption in the pores of the activated carbon and chemical reaction with the impregnant. This method is highly effective because it involves chemical decontamination of the warfare agents. The ASZM- TEDA carbon provides a high level of protection against all the chemical agents listed in FM 3-9 entitled "Potential Military Chemical/Biological Agents and Compounds". The vapor filtration performance of the adsorbent primarily depends on two factors like vapor pressure of warfare agents and reaction chemistry (including kinetics) of decontamination reaction. Chemicals with low vapor pressure are effectively filtered by physical adsorption alone. As a general rule of the thumb, chemicals with a vapor pressure below 10 mmHg (at the temperature of the filter) are effectively removed by physical adsorption into the pores of the activated carbon. As one considers the higher vapor pressure of chemicals the ability of the sorbent to remove the contaminant by physical adsorption alone decreases, in such cases, reaction with the impregnant is necessary for effective overall filtration performance. The filtration efficiency for chemical vapors by the NBC filters is generally 99.999% [49].This level of protection has to be provided by adsorbent at all ambient levels of temperature and humidity except when near 100% relative humidity. The entry of moisture in the adsorbent layer deteriorates its performance against chemical warfare agents. An NBC adsorptive filter does not provide significant protection against vapors of many chemicals with vapor pressures greater than 100mmHg. Exceptions would be the organic chemicals which react with the impregnant on the carbon surface to produce breakdown products which are either non-hazardous or are retained by the adsorbent.

V. THEORETICAL ASPECTS OF FILTRATION AND DECONTAMINATION OF WARFARE AGENTS

Particulate Filtration

Particulate filtration serves the suspended particulates from air stream by the virtue of size, shape and charge of particulate, on the other hand, adsorptive filtration removes gases or vapors from air by adsorption of high diffusive molecules.

The particulate filtration can be characterized by the pressure drop Δp and the efficiency E of the filter. The pressure drop Δp of a filter can be defined by

$$\Delta p = p_1 - p_2$$

(Where p_1 and p_2 stand for pressures at measurement points 1 and 2 respectively)

The filter efficiency E can be defined by

$$E = \frac{G_1 - G_2}{G_1}$$

Where G_1 is the flux of particles into the filter, G_2 the flux of particles from the filter The related quantity is the penetration of the filter P, which can be defined by

$$P = 1 - E$$

For comparison of different filters, the filter quality Q, is often used, which is defined by

$$Q = \frac{-\ln P}{\Delta p}$$

When considering the distribution of particulate sizes, another approach is also used to compare the quality of different filters. It is defined by

$$P = \left(\frac{\theta}{\theta + \Delta p} \right)^{\gamma} \quad (\mu = \frac{\gamma}{\theta}, \; \sigma = \frac{\sqrt{\gamma}}{\theta})$$

where μ is the mean value of different size of particulate, σ is their standard deviation, θ is another parameter.

In order to solve the application problems it is necessary to express both the pressure drop and the filter efficiency as a function of the quantities, which describe the properties of the particles, dispersing fluid and filter.

Flow Field and Pressure Drop in Porous Filters

There are two theories of particulate filters. The first is the channel theory, wherein the porous membrane structure can be modeled as a system of capillaries and the fluid flow through a circular capillary can be described by Poiseuille's Law. This theory is more appropriate for high packing-density filters. The second is the drag theory, wherein the porous membrane structure can be considered as a realistic geometric model, which is simple enough to calculate the velocity field. By the velocity distribution in the porous membrane structure, the drag force acting on a small piece of representative defined as structural unit in membrane structure can be determined for a given pressure drop.

A certain structure of a filter has been modeled by Piekaar and Clarenburg [57], Wilkinson and Davies [58] where the airflow adopted a certain flow pattern. Once the flow pattern is known, the pressure drop across the filter can be calculated. From this information the behavior of entrained particles in the membrane structure can be derived, leading to a better understanding of particle capture mechanisms and enabling to calculate values of single fiber efficiency.

The behavior of the airflow in a filter media can be affected by four of its intrinsic properties: mass, viscosity, elasticity, and molecular properties. Here, we follow the pathway that consider an incompressible, viscous, steady flow and then bring into correction for the molecular effect.

Fluid Flow Around an Isolated Fiber

Filter should not only sieve out large particles, but also could capture particles that are far too smaller than the interfiber spaces. Therefore, particle capture mechanism must consider just one fiber; and for this reason, single fiber theory must be considered firstly.

The starting point for calculation of the velocity field is Oseen's approximation of the Navier-Stokes' equation. The exact solution for Oseen's equations for a cylinder was obtained by Bairstow et al. [59]. The approximation arrived by Lamb [60] is usually employed. And starting from a different approximation of the velocity field around a cylinder, Davies [61] also obtained the same result.

Fluid Flow through Ordered System of Fibers

Since the effect of nearby fibers can not be neglected, it will be more appropriate to consider the fluid flow in a system of fibers. Depending upon the order of arrangement of fibers, direction of flow field and porosity of membrane structure, fluid flow various.

One-dimension Array of Parallel Fibers

For high-porosity system, the velocity field and drag on a single cylinder in a high-porosity row of parallel, equidistant circular fibers was investigated by Tamada and Fujikawa [62, 63], using Oseen's approximations and simplified by Miyagi [64]. For a low-porosity system, Keller [65] gave a theoretical discussion.

Two-dimension Array of Parallel Fibers

(1) High-porosity system
(a) Transverse flow

    The cell models for transverse flow are discussed in detail by Happel and Brenner [66]. Each cylinder is assumed to be surrounded by a concentric circular fiber and some of the boundary conditions are specified on the surface of this cell. Kuwabara [67] assumed that vorticity vanishes at the cell surface and Happel [68] assumed that the velocity at the cell surface is zero. The velocity field in high-porosity system of parallel cylinders for a square arrangement of cylinders was investigated by Hasimoto [69]. A different approach to calculation of the velocity field in a system of cylinders was suggested by Spielman and Goren [70].

(b) Longitudinal flow

The velocity field, for fluid flow parallel with the axes of fibers, has been investigated by Happel for a unarranged structure [68]; Emersleben for a square structure [71]; by Sparrow and Loefler for a triangular arrangement [72].

(2) Low-porosity system

Approximation of the velocity field for transverse flow in low-porosity systems of parallel cylinders has been described by Fuchs [73] and later by Keller [74].

Fluid Flow through Random System of Fibers

Moreover, all the research work above pertained to modeling of fiber orientations in porous membrane structure and fluid flow around the fiber do not consider realistic structure fibrous membrane. For instance: (1) diameters of fibers in the filter have a distribution (2) fibers are non-parallel in fibrous structure (3) interfiber distance greatly varies in the fibrous structure etc. There is a need to solve this complex problem by considering three dimensional structure of fibrous media and distribution of fiber diameter in the given structure.

Langmuir [75] investigated a system of parallel cylinders to account for the nonparallel orientation of fibers with respect to the gas flow. Iberall [76] assumed that cylindrical fibers are equi-partitioned in three perpendicular directions, one of which is the direction of flow. Reynolds number dependent pressure drop was determined by the application of Lamb's equation for the drag of isolated cylinder. Fardi and Liu calculated the flow pattern and pressure drop across a porous system with rectangular fibers by numerical methods [77]. Brown used a variation method to give arise to the lowest rate of dissipation of energy by viscous drag as an alternative both to numerical methods and to the method of solving a flow equation, then derived the stream function indirectly [78]. Later he generalized this method to describe the flow through pleat filters [79]. Yu and Soong quantified the flow through heterogeneous filter in directions perpendicular to the flow by dividing the filter into sections parallel to the flow direction [80]. Heterogeneous filters in both directions parallel and perpendicular to the flow was investigated by Lajos based on discrete elements in two-dimension and three-dimension [81].

Empirical / Semiempirical Equations

Some empirical / semiempirical equations were suggested by Davies [82], Sullivan [83], Silverman and First [84]. Blasewitz and Judson [85], Whitby et. al [86] and others, which are summarized by Chen [87] and Billings [88]

Knudsen Region Correction

Natanson calculated the velocity around an isolated, infinitely long cylinder placed perpendicular to gas flow by taking into account the gas slipping at the surface of cylinder and derived the force acting on unit length of the cylinder [89]. Pich [90] generalized Kuwabara's boundary conditions in order to include the slip effect and derived an equation describing the velocity field in a system of parallel cylinders at low Knudsen number. Based on this velocity field, he derived the equation of pressure drop. Spielman and Goren came theoretically to the same conclusion using the Brinkman model [91]. Wheat, Werner and Clarenburg [92] suggested empirical formulas, using the Knudsen-Webber correction [93].

Filtration Mechanisms and Estimation of Efficiency

Capture mechanisms of particulates in fibrous porous media include various mechanisms like diffusional deposition (which the combined action of airflow and Brownian motion brings a particle into contact with a fiber), direct interception (which involves a particle following a streamline and being captured if the particulate comes into contact with the fiber), inertial impaction (which capture is effected b the deviation of a particle from a streamline because of its own inertia), electrostatic deposition (which the electrostatic attractive force between the airborne particles and the fiber rises to a primary position) and gravitational settling.

Each of the above mechanisms is described by one or several dimensionless parameters, the numerical value of which determines the intensity of the individual mechanisms in the filter performance. Each dimensionless parameter corresponds to a capture coefficient that quantitatively describes the rate of particle retention by fibrous media due to the given mechanism. If several mechanisms are operating simultaneously, the filter efficiency is an unknown function of partial capture coefficients.

$$E = f(E_D, E_R, E_I, ...)$$

Where E is the total capture efficiency, E_D is the capture coefficient due to diffusional deposition, E_R is the capture coefficient due to direct interception, E_I is the capture coefficient due to inertial impaction.

Diffusion Mechanism

The capture coefficient E_D, describing the particle deposition on a single cylinder or in a system of cylinders due to particle diffusion, is a function of the Peclet number Pe, which can be defined by

$$Pe = ReSc = \frac{d_f U_0}{D}$$

The case of the isolated cylinder is discussed by Stechkina [94] for Pe<<1, Re<1; by Langmuir [75], Friedlander [95], Natanson [96], Torgeson [97] and Stechkina [98] for Pe>>1, Re<1; by Boussinesq [99], Lewis and Smith [100], Stairmand [101] and Natanson [96].

The first calculation of diffusion deposition in a system of parallel cylinders was reported by Fuchs and Stechikina using the Natanson's equation and employing the Kuwabara-Happel velocity field [102]. Spielman and Goren adapted Natanson's solution to their velocity field for different structure of filters [103].

Experiments on diffusion deposition have been reported in two model filters by Kirsch and Fuchs [104] and in real filters by Sadoff and Almolf [105]. These findings lead to the conclusion that the capture coefficient is related exponentially to filter solidity by the index of −0.4. On the other hand, Kirsch and Fuchs [104] concluded that compressing the filter does not change E_D.

Direct Interception Mechanism

The mechanism of direct interception is characterized by a dimensionless parameter N_R, which is equal to the ratio of d_p to d_f. The capture coefficient due to direct interception E_R is a function of N_R. The potential flow around an isolated cylinder was investigated by Natanson [89] and Gillespie [106]. The vicous flow through a series of cylinders was investigated by Langmuir [107] and Pich [108] and Stechkina et al. [109] with different hydrodynamic factors.

Experimental investigation of the direct interception mechanism has been reported by Radushkevich and Kolganov [110] and concluded that E_R increases linearly with N_R with a coefficient less than 2.

Inertial Mechanism

In continuum region, the capture coefficient E_{IR} is a function of Reynolds number of cylinder Re, interception parameter N_R, inertia parameter Stk, and $\phi*$ (accounts the conditions where velocities or particles are very high that particle drag cannot be described by Stokes' law), i.e. $E_{IR}= f(Re, N_R, Stk, \phi*)$. When particle diameter can be neglected in comparison with the cylinder diameter, then the coefficient E_{IR} deduces to the capture coefficient E_I describing pure inertial impaction., so that $E_I=f(Re, Stk, \phi*)$. Furthermore, for Stokes particles, $E_I=f(Re, Stk)$; and for potential flow, $E_I=f(Stk)$.

Impaction on isolated cylinder in viscous flow has been studied for different Re by Davies and Peetz [82, 111], which shows that the capture coefficient is the lowest in viscous flow for any value of Stk. Yoshioka et al. calculated the capture coefficient E_{IR} for Re=0.2, 0.5, 1.0 for $0.06<N_R<1$ and $0<Stk<\infty$, using Lamb's velocity field [112], and then extended for the whole range of Reynolds numbers as a function of Re, Stk, and N_R [113] Householder and Goldschmit calculated the capture coefficient E_{IR} for Re=0.2 for $N_R=1\sim7$ as a function of Re, N_R and ρ_p/ρ_g, using Davies' approximation for the velocity field around a cylinder [114].

For a cylinder system, Dawson calculated the capture coefficient E_{IR} for $0<Stk<20$, $0.01<N_R<0.2$ and $0.005<\beta<0.2$ using the Spielman-Goren velocity field and found E_{IR} is a increasing function of all three parameters [115]. Harrop and Stenhouse calculated the capture coefficient E_{IR} as a function of Stk at $N_R=0.05$ and β of 0.01, 0.03, 0.06 and 0.11 using the Happel's velocity field and found E_{IR} is a increasing function of all three parameters [116].

Stechikina et al., using Kuwabara's velocity field and assuming Stk<<1, calculated the capture coefficient E_{IR} for $0.01 < N_R < 0.4$ and $0.0035 < \beta < 0.111$ [109].

Electrostatic Mechanisms

Three cases of coulombic attraction between charged particle and charged fiber, neutral particles and charged fiber, charged particles and neutral fiber are described by Gillespie [106] and Natanson [96]. Different expressions of dimensionless parameter N_E due to the above three cases are given by Ranz and Wong [117] and Pich [118].

External Electric Field Absent

The capture coefficient in the case of charged particle and charged fiber E_{Qq} was derived by Kraemer and Johnstone [119], Natanson [96] and Torgeson [120]. Levin derived a general equation describing the deposition of charged particles on charged cylinders of arbitrary shape [121]. The capture coefficient in the case of neutral particles and charged fiber E_{q0} was derived by Natanson [96]. The capture coefficient in the case of charged particles and neutral fiber E_{q0} was derived by Natanson and Whitby and Liu [122]

Selective Characteristic

The selective characteristic of a filter is defined as a dependence of the capture coefficient or particle size. This dependence has been studied theoretically by several authors [107, 109, 123-125], .Total pressure drop Δp across a unit volume of a filter with a uniform thickness is the total force on the fibers [126, 127].

VI. DESIGN AND DEVELOPMENT OF CANISTERS

Filter designers have a responsibility to provide suitable designs for the canister, which should increase the level of protection and decrease the air flow resistance. Rigorous optimization of the level of protection needs to be undertaken without compromising in the air flow resistance. Before proposing any new design or incorporating change in the existing design, it is necessary to understand how the physical dimensions of the particulate filter and adsorbent bed affect the level of protection and air flow resistance. The particulate filter used for the military grade protective respiratory mask should have retention efficiency above to 99.97 % for liquid droplets (challenge particles of DOP) and solid particles (challenge particles of NaCl) of 0.3 microns mass median aerodynamic diameter. Therefore, particulate filter should be of High Efficiency Particulate Air (HEPA) grade (MERV rating from 17 to 20). At the same time, the particulate filter (of above specifications often designated as P100) should preferably offer air resistance below 160 Pa at air flow rate of 85 liter/min. The filter which meets the former criterion often fails to meet later one. In order to meet later criterion, canister manufactures are folding the HEPA grade filter in a variety of configurations or arrangements in given space in the canister. The folding (called as pleating) of particulate filter considerably increases surface area thereby reduces the pressure drop across it and helps the mask wearer to breath normal without increasing efforts during breathing. This also permits use of more efficient grade of particulate filter. The pleating arrangement also increases the apparent thickness of the particulate filter medium relative to the angle of approaching particles.

The pleating of filter is an important advance in the design and development of particulate filter and is not clearly discussed in the open literature. Canister manufactures keep this information as a trade secret. The material of filter media (more particularly fibers) should meet the following requirements:

- Filter media should facilitate easy bending so as to pleat the filter.
- Filter media should be sufficiently rigid to withstand the specific pleat geometry during course of filtration. In another words, air flow during filtration should not affect geometry of pleated particulate filter.
- Filter media should be sufficiently water repellent so as to minimize accumulation of water droplets/mist on its surface (exposed to ambient air) and helps to keep low pressure drop across the filter during course of filtration.

Water repellent micro glass fibrous material is of low pressure loss type; furthermore it posses high particle holding capacity, hence widely used for the manufacturing of particulate filter. HEPA filter media of 0.56 mm thick was used for the preparation of pleated particulate filter [128]. The particulate filter can be mounted in the canister in variety of arrangements. Most preferred arrangement is shown in Figure 4 and Figure 5. The annular filtering assembly is formed from a thin glass fibrous media folded to provide a number of circumferentially spaced radially extending pleats and inner edges of the pleats are bonded together at central opening as shown in Figure 5. This arrangement considerably reduces the pressure drop across the filter; furthermore it helps to utilize area of filter optimally in a given space in the canister [129], hence widely preferred in most of the canisters.

In pleated arrangement, area of filter can be increased by increasing number of pleats. However, there is practical limit to this due to the diameter of central opening within the pleated annular filter. For a given diameter of the pleated filter, the maximum numbers of pleats (n) can be determined from the following equation [128].

$$n = \frac{\pi d}{4t}$$

Where, "d" is the filter diameter and "t" is the filter thickness.

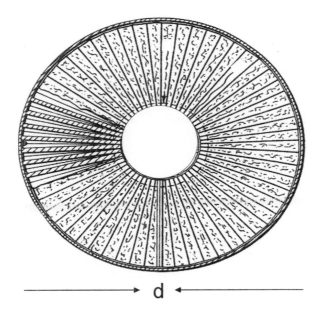

Figure 4. Arrangement of Pleats in a Particulate Filter (Top View)

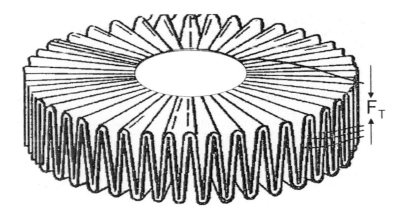

Figure 5. Arrangement of Pleats in a Particulate Filter (Side View)

It was found that when filter was pleated by using above formula, it did not give the lowest possible air flow resistance [128]. This may be due to close packing of pleats, which drive considerable amount of air over the surface of pleated filter rather than passing through it. So, air has to overcome additional resistance due to the friction before passing through the filter media. This increases the pressure drop across the filter media while filtering the air.

For a typical filter media of 0.56 mm thick and diameter in the range of 75 to 120 mm and pleat height in the range of 10 to 27 mm, optimum numbers of pleats (N) to achieve minimum air flow resistance can be arrived by the following empirical formula [128].

$$N = 14d + \frac{5d}{\sqrt{F_T}}$$

Where, "d" is a numerical value equal to the diameter of annular filter element in inches and "F_T" is a numerical value equal to pleat height or depth in inches.

Figure 6 shows "V-shaped" pleat. Pleat geometry can be described by distance between two consecutive pleats (F_B), pleat height (F_T) and angle between the edges of filter media in the pleat (α) as shown in the figure 6.

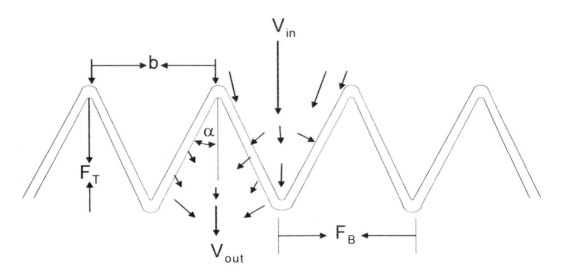

Figure 6. 'V' Shaped Pleat Geometry

The effect of pleat geometry on the pressure drop across the filter media can be studied by considering the following three types of pressure drops:-

1. Pressure drop inside the pleat (ΔP_F) due to friction losses and dynamic pressure gain;
2. Pressure drop while entering and leaving the pleat due to contraction (ΔP_E) and expansion (ΔP_A) in cross sectional area;
3. Pressure drop (ΔP_M) while flowing through filter medium due to material properties and its packing density and flow velocity.

Caesar and Schroth [130] derived equations for the estimation of the above pressure drops, these equations can be solved either analytically or numerically. The total pressure drop across the pleated filter can be determined by summation of the estimated pressure drops (ΔP_F, ΔP_E, ΔP_A and ΔP_M). Optimal pleating can reduce the air flow resistance by 35 to 50 % of unpleated filter.

VII. POTENTIAL ROLE OF NANOTECHNOLOGY IN DESIGNING A PROTECTIVE SYSTEM

Recent terrorist strikes prove that chemical and biological attacks are more than just an academic possibility. Because of the deadly threat that is posed by the chemical and biological agents, enormous efforts will need to be focused on the protection of military and civilian personnel. Current decontamination protocols, including the use of incineration and chemical decontamination solutions that may be ideal for decommissioning chemical stockpiles or decontaminating large areas after chemical or biological exposure are not effective for the protection of personnel. The development of a new generation of biomaterials is required that can simultaneously act as a barrier, a reporter, and a decontaminator for both chemical and biological weapons. Such materials should be active on contact with an agent and retain activity over long periods of time.

Several current lines of research are pursuing the development of self decontaminating materials that offer, a passive means of protecting, personnel and equipment from chemical and biological agents. Currently, these materials do not have the ability to sense the presence of the agent. New materials that are selective and specific are on the horizon. With future advances in biotechnology and material science, we can expect these "smart materials" to play an integral role in personal protections. These types of materials will find uses not only in the defense industry, but in the biomedical, food, and chemical industries as well. The merging of biotechnology with materials science offers a wide range of possibilities for the design of advanced materials that are only now being investigated.

Collective Protection

The protection offered against the entry of all particulate airborne contaminants and the gaseous toxins is called collective protection. Most of the face mask canisters and cartridges offer total or collective protection. The non-powered air purifying type respirators shield the user from both biological and chemical warfare agents, and hence they also come under the collective protection category.

Particulate Arrestors

High-efficiency particulate air (HEPA) filters, formerly called high-efficiency particulate arrestors, are a further extension of extended-surface media filters. HEPA filters are incorporated in a face mask to offer protection against the entry of particulate matter and biological warfare agents. HEPA filters were originally developed during World War II to prevent discharge of radioactive particles from nuclear reactor facility exhausts. They have since become a vital technology in industrial, medical, and military clean rooms and have grown in popularity for use in portable residential air cleaners. A HEPA filter has been traditionally defined as an extended-surface dry-type filter having a minimum particle removal efficiency of 99.97% for all particles of 0.3　m diameter with higher efficiency for both larger and smaller particles. To qualify as a "true" HEPA, the filter must allow no more than 3 particles out of 10,000 to penetrate the filtration media. The filtering media of a HEPA filter is made of submicron glass fibers in a thickness and texture very similar to blotter paper. More recently, filters made in the same physical style using less efficient filter paper are being referred to as HEPA filters or "HEPA-type" filters. Their actual efficiency may be 55% or less at 0.3 microns. [131]

Triboelectric Filters

Triboelectric filters incorporate mechanical filters combined with an electrostatic precipitator or an ion generator in an integrated system or single self-contained device. An example of a triboelectric filter is the "electret" media filter which uses permanently charged media fabricated into either flat panel filters or extended media filters. A the medium filter, made from synthetic fibers, are inherently charged in the manufacturing process and retains a charge which attracts airborne particles that are trapped and retained within the fibers in the conventional methods of impingement and diffusion of other dry-type filters. However, this being a media filter, it presents resistance to airflow which increases as the filter becomes soiled. The filter must, therefore, be replaced periodically. The advantages of an "electret" filter are the filter's relatively low energy cost and their high efficiency when clean. The disadvantages are high maintenance costs due to frequent need to replace filters and efficiency that drops with use. [132]

Another category of triboelectric filters, although not yet available commercially, is the electrostatically enhanced filters. In this type of interaction, an electric field is actively superimposed on fibrous, media-based air filters. The principle underlying this technology is electrostatic precipitation superimposed on other capture mechanisms such as impaction, sedimentation, or diffusion. Under experimental conditions, this technology generally leads to increased filtration efficiency, relative to media-based filters alone, especially under low-flow velocity conditions. Experimental data have been obtained for different pollutants such as latex aerosols, dioctylphthalate (DOP) smoke, and two different kinds of laboratory generated dust. Certain advancement would be to incorporate these charged HEPA filters in face masks, so that, higher capture efficiency is obtained. Normally particles of size less than 0.3 microns are not captured by HEPA filters. When the HEPA material is electrostatically charged, it would attract and capture particles which are smaller than its pore size. This phenomenon could be very useful in capture of viruses which usually are sub micron in nature. [133]

Modification of Surface Properties

Another breakthrough in the capture of particulate material is by varying the surface properties of the filter. Usually HEPA filters are made of glass fibers which are slightly hydrophobic in nature and do not allow retention of moisture. By making the surface more hydrophobic, moisture capture could be totally avoided thereby making the filtration of particulate more efficient. Under normal circumstances when water gets deposited in the form of vapor or moisture onto the filter it clogs the pores or attracts large dust particles which lead to clogging of the filter within a short time. In order to avoid this from happening inside the face mask canister, it is proposed that the filter material be made of material which is highly hydrophobic in nature, such as Teflon, PET etc. alternately, the filter could be made of glass fibers, but a final coating of one of the above mentioned polymers could be given to the filter so as to enable the surface hydrophobic. Moisture retention and clogging are critical constraints faced in a canister as they not only decrease the filtration efficiency but also increase the pressure drop and resistance to breathing making the user more uncomfortable. [134]

Hybrid Filters

Fiber size has always been of interest in filtration applications. It is widely believed that finer fibers can give better removal efficiencies. Synthetic melt blown fabrics and microglass fibers have been the materials of fabrication for the particulate arrestors. They are available up to 0.25 microns in diameter. Due to fabrication constraints fibers of smaller scale are not used. The innovation in polymer fabrication techniques has given rise to fibers of finer diameter, called nanofibers. By a well known technique [135] called electrospinning it is possible to fabricate fibers of diameters typically even less than 0.1 μm. But since these polymer fibers do not possess requisite mechanical strength, it is recommended that they can be blended with the glass microfibers in a layer by layer deposition technique. Therefore it now becomes possible to have glass fibers which are electrostatically charged and a layer of super-hydrophobic polymer nanofibers. It has been proven that certain surface properties such as water repellence improve when size goes down to nano-scale. Therefore polymers which are slightly hydrophobic act extremely hydrophobic when they are spun into nanofiber form, and vice versa.

Another new technique adopted is the "islands in the sea" technique of fabrication. The smaller fibers are spun with a dissolvable sea, which must be removed leaving the island. The sea can be any polymer which is dissolvable in organic solvents or water. The island forms the glass microfibers. Commercially available fibers have offered 37 islands of Nylon in an alkali soluble co-polyester sea. The fibers produced by this technique are normally micron sized with diameters ranging up to 6 μm. [136]

Electric charging and decay of residual charges on electrospun fibers of two electrically dissimilar polymers were studied in an effort to enhance the filtration properties of the electrospun filter media. PS and PAN were electrospun individually in a single component fashion and deposited in a layer by layer configuration. It was found that the residual charge of the layer by layer configuration increased over a 2 h period when the fibrous web was laid on a conducting surface and then diminished over a 24 h period to a relatively high charge plateau value of 346 V. The residual charge decayed by 80% over a 24 hour time period, which makes this configuration highly appropriate for use in face masks as the mission duration rarely exceeds 8 hours. Very high filtration efficiencies of 99.9999% could be observed for this configuration. [137]

The production processes and quality control of electrospinning nanofiber webs present some special challenges. The electrospinning process itself has some important technical parameters that need to be understood and controlled. Quality control of the nanofiber web is also important because of the small fibers and low basis weights, traditional on-line QC techniques may not be appropriate and new methods need to be deployed. [138]

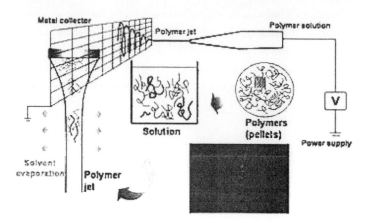

Figure 7. Electrospinning Apparatus Set-up

Recently pathogen air filter systems have been proposed wherein the porous nanofilter media is enveloped with an electronic field that causes the airborne particles to move about in churning motion perpendicular to the air flow direction without ionization, thus significantly enhancing the London-Van der waals interaction resulting in a super-efficient air filtration and purification system to effectively capture bacteria and viruses. The same methodology could be well adopted in HEPA used in canisters. Unlike traditional filters, the nanofibers are known to provide the minimal pressure drop even in reduced flow rates which would result not only in higher filter efficiency but also in higher energy efficiency. It was proven that by replacing the nanofilters in commercial filtration applications, about 35% of HVAC energy consumption could be avoided. In the case of face masks with facilitated breathing (powered type) reduced pressure drop is a vital factor in design. As for the non-powered canisters are concerned, the reduced resistance to breathing

Gas Adsorbent

Compared to particulate control, gas phase pollution control is a relatively new and complex field. Neither mechanical nor electronic filters effectively remove gases and associated odors. Air cleaning units are often equipped with a chemical filter designed to remove pollutant gases from the air. Two types of gas phase capture and control are physical adsorption and chemical absorption (also called Chemisorption). Both are used for removing certain solvent vapors, odors, and low concentrations of gases and vapors in indoor air. Physical adsorption results from the electrostatic interaction between a molecule of gas or vapor and a surface. For example, in the adsorption of air, N_2 is physically adsorbed and is easily desorbed without affecting the adsorbent. Solid adsorbents such as activated charcoal and several other materials such as silica gel, activated alumina, zeolites, porous clay minerals, and molecular sieves are useful as adsorbents due to their large internal surface area, stability, and low cost.

Chemisorption, on the other hand, occurs when the sorbent attracts gas molecules onto the surface of the sorbent. Chemisorption involves electron transfer and is essentially a bond-forming chemical reaction between the adsorbing surface and the adsorbed molecule.

Chemical reaction can occur when the molecules absorb, or go into solution with elements of the substrate or with other reactive reagents which are manufactured into the sorbate. This enables the sorbent to form chemical bonds with the contaminant molecule which binds it to the sorbent substrate or converts it into more benign chemical compounds. Other more complex reactions result in compounds that bind to the sorbent substrate. Once bound, the contaminant is chemically altered and cannot escape back into the air stream. Chemisorption is usually slower than physical adsorption because of the complexity of the process. It is also not reversible as the active reagent component is consumed through the chemisorption process. [140]

Activated charcoal is a widely used adsorbent. The activation process etches the surface of the carbon to produce submicroscopic pores and channels where adsorption can occur. These pores provide the high surface area-to-volume ratio necessary for a good sorbent. Another advantage of charcoal is that it is non-polar, permitting adsorption of organic gases from air with high moisture content.

There are several disadvantages to the use of activated charcoal. Although relatively small quantities of activated charcoal have been reported to reduce odors in residences, many pollutants affect health at levels below odor thresholds. Activated carbon adsorbs some gaseous indoor air pollutants, especially volatile organic compounds, sulfur dioxide, and ozone, but it does not efficiently adsorb volatile, low molecular weight gases such as formaldehyde and ammonia. Because the rate of adsorption (i.e., the efficiency) decreases with the amount of pollutant captured, gaseous pollutant air cleaners are generally rated in terms of the adsorption capacity (i.e., the total amount of the chemical that can be captured). All adsorbents have limited adsorption capacities and thus require frequent maintenance. Another problem with the use of traditional adsorption beds is that there is no means to determine the effective residual capacity of activated carbon while it is in use. Additionally, there is concern that sorbent filters, when saturated, may re-emit trapped pollutants. [141]

Recent developments in the gas phase sorbent filter field have yielded advanced products for use in residential HVAC systems as well as in portable air cleaners. This technology utilizes smaller, more active sorbent particles of carbon, permanganate/alumina, or zeolite which are incorporated into a fabric matte. The resulting matrix of fiber and active sorbent particles combines particulate filtration and gas phase filtration into one filter. The particles are situated evenly throughout the fabric containment matrix which assures good airflow and thorough contact with the air stream.

One manufacturer reports substantial sorption capacity increase over a similar weight of larger pelletized charcoal. The whole filter cartridge is disposable to facilitate servicing. Like other gas phase sorbent filters, their useful service life varies according to indoor pollution concentrations. Unlike the more bulky traditional sorbents, they are considerably more economical. Also, because they have particulate arrestance capability comparable to the generic pleated particulate filter, no prefilter is required and the cartridge can be changed based upon static pressure increase. [142]

Shape Factor

Most sorbents are manufactured and applied in pellet form. This makes it possible to create gas phase filters which are sorbent mixtures of two or more materials. Usually, compound mixtures more effectively remove odors and gases than charcoal alone. Additionally, filter manufacturers can include in their products specific adsorbents to target particular odors or gases. The recent "hi-tech" matrix-type sorbent can employ mixtures of sorbent types, which allows more effective removal of a much broader range of pollutants than is possible with a single type of sorbent. [141]

Activated carbon was chosen as the sorbent material for filters used in face masks due to its high surface area. The BET surface area of the charcoal which is commonly used in the face masks typically lies in the range of 100-400 m^2/g. They ensure complete protection from the Organophosphorus and other warfare compounds for a maximum time period of 8 hours continuously. [143]

Nanotubes to Nanofibers

A subtle improvement in the activated carbon bed used in the face mask was to replace the carbon filler material with activated carbon fibers. Carbon nanofibers are state-of-the-art in the adsorbent technology. These fibers have a high aspect ratio and a BET surface area of approximately 600 m^2/g. Considerable researches have been carried out in the adsorption studies of Organophosphorus vapors onto activated carbon fibers and they have proven successful when tested with DMMP (a nerve gas simulant). The studies show that activated carbon fibers have micro porous structure which facilitates adsorption of toxic gases and other compounds. A technique for the production of carbon fibers is the vapor growth method which is very similar to CVD. Studies indicate that carbon fibers can also prevent the entry of aerosol and bacterial micro particles. A certain advantage in replacing the filler charcoal particles with fibers is that there is a reduction in pressure drop and resistance to breathing. The constraint encountered here is that, there is so far no method to produce continuous fibers on a large scale. The maximum length achieved lies in the range of couple of millimeters. This again imposes a limit to the reduction achievable in pressure drop across the filter as stacking is required. [144]

Impregnation

Another milestone in adsorption filter technology is impregnation of metal nanoparticles onto carbon particles and nanofibers. Some of the features possessed by these fibers which make them suitable for this purpose are large surface area, higher diffusional resistance, low pressure drop across the filters. Some activated carbon fibers were impregnated with metal nanoparticles like Ag, Au or Cu and the adsorption was carried out. The adsorption capacity of the activated carbon fibers was found to be 7 times higher than normal activated carbon 12 X 30 mesh particles. Carbon micro fibers could find potential use in the gas masks and protective clothing which are specifically prepared for the military personnel for protection against chemical warfare agents. [145]

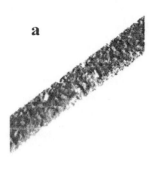

Figure 8. SEM Image of (a) Single Carbon nanofiber, (b) Carbon Nanofiber Membrane

Other studies indicate special treatments done to the carbon nanofibers to increase the number of surface active sites. The fibers were treated with reagents which had affinity for the target molecule. The reagents penetrated the pores of the fiber and helped in the decomposition of the toxic gas. Thus not only adsorption, but also decomposition was enabled using activated carbon fibers.

Temperature Effects

Temperature plays a vital role in adsorption of gases. The rate of adsorption falls with increase in temperature. The exact dependence of temperature on rate of adsorption depends on the adsorbent and the fiber characteristics. On an average, an increase in temperature of about 20-25°C will bring about a decrease in adsorption efficiency by 33%. The data of temperature Vs amount of gas adsorbed is particularly useful for face mask canisters because, the effect can be reversed by increasing temperature and the adsorbent can be re-used. Also, the effect of moisture and other vapors can be reversed to achieve higher filtration efficiency by treating the adsorbent at higher temperature after use. [146]

Sensors

A recent breakthrough is to attach SAW resonators onto the adsorbents. It is always a constraint to detect the amount of toxin present and estimate the useful service life of the face mask. A solution to the abovementioned problem was proposed. SAW resonators exhibit superior selectivity for detection of very low levels of nerve and blister agents. Due to their solid state design and the SAW chemical sensors are extremely reliable and can detect most chemical warfare agents even when present in minute quantities. It has been proposed to attach these piezoelectric materials onto carbon nanofibers for use in canisters. An assay performed after a period of time would give information to the user about the level of contaminant he has been exposed to and the total active life of the canister remaining. [147]

Selectivity Issues

Selectivity issues and the effects of co-adsorption also have been addressed for carbon nanofiber based adsorbents. Experiments were performed with CK (Cyanogen Chloride) and PS (Chloropicrin). The activated carbon fibers were challenged with equal concentrations of both these gases and their interference was studied. It was concluded that at low concentration regimes, there is no observable interference. The presence of water / moisture however indicates considerable interference in the adsorbed quantities of toxins. Presence of moisture slows down and drastically reduces adsorption while different gases do not interfere with adsorption of each other. [148]

Emerging Catalytic Technologies

Photo-catalytic metal particles are also impregnated onto carbon fibers and used in air purification systems. These particles absorb photons of ultraviolet light and drive oxidation and reduction reactions on the catalyst surface and enhances decomposition rate. Some of the metal particles which have been impregnated upon activated carbon are as follows:

Table 4. Metal Impregnants on Charcoal

Impregnant	% Loading in charcoal
Copper as cupric carbonate	5
Silver in elemental form	0.05
Zinc as zinc carbonate	5
Molybdenum as ammonium di-molybdate	2
Triethylenediamine	3

TiO_2 metal nanoparticles are of increasing interest for impregnation upon carbon fibers and adsorbents in canisters. This is due to the anti-bacterial properties which Ti possesses. The metal nanoparticles can act on oncoming bacterial and viral particles and enable them inactive. This approach was particularly suggested for face masks to shield from SARS virus, nevertheless, is of considerable importance in the department of defense for the fabrication of protective masks. [149]

Other molecules which are being considered for impregnation/attachment to the filter surface are the biocatalysts (enzymes). These enzymes form powerful oxidizing or reducing agent mediators and help decompose highly toxic warfare agents such as the mustard and the nerve gases. Various ways of immobilization of these enzymes have been proposed onto fibers (HEPA as well as carbon) so as to protect the wearer from harmful gases. Some of the enzymes well known to act from this perspective are the Organophosphorus hydrolase, Acetylcholine esterase, Sarinase, etc; A prominent problem in this approach is that these enzymes are highly sensitive to temperature effects and degrade when the temperature exceeds $60^{\circ}C$. They also degrade with time. Hence the shelf life of the biological filters is very short [150].

The nanoparticles of Al_2O_3, CaO, MgO, TiO_2 and ZnO, in the size range of 2 to 10 nm and having specific surface area of 90 to 600 m^2/g estimated by BET method, have been employed for de-contamination of chemical warfare agents.

VIII. Conclusion

Although a number of techniques have been evolved, there exist many limitations with their usage. Carbon particles are difficult to handle. Although available in abundance, they do not possess any selectivity towards adsorption unless mediated by a carrier compound. The adsorption is purely physical, without any decontamination. Very high pressure drop and subsequent resistance offered to breathing are the main practical constraints in using these materials in canisters.

The improved version of activated carbon, viz. nanofiber was quite apt for canisters, as it provided lower resistance to breathing. But there was yet another constraint imposed, which was their fabrication methodology. As there is no single technique which can grow carbon nanofibers in large quantity, this imposes a major restriction to their use.

Polymer materials are considered as replacement for the carbon adsorbents. Since they arc highly versatile in many aspects polymeric materials form niche replacement. By adoption of technique known as electrospinning which was mentioned earlier, it is possible to fabricate nanoscale fibers with high aspect ratios and large surface area. Functionalization of the polymers is possible which leads to interesting properties. [151]

Novel fabrication techniques are also being explored. For e.g. a company has come up with the method of producing nanofibers without applying electric charge. The expected applications of such fiber mats are air and liquid filtration membranes. Electrospinning, carding, dry and air laying, melt blowing are some of the well known processes which are at the moment available for the production of polymer non woven sub micron size fibers. Each technology offers its unique properties that can be used by the filter design engineer to meet the expectation of the end user.

By choosing the right polymer, a highly porous structure can be obtained. Researchers are currently trying to make nanofibers which are functionalized for capturing and decomposition of a particular type of gas, such as nerve gas, etc. The polymer is functionalized with the necessary nucleophilic agents that are capable of capturing and decomposing the nerve gases. Functional derivatives of oximes, chloramines, etc and formulations like ICD 2701 which have a history of decontaminating warfare agents are functionalized onto the polymer and spun into filters. These filters would not only adsorb the warfare agent but also aid in its decontamination, thereby taking the protection level to one step further. Also biological molecules such as enzymes can be immobilized onto the polymer nanofibers with ease. They would aid in degrading chemical toxins. The idea of functionalized nanofibers for selective capture and decomposition is a futuristic one and much depends on the surface chemistry of the fibers with the functional moieties. More recent breakthroughs show the success in fabrication of ceramic nanofibers. They are also highly porous structures and can be functionalized for selective capture. [152]

Both ceramic and polymer nanofibers are light in weight and offset the constraint faced due to weight in a typical canister and thereby provide maximum comfort to the wearer.

Whilst the success of these projects are still under investigation, nevertheless, it shows the never ending quest for finding better suited materials for the best protection.

IX. Acknowledgement

This work is supported by the Defense Science and Technology Agency (DSTA), Government of Singapore under Grant No. WBS R-398-000-027-422.

X. References

[1]   NATO Handbook on the Medical Aspects of NBC Defensive Operations, Amed. P-6(B), Part II Biological, February 1, 1996

[2]   E Raber, A Jin, K Noonan, R McGuire, RD Kirvel. Decontamination issues for chemical and biological warfare agents: how clean is clean enough? *International Journal of Environmental Health Research 2001;* 11(2): 128-48.

[3]   *https://chemdef.apgea.army.mil* (An official web site of the United states Army medical research institute of chemical defense, accessed on 3rd October 2006)

[4]   Dunn MA, Sidell FR. Progress in medical defense against nerve agents. *The journal of the American Medical Association 1989;* 262(5):649-52.

[5]   GL Gresham, GS Groenewold, JE Olson. Identification of the nitrogen-based blister agents bis(2-chloroethyl)methylamine (HN-2) and tris(2-chloroethyl)amine (HN-3) and their hydrolysis products on soil using ion trap secondary ion mass spectrometry. *Journal of Mass Spectrometry 2000;* 35(12):1460-69.

[6]   Morrison R.W. Overview of current collective protection filtration technology. A paper presented in NBC Defense collective protection conference 2002 *(http://www.natick.army.mil/soldier/jocotas/ColPro_Papers/Morrison.pdf* accessed on 3rd October 2006).

[7]   Greg Hanson. Chemical Warfare Agents. *III-YearSeminarat University of Wisconsin Madiason 2003* (http://www.chem.wisc.edu/areas/organic/studsemin/hanson/hanson-abs.pdf accessed on 3 rd October 2006).

[8]   T Cassagne, HJ Cristau, G Delmas and M Desgranges. Destruction of chemical warfare agents VX and soman by alpha-nucleophiles as oxidizing agents. *Heteroatom Chemistry 2001,* 12(6): 485-90.

[9]   NATO Handbook on the Medical Aspects of NBC Defensive Operations, Amed. P-6(B), Part-I Nuclear, Chapter 1 *(http://www.fas.org/nuke/guide/usa/doctrine/dod/fm8-9/2ch1.htm* accesed on 3rd October 2006).

[10]   SV Mello, M Mabrouki, X Cao, RM Leblanc, TC Cheng and JJ DeFrank. Langmuir and Langmuir-Blodgett films of organophosphorous acid anhydrolase. *Biomacromolecules 2003,* 4(4): 968-973.

[11]   Greenfield, R. A., B. R. Brown, J. B. Hutchins, J. J. Iandolo, R. Jackson, L. N. Slater and M. S. Bronze. Microbiological, biological, and chemical weapons of warfare and terrorism. Am. J. Med. Sci. 2002, 323:326-340

[12]   An official website of Research area directorate IV, US. Army Medical Research and Material Command (*www.medchembio.detrick.army.mil* accessed on 3 rd October 2006).

[13]   Paddel, B.M. Biosensors for chemical and biological agents of defense interest. Biosensor and Bioelectronics 1996; 11:1079-113.

[14]   Doney, B.C., D.W. Groce, D.L. Campbell, M. F. Greskevitch, W.A. Hoffman, P. J. Middendorf, G. Syamlal, and K. M. Bang. Private sector respirator use in the United States: An overview of findings, *Journal of Occupational and Environmental Hygiene 2005*, 2: 267–276.

[15]   A web site of Inter-American Security Products, Inc (*www.interamer.com/Masks2.htm* accessed on 3 rd October 2006).

[16]   A web site of saftely system corporation, Tactical equipment specialist (*www.safetysystemscorp.com* accessed on 3 rd October 2006).

[17]   Legare, Pierre; Pike, D.W. Filter sealing apparatus *U.S. Patent No. 5,062,874 (* date of publication 5 th November 1991).

[18]   *www.approvedgasmasks.com/filter-scott.htm* (accessed on 3 rd October 2006).

[19]   Maruscak, John; Legare, Pierre; Welch, Jr., Thomas C. Plastic scrim. *U.S. Patent No: 5,038,775* (date of publication 13th August 1991).

[20]   Smith, Simon J.; Hern, Jamie A. Broad spectrum filter system for filtering contaminants from air or other gases. *U.S. Patent No: 6,344,071* (date of publication 5th February 2002).

[21]   Koslow, Evan E. Air purifying filter systems for building air supply and respirators useful against NBC attacks. *U.S. Patent No: 6,840,986* (date of publication 11th January 2005).

[22]   Grove, Corey M.; Chase, Stephen E.; Hofmann, Jeffery S. Chemical/biological special operations mask. *U.S. Patent No: 6,763,835* (date of publication 20th July 2004).

[23]   Edward J. Poziomek, Raymond A. Mackay and Richard P. Barrett. Electron spin resonance studies with copper/silver/chromium impregnated charcoals. *Carbon 1975*, 13: 259-262.

[24]   G.K. Prasad, Beer Singh. Reactions of sulphur mustard on impregnated carbons. *Journal of Hazardous Materials 2004*; 116:213–217.

[25]   Brey, Larry A.; Smith, Simon J.; Weagle, Glenn E. Broad spectrum filter system including tungsten-based impregnant and being useful for filtering contaminants from air or other gases. *U.S. Patent No: 20040261385* (date of publication 30th December 2004).

[26]   Liang, Septimus H.; Harrison, Brian H.; Pagotto, Jack G. Reduced pressure sublimation of amine compounds on activated carbons. US Patent No. 5,145,820 (date of publication 8th September 1992).

[27]   US Patent No: 2004058637.

[28]   Lee, Hoo-Kun; Park, Seong-Won; Ro, Seung-Gy; Park, Hyun-Soo. Reusable canister for a gas mask. *U.S Patent No: 6,146,449* (date of publication 14th November 2000).

[29]   Newton, Richard A. Frustum layered canister. U.S. Patent No: 5,660,173 (date of publication 26 Agugust 1997).

[30]   www.waterlink.com/index.cfm.

[31]   Weiss RA, Weiss MP, Church JK Jr, Strawbridge JB, Decker RW II, Martin FA. Chemical Warfare Respiratory Protection: Where We Were and Where We Are Going.

Unpublished report of US Army Chemical Research Development and Engineering Center; Aberdeen Proving Ground, MD. (accessed on *https://ccc.apgea.army.mil/sarea/products/textbook/Web_Version/chapters/chapter_16 .htm* on 3rd October 2006).

[32]   Phillips YY. Colonel, Medical Corps, US Army; Chief, Department of Medicine, Walter Reed Army Medical Center, Washington, DC. Personal communication, July 1996   (accessed   on *https://ccc.apgea.army.mil/sarea/products/textbook/Web_Version/chapters/chapter_16 .htm* on 3rd October 2006).

[33]   A web site of SEA group (a leading manufacturer of respiratory equipments in Australia) www.sea.com.au/docs/articles/nswfb_firedrill.pdf   (accessed on 3 rd October 2006).

[34]   L.L. Elsberg, J.L. Mcmanus and D.C. Strack, Face mask filtration media with improved breathability. *PCT application WO 0241717* (date of publication 30 may 2002).

[35]   Japanese standard for gas mask, article 7, Ministry of Labor Notification No. 68 of September 26, 1990, with latest amendments, Labor and welfare Notification No. 299 of   September   18,   2001,   Govt.   of   Japan (*http://www.jicosh.gr.jp/english/law/GasMask/index.html* accessed on 3 rd October 2006).

[36]   Military standard (US): Filter units, protective clothing, gas mask components and related products: Performance-test methods (with changes 1 thru 4) Document No. MIL-STD-282(4).

[37]   Military standard (US): FILTER CANISTER TESTS - Performance Specification, Canister, Chemical-Biological Mask C2A1, 1 July 1997. Document No. M10: MIL-PRF-51560A (EA).

[38]   Respiratory Protective Devices - Gas Filter(s) and Combined Filter(s) - Requirements, Testing, Marking, PREN 14387, European committee for standardization.

[39]   C-87-040-000/MS-001 Department of National Defense Respiratory Protection Program, Government of Canada.

[40]   Statement   of   Standard   for   Full   Facepiece   Air   Purifying   Respirators (*http://www.cdc.gov/niosh/npptl/standardsdev/cbrn/apr/standard/aprstd-a.html.*, accessed on 4th October 2006).

[41]   Regulations   (Standards   -   29   CFR)   Respiratory   Protection.   -   1910.134 (*http://www.osha.gov/pls/oshaweb* , accessed on 4th October 2006).

[42]   NIOSH CBRN Respirator Standards Development for Full facepiece air purifying respirators (APR) to protect emergency response workers against CBRN agents, (*http://www.cdc.gov/niosh/npptl/standardsdev/cbrn/apr* accessed on 4th October 2006).

[43]   A web site of Filter Science, Phoenix, Arizona (*http://www.filterscience.com/gas-masks_safe-room_science.html* accessed on 4th October 2006).

[44]   Worst case" aerosol testing parameters: I. Sodium chloride and dioctyl phthalate aerosol filter efficiency as a function of particle size and flow rate. *American Industrial Hygiene Association Journal 1989*; 50(5):257-264 and erratum in: *American Industrial Hygiene Association Journal* 1989; 50(9): 424.

[45]   *http://emc.ornl.gov/CSEPPweb/data/GuidanceDocuments/CSEPPPlanningGuidance/*
        AppxE-25Aug00.doc.

[46]   Mulchi, Charles L. Air-pollution filter and face mask. *US Patent No. 4,141,730* (date
        of publication 27 Feb. 1979).

[47]   Yaakov Suzin, Ido Nir and Doron Kaplan. The effect of flow pattern on adsorption of
        dimethyl methyl phosphonate in activated carbon beds and canisters. *Carbon 2000*;
        38:1129-1133.

[48]   Personal   protective   equipment: Trainee   objectives
        (*http://www.tfhrc.gov/hnr20/lead/sect4/sect4.htm* accessed on 4th October 2006).

[49]   Morrison, R.W. Overview of current collective protection filtration technology, *A
        paper presented in NBC Defense collective protection Conference 2002*, USA.

[50]   Caesar, T. and Schroth, T. The influence of pleat geometry on the pressure drop in
        deep-pleated cassette filters, *Filtration+Separation 2002;* November: 49-54.

[51]   A product information of hollingsworth-vose, USA (*http://www.hollingsworth-
        vose.com/products/high_efficiency_air_liquid_filtration/hepa/hepa_ulpa_cleanroom.ht
        m* accessed on 4 th October 2006).

[52]   Capon, Andrew; Friday, David K.; Davis, Brian E.; Pike, David W.; Dunn, Gary M.
        Self-sealing filter connection and gas mask filter assembly incorporating the same.
        U.S. Patent No: 6,860,267 (date of publication 1st March 2005).

[53]   Morgan WP. Psychological problems associated with the wearing of industrial
        respirators: A review. *Am Ind Hyg Assoc J.* 1983; 44 (9):671-676.

[54]   G.K. Prasad, Beer Singh. Reactions of sulphur mustard on impregnated carbons.
        Journal of Hazardous Materials 2004; 116:213-217

[55]   Krishnan, P.N., Katz, S.A., Birenzvige, A and Salem, H. The role of chromium in ASC
        whetlerite. *Carbon 1988;* 26: 914.

[56]   J. A. Baker and E.J. Poziomek. Effect of Amine Treatments on the Chemical
        Reactivity of Copper/Silver/Chromium Impregnated Charcoals, *Carbon 1975*; 13: 347-
        348.

[57]   H. W. Piekaar and L. A. Clarenburg. Aerosol filters—Pore size distribution in fibrous
        filters. *Chemical Engineering Science 1967*; 22: 1399-1408.

[58]   Wilkinson, E. T. and Davies, G. A. A stochastic model for the filtration of dilute
        suspensions using non-woven cloths. *Canadian Journal of Chemical Engineering
        1985*; 63: 891-902.

[59]   L. Birstow, B. M. Cove and E. D. Lang. The Resistance of a Cylinder Moving in a
        Viscous Fluid. *Philosophical Transaction of the Royal Society of London, Series A
        1923*; 223:383-432.

[60]   H. Lamb. *Hydrodynamics.* 6th ed., Published by the Press Syndicate of the University
        of Cambridge, Cambridge 1932.

[61]   C. N. Davies, Proc. Phys. Soc. (London), Sect. B, 63,288 (1950).

[62]   K. Tamada and H.Fujikawa, *Quaterly Journal of Mech and Applied Math 1957*;10:
        425.

[63]   K. Tamada and H.Fujikawa. The steady flow of viscous fluid at low Reynolds numbers
        passing obliquely through a plane grid made of equal parallel circular cylinders.
        Journal of the Physical Society of Japan 1959; 14(2):202-216.

[64]   T. Miyagi. Viscous flow at low Reynolds numbers past an infinite row of equal
        circular cylinders. *Journal of the Physical Society of Japan 1958;* 13(5) :493-498.

[65] J. B. Keller. Viscous flow through a grating or lattice of cylinder. *Journal of Fluid Mechanics 1964*; 18:94-96.

[66] J. Happel and H. Brenner. Low Reynolds Number Hydrodynamics, Prentice-Hall, Engelwood Cliffs, New Jersy 1965.

[67] S. Kuwabara. Impulsive motion of a circular cylinder in a viscous fluid at small Reynolds Numbers. *Journal of the physical Society of Japan 1961;16(9):1762-1770.*

[68] J. Happel. Viscous flow relative to arrays of cylinders. *AIChE J.1959;* 5(2):174-177.

[69] H. Hasimoto. On the periodic fundamental solutions of the Stokes equations and their application to viscous flow past a cubic array of spheres. *Journal of Fluid Mechanics 1959*;5, 317-328.

[70] Lloyd Spielman and Simon L. Goren. Model for Predicting Pressure Drop and Filtration Efficiency in Fibrous Media, *Environmental Science and Technology* 1968; 22(4):279-287.

[71] O. Emersleben, *Phys. Verh.,* 6, 150 (1955).

[72] E. M. Sparrow and A. L. Loefler. Longitudinal laminar flow between cylinders arranged in regular array. *AIChE J. 1959;* 5(3):325-330.

[73] N. A. Fuchs, *The Mechanics of Aerosols,* Pergamon, Oxford, 1964.

[74] J. B. Keller. Viscous flow through a grating or lattice of cylinders. *Journal of Fluid Mechanics 1964*;18:94-96.

[75] Langmuir, OSRD Report, No. 347 (1931).

[76] Arthur S. Iberall, "Permeability of Glass Wool and other highly Porous Media," *Journal of Research of the National Bureau of Standards 1950;* 45:23-30.

[77] Fardi, B. and Liu, B. Y. H. Flow field and pressure drop of filters with rectangular fibres. *Aerosol Sci. Technol.* 1992; 17:36-44.

[78] Brown. R. C. A many fibre model of airflow through a fibrous filter. *J. Aerosol Sci.,*1984; 15(5): 583-593.

[79] Brown. R. C. The use of the variational principle in the solution of Stokes flow problems in fibrous filters. *J. Phys. D.,* 1983; 16:743-754.

[80] Yu, C. P. and Soong, T. T. A radom cell model for pressure drop prediction in fibrous filters. *J. Appl. Mech, Transactions of the ASME 1975*; June:301-304.

[81] Lajos, T. The effect of inhomogeneity on flow in fibrous filters. *Staub Reinhalt. Luft.,1985*; 45 (1): 19-22.

[82] C. N. Davies. The separation of airborn dust and particles. *Proceedings of Institute of the Mechnical Engineers Series B 1952*;1:185.

[83] R. R. Sullivan. Further Study of the Flow of Air Through Porous Media. *Journal of Applied Physics 1941;12(6):503-508 and* R. R. Sullivan. Specific Surface Measurements on Compact Bundles of Parallel Fibers. *Journal of Applied Physics 1942;*13(11):725-730.

[84] L. Silverman and M. First. Edge and Variable Compression Filters for Aerosols. *Industrial and Engineering Chemistry 1952*; 44: 2777-1783.

[85] A.G. Blasewitz and B.F. Judson. *Chemical Engineering* Progress 1955; 51(1):6J-11J.

[86] K. T. Whitby, R. C. Jordan, and A. B. Algen, *ASHRAE J.,* 4, 79 (1962).

[87] Chen, C. Y. Filtration of Aerosols by Fibrous Media. *Chemical Review 1955;* 55:595-623.

[88] E. Billings, Ph. D. thesis, California Institute of Technology, Pasadena, 1966.

[89] G. L. Natanson, *Kolloid. Zh.* Vol. 24, 52 (1962).

[90]   J. Pich, in Aerosol Science (C. N. Davies, ed.), Academic, New York, 1966.

[91]   Lloyd Spielman and Simon L. Goren, "Model for Predicting Pressure Drop and Filtration Efficiency in Fibrous Media", *Environmental Science and Technology,* Volume 2, Issue 4, 279-287, 1968.

[92]   J. A. Wheat, *Can. J. Chem. Eng.,* 41, 67 (1962).

[93]   R. M. Werner and L. A. Clarenburg. Aerosol Filters. Pressure Drop across Single-Component Glass Fiber Filters. *Industrail Engineering Chemistry Process Design and. Development 1965;* 4(3): 288-293.

[94]   B. Stechkina, *Inzh. Fiz. Zh.,* 7, 128 (1964).

[95]   S. K. Friedlander. Mass and heat transfer to single spheres and cyl-. inders at low Reynolds numbers. *AIChE J. 1957; 3(1):*43-48.

[96]   G. L. Natanson. Diffusive deposition of aerosols on a cylinder in a flow in the case of small capture coefficients. *Dokl. Akad. Nauk SSSR 1957;*112: 100.

[97]   W. L. Torgeson, in General Mills, Rept. 1890 (1958).

[98]   B. Stechkina, Dokl. Akad. Nauk SSSR, 167, 1327 (1966).

[99]   J. Boussinesq, Theorie Analytique de Chaleure, Vol. II, Paris, 1903.

[100] W. K. Lewis and J. M. Smith, OSRD Report, No. 1251 (1942).

[101] J. Stairmand. Dust collection by impingement and diffusion. *Transcation of Institute of Chemical Engineers 1950;* 28:130-139.

[102] N. A. Fuchs and I. B. Stechikina, *Ann. Occup. Hyg.* 6, 27 (1963).

[103] L. Spielman and S. L. Goren. Model for predicting pressure drop and filtration efficiency in fibrous media.*Environ. Sci. Techno 1968;* 2:279-87.

[104] A. Kirsch and N. A. Fuchs. Studies on Fibrous Aerosol Filters. III. Diffusional Deposition of Aerosols in Fibrous Filters. *Annals of Occupational Hygenie 1968;*11: 299.

[105] H. L. Sadoff and J. W. Almolf. Testing of Filters for Phage Removal. *Industrial and Engineering Chemistry 1956;* 48:2199-2203.

[106] T. Gillespie. The role of electric forces in the filtration of aerosols by fiber filters. *Journal of Colloid Science 1955;*10:299-314.

[107] Langmuir, I. 1942. OSRD Report No. 865.

[108] J. Pich, Staub, 26, 267 (1966).

[109] Stechkina IB, Kirsch AA, Fuchs N A. Studies on fibrous aerosol filters. IV. Calculation of aerosol deposition in the model filters in the range of maximum penetration. *Ann.Occup.Hyg.1969*;12(1):1-8.

[110] L. V. Radushkevich and V. A. Kolganov. Experimental study of the deposition of flowing highly dispersed aerosols on thin cylinders. *Journal of Colloid and Interface Science 1965; 29:*55-65.

[111] N. Davies and C. V. Peetz. Impingement of Particles on a Transverse Cylinder. *Proceedings of the Royal Society of London. Series A, Mathematical and Physical Sciences 1956*; 234(1197):269-295.

[112] N. Yoshioka, H. Emi, and M. Fukushima, *Kagaku Kogaku,* 31, 157 (1967).

[113] N. Yoshioka, H. Emi, H. Matsumura, and M. Yasunami, *Kagaku Kogaku,* 33, 381 (1969).

[114] M. K. Householder and V. M. Goldschmit. The impaction of spherical particles on cylindrical collectors. *Journal of colloids and Interface Science 1969;* 31:464-478.

[115] S. V. Dawson, D. Sc. Thesis, Harvard University, Boston, Mass., 1969.

[116] J. A. Harrop and J. I. T. Stenhouse. The theoretical prediction of inertial impaction efficiencies in fibrous filters. *Chemical Engineering Science 1969*; 24: 1475-1481

[117] W. Ranz and J. Wong. Impaction of Dust and Smoke Particles on Surface and Body Collectors. *Industrial and Engineering Chemistry 1952;* 44:1371-1381.

[118] J. Pich, in Aerosol Science (C. N. Davies, ed.), Academic, New York, 1966.

[119] Herbert F. Kraemer and H. F. Johnstone. Collection of Aerosol Particles in Presence of Electrostatic Fields. *Industrial and Engineering Chemistry 1955;* 47: 2426-2434.

[120] W. L. Torgeson, in General Mills, Rep. No. 1919 (1960).

[121] L. M. Levin, Izv. Akad. Nauk SSSR, Ser. Geofiz., No. 7, 1073 (1959).

[122] K. T. Whitby and Y. h. Liu, in Aerosol Science (C. N. Davies, ed.), Academic, new york, 1966.

[123] S. K. Friedlander. Theory of Aerosol Filtration. *Industrial and Engineering Chemistry 1958;* 50: 1161-1164.

[124] J. Pich, *Zdrav. Tech. Vzduchotech.*, 4, 119 (1961).

[125] K. T. Whitby. Calculation of the clean fractional efficiency of low media density filters. *ASHRAE J. 1965;* 7:.56-65.

[126] Arthur S. Iberall. Permeability of Glass Wool and other highly Porous Media. *Journal of Research of the National Bureau of Standards 1950;* 45:1950, 23-30.

[127] Fuchs, N.A. and Kirsch, A. A. Studies on fibrous Aerosol filters-II. Pressure Drops in Systems of parallel Cylinders. *Annals of Occupational Hygiene 1967;* 10: 23-30.

[128] Ackley, Mark W.; Szafranski, Brian D. Particulate air filter assembly. *US patent No. 4,548,626* (date of publication 22 October 1985).

[129] Robert David Lewis and Coloma Mich. Filter assembly. *US Patent No. 3,803,817* (date of publication of patent 16 April 1974).

[130] Caesar, T. and Schroth, T. The influence of pleat geometry on the pressure drop in deep-pleated cassette filters, *Filtration+Separation 2002;* November:49-54.

[131] Jeff Dugan and Ed Homonoff. Synthetic Split Microfiber Technology for Filtration. *Fiber Innovation Technology Publications (www.fitfibers.com* accessed on 3rd October 2006).

[132] Heidi L. Schreuder-Gibson and Phil Gibson. The effect of co-operative charging of electrospun nanofibers of electrically dissimilar polymers on filtration properties, *International Nonwovens Journal 2004;* 12(2): 39-45.

[133] The website of the US Global nanospace. *Nanofilter Pathogen air filter purifying systems (www.usgn.com* accessed on 3rd October 2006).

[134] Stephen Martin and Ernest Moyer. Electrostatic Respirator Filter Media: Filter Efficiency and Most Penetrating Particle Size Effects. *Applied Occupational and Environmental Health Hygiene 2000;* 15 (8): 609-17

[135] Audrey Frenot and Ioannis Chronakis, Polymer Nanofibers assembled by electrospinning. *Current Opinion in colloid and interfacial science 2003;* 8: 64-75.

[136] David Adam. A fine set of threads, *Nature 2001;* 411: 236.

[137] Montefusco Francesca, The use of nonwoven in air filtration, *Filtration & separation* 2005; 42(2): 30-31.

[138] Sergey V. Fridrikh, Jian H. Yu, Michael P. Brenner, and Gregory C. Rutledge. Controlling the Fiber Diameter during Electrospinning. *Physical Review letters 2003;* 90: 144502.

[139] Timothy K. Grafe and Kristine M. Graham, Nanofiber webs from electrospinning, available online at *www.donaldson.com* accessed on 3rd October 2006.

[140] H Marsh and H.G Campbell. The characterisation of microporous carbons by adsorption from liquid and vapour phases. *Carbon 1971;* 9: 489-98.

[141] Website *www.lugunsa.org* accessed on 3rd October 2006.

[142] P A Barnes, E A Dawson, P R Norman & M J Chinn. Activated carbon filter, method for the manufacture thereof and process for the separation of noxious gases. *British Patent No.GB2344814 (date of publication 2001).*

[143] Mathew C. Middlebrooks, Importance of humidity on the performance of gas phase filtration. (http://www.bbafiltration.com/pdf/INDAFiltration2001paper.PDF accessed on 3rd October 2006).

[144] MJG Linders, LJP van den Broeke, F. Kapteijn and JA Moulijn, Effect of the adsorption isotherm on one- and two-component diffusion in activated carbon, *Carbon 1997;* 35(9): 1415-1425

[145] Filtration of airborne chemical and biological agents in military applications: State of the art and emerging technologies, (*www.myclex.com* accessed on 3rd October 2006).

[146] Seong-Ryeol Choi, Ki-Hwan Kim, Hee-Seung Yoon, Seung-Kon Ryu and D.D.Edie, Adsorption of DMMP on activated carbon fibers. (http://acs.omnibooksonline.com/papers/2001_P1.05.pdf accessed 3rd October 2006).

[147] A website of MSA, USA (*www.msagasdetection.com* accessed on 3rd October 2006).

[148] Jayesh Doshi, Environmental Benefits: Development of High Surface Area Material and Filter Media, *Nanotechnology and the Environment: applications and implications STAR progress review workshop 2002:* 68.

[149] Morinobu Endo, Yoong Ahm Kim, Masay Ezaka, Koji Osada, Takashi Yanagisawa, Takuya Hayashi, Marucio Terrones, and Mildred S. Dresselhaus, Selective and Efficient Impregnation of Metal Nanoparticles on Cup-Stacked-Type Carbon Nanofibers. *Nano Letter;, 2003* 3(6): 723 -726.

[150] Cowsar, Donald R.; Dunn, Richard L.; Casper, Robert A. Process for decontaminating military nerve and blister agents. *US Patent 4784699, (date of publication 15 November 1988).*

[151] Luzinov, Hybrid Polymer Nanolayers for Surface Modification of Fibers, *NTC Annual Report 2003 (http://www.ntcresearch.org/pdf-rpts/Bref0602/M01-CL03-02.pdf* accessed on 5 October 2006).

[152] Fred Tepper and Leonid Kaledin, Nanofiber Biological Filter, from US army website (*www.natick.army.mil* accessed on 3rd October 2006).

In: Bioterrorism: Prevention, Preparedness and Protection
Editor: J. V. Borrelli, pp. 125-137

ISBN 1-60021-180-1
© 2007 Nova Science Publishers, Inc.

Chapter 4

BIOTERRORISM: THE CENTERS FOR DISEASE CONTROL AND PREVENTION'S ROLE IN PUBLIC HEALTH PROTECTION[*]

Janet Heinrich

This article presents an analysos of the CDC's research and preparedness activities on bioterrorism and augments our previous work on combating terrorism.[1] Specifically, we will focus on CDC's research and preparedness activities on bioterrorism, and remaining gaps that could hamper the response to a bioterrorist event.

In summary, CDC has a variety of ongoing research and preparedness activities related to bioterrorism. Most of CDC's activities to counter bioterrorism are focused on building and expanding public health infrastructure[2] at the federal, state, and local levels. These include funding research on anthrax and smallpox vaccines, increasing laboratory capacity, and building a national pharmaceutical stockpile of drugs and supplies to be used in an emergency. Since CDC's bioterrorism program began in 1999, funding increased 43 percent in fiscal year 2000 and an additional 12 percent in fiscal year 2001. While the percentage increases are substantial, they reflect only a $73 million increase in overall spending because many of the activities initially received relatively small allocations. Gaps in CDC's activities could hamper the response to a bioterrorist attack. For instance, laboratories at all levels can quickly become overwhelmed with requests for tests. In addition, there is a notable lack of training focused on detecting and responding to bioterrorist threats.

BACKGROUND

---

[*] Extracted from http://www.gao.gov/new.items/d02235t.pdf.
[1] See the list of related GAO products at the end of this statement.
[2] The public health infrastructure is the underlying foundation that supports the planning, delivery, and evaluation of public health activities and practices.

Although many aspects of an effective response to bioterrorism are the same as those for any form of terrorism, there are some unique features. For example, if a biological agent is released covertly, it may not be recognized for a week or more because symptoms may not appear for several days after the initial exposure and may be misdiagnosed at first. In addition, some biological agents, such as smallpox, are communicable and can spread to others who were not initially exposed. These characteristics require responses that are unique to bioterrorism, including health surveillance,[3] epidemiologic investigation,[4] laboratory identification of biological agents, and distribution of antibiotics to large segments of the population to prevent the spread of an infectious disease. However, some aspects of an effective response to bioterrorism are also important in responding to any type of large-scale disaster, such as providing emergency medical services, continuing health care services delivery, and, potentially, managing mass fatalities.

The burden of responding to bioterrorist incidents falls initially on personnel in state and local emergency response agencies. These "first responders" include firefighters, emergency medical service personnel, law enforcement officers, public health officials, health care workers (including doctors, nurses, and other medical professionals), and public works personnel. If the emergency requires federal disaster assistance, federal departments and agencies will respond according to responsibilities outlined in the Federal Response Plan.[5]

Under the Federal Response Plan, CDC is the lead Department of Health and Human Services (HHS) agency providing assistance to state and local governments for five functions: (1) health surveillance, (2) worker health and safety, (3) radiological, chemical, and biological hazard consultation, (4) public health information, and (5) vector control.[6] Each of these functions is described in table 1.

Table 1. CDC's Functions under the Federal Response Plan

Function	Description of function
Health surveillance	Assist in establishing surveillance systems to monitor the general population and special high-risk population segments; carry out field studies and investigations; monitor injury and disease patterns andpotential disease outbreaks; and provide technical assistance and consultations on disease and injury prevention and precautions.
Worker health and safety	Assist in monitoring health and well-being of emergency workers; perform field investigations and studies; and provide technical assistance and consultation on worker health and safety measures and precautions.
Radiological,	Assist in assessing health and medical effects of radiological, chemical,

---

[3] Health surveillance systems provide for the ongoing collection, analysis, and dissemination of data to prevent and control disease.

[4] Epidemiological investigation is the study of patterns of health or disease and the factors that influence these patterns.

[5] The Federal Response Plan, originally drafted in 1992 and updated in 1999, is authorized under the Robert T. Stafford Disaster Relief and Emergency Assistance Act (Stafford Act; P.L. 93-288, as amended). The plan outlines the planning assumptions, policies, concept of operations, organizational structures, and specific assignment of responsibilities to lead departments and agencies in providing federal assistance once the President has declared an emergency requiring federal assistance.

[6] A vector is a carrier, such as an insect, that transmits the organisms of disease from infected to noninfected individuals.

chemical, and biological hazard consultation	and biological exposures on the general population and on high-risk population groups; conduct field investigations, including collection and analysis of relevant samples; advise on protective actions related to direct human and animal exposure, and on indirect exposure through radiologically, chemically, or biologically contaminated food, drugs, water supply, and other media; and provide technical assistance and consultation on medical treatment and decontamination of radiologically, chemically, or biologically injured or contaminated victims.
Public health information	Assist by providing public health and disease and injury prevention information that can be transmitted to members of the general public who are located in or near areas affected by a major disaster or emergency.
Vector control	Assist in assessing the threat of vector-borne diseases following a major disaster or emergency; conduct field investigations, including the collection and laboratory analysis of relevant samples; provide vector control equipment and supplies; provide technical assistance and consultation on protective actions regarding vector-borne diseases; and provide technical assistance and consultation on medical treatment of victims of vector-borne diseases.

Source: The Health and Medical Services Annex in the Federal Response Plan. April 1999.

HHS is currently leading an effort to work with governmental and nongovernmental partners to upgrade the nation's public health infrastructure and capacities to respond to bioterrorism.[7] As part of this effort, several CDC centers, institutes, and offices work together in the agency's Bioterrorism Preparedness and Response Program. The principal priority of CDC's program is to upgrade infrastructure and capacity to respond to a large-scale epidemic, regardless of whether it is the result of a bioterrorist attack or a naturally occurring infectious disease outbreak. The program was started in fiscal year 1999 and was tasked with building and enhancing national, state, and local capacity; developing a national pharmaceutical stockpile; and conducting several independent studies on bioterrorism.

CDC's RESEARCH AND PREPAREDNESS ACTIVITIES ON BIOTERRORISM

CDC is conducting a variety of activities related to research on and preparedness for a bioterrorist attack. Since CDC's program began 3 years ago, funding for these activities has increased. Research activities focus on detection, treatment, vaccination, and emergency response equipment. Preparedness efforts include increasing state and local response capacity, increasing CDC's response capacity, preparedness and response planning, and building the National Pharmaceutical Stockpile Program.

---

[7] Beyond CDC, other offices and agencies within HHS are involved in this effort, including the Agency for Healthcare Research and Quality, the Food and Drug Administration, the National Institutes of Health, and the Office of Emergency Preparedness.

Trends in CDC's Funding for Bioterrorism Activities

The funding for CDC's activities related to research on and preparedness for a bioterrorist attack has increased 61 percent over the past 2 years. See table 2 for reported funding for these activities.

Funding for CDC's Bioterrorism Preparedness and Response Program grew approximately 43 percent in fiscal year 2000 and an additional 12 percent in fiscal year 2001. While the percentage increases are significant, they reflect only a $73 million increase because many of the programs initially received relatively small allocations. Approximately $45 million of the overall two-year increase was due to new research activities.

Relative changes in funding for the various components of CDC's Bioterrorism Preparedness and Response Program are shown in Figure 1. Funding for research activities increased sharply from fiscal year 1999 to fiscal year 2000, and then dropped slightly in fiscal year 2001. The increase in fiscal year 2000 was largely due to a $40.5 million increase in research funding for studies on anthrax and smallpox. Funding for preparedness and response planning, upgrading CDC capacity, and upgrading state and local capacity was relatively constant between fiscal year 1999 and fiscal year 2000 and grew in fiscal year 2001. For example, funding increased to upgrade CDC capacity by 47 percent and to upgrade state and local capacity by 17 percent in fiscal year 2001. The National Pharmaceutical Stockpile Program experienced a slight increase in funding of 2 percent in fiscal year 2000 and a slight decrease in funding of 2 percent in fiscal year 2001.

Table 2. Reported Funding for CDC's Bioterrorism Preparedness and Response Program Activities (Dollars in millions)

Program/initiative[a]	Fiscal year 1999	Fiscal year 2000	Fiscal year 2001
Research activities			
Research and development	0	$40.5	$42.9
Independent studies[b]	$1.8	$7.7	$2.6
Worker safety	0	0	$1.1
Preparedness activities			
Upgrading state and local capacity	**$55.0**	**$56.9**	**$66.7**
Preparedness planning	$2.0	$1.9	$5.8
Surveillance and epidemiology	$12.0	$15.8	$16.1
Laboratory capacity	$13.0	$9.5	$12.8
Communications	$28.0	$29.7	$32.0
Upgrading CDC capacity	**$12.0**	**$13.9**	**$20.4**
Epidemiologic capacity	$2.0	$1.8	$4.0
Laboratory capacity	$5.0	$7.6	$11.4
Rapid toxic screening	$5.0	$4.5	$5.0
Preparedness and response planning	$1.0	$2.3	$9.2
Building the National Pharmaceutical Stockpile Program	**$51.0**	**$51.8**	**$51.0**
Total	**$120.8**	**$173.1**	**$193.9**

[a] CDC also received funding in fiscal year 1999, fiscal year 2000, and fiscal year 2001 for bioterrorism deterrence activities, such as implementing regulations restricting the importation of certain biological agents. That funding is not included here.

[b] For instance, $1 million was specified in the fiscal year 2000 appropriations conference report for the Carnegie Mellon Research Institute to study health and bioterrorism threats.

Note: We have not audited or otherwise verified the information provided.

Source: CDC.

Research Activities

CDC's research activities focus on detection, treatment, vaccination, and emergency response equipment. In fiscal year 2001, CDC was allocated $18 million to continue research on an anthrax vaccine and associated issues, such as scheduling and dosage. The agency also received $22.4 million in fiscal year 2001 to conduct smallpox research. In addition, CDC oversees a number of independent studies, which fund specific universities and hospitals to do research and other work on bioterrorism. For example, funding in fiscal year 2001 included $941,000 to the University of Findlay in Findlay, Ohio, to develop training for health care providers and other hospital staff on how to handle victims who come to an emergency department during a bioterrorist incident. Another $750,000 was provided to the University of Texas Medical Branch in Galveston, Texas, to study various viruses in order to discover means to prevent or treat infections by these and other viruses (such as Rift Valley Fever and the smallpox virus). For worker safety, CDC's National Institute for Occupational Safety and Health is developing standards for respiratory protection equipment used against biological agents by firefighters, laboratory technicians, and other potentially affected workers.

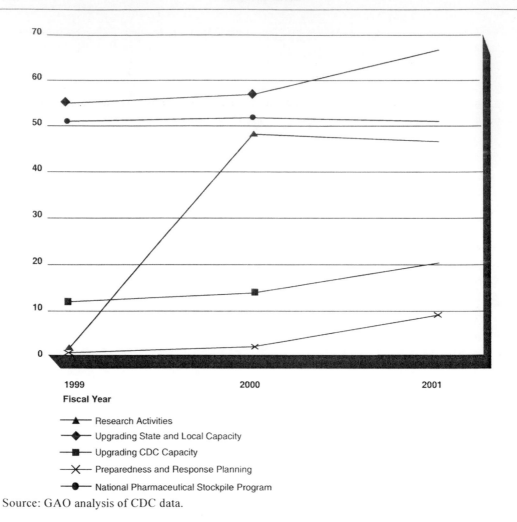

Source: GAO analysis of CDC data.

Figure 1. CDC's Bioterrorism Preparedness and Response Program Funding

Preparedness Activities

Most of CDC's activities to counter bioterrorism are focused on building and expanding public health infrastructure at the federal, state, and local levels. For example, CDC reported receiving funding to upgrade state and local capacity to detect and respond to a bioterrorist attack. CDC received additional funding for upgrading its own capacity in these areas, for preparedness and response planning, and for developing the National Pharmaceutical Stockpile Program. In addition to preparing for a bioterrorist attack, these activities also prepare the agency to respond to other challenges, such as identifying and containing a naturally occurring emerging infectious disease.

Upgrading State and Local Capacity

CDC provides grants, technical support, and performance standards to support bioterrorism preparedness and response planning at the state and local levels. In fiscal year 2000, CDC funded 50 states and four major metropolitan health departments for preparedness and response activities. CDC is developing planning guidance for state public health officials to upgrade state and local public health departments' preparedness and response capabilities. In addition, CDC has worked with the Department of Justice to complete a public health assessment tool, which is being used to determine the ability of state and local public health agencies to respond to release of biological and chemical agents, as well as other public health emergencies. Ten states (Florida, Hawaii, Maine, Michigan, Minnesota, Pennsylvania, Rhode Island, South Carolina, Utah, and Wisconsin) have completed the assessment, and others are currently completing it.

States have received funding from CDC to increase staff, enhance capacity to detect the release of a biological agent or an emerging infectious disease, and improve communications infrastructure. In fiscal year 1999, for example, a total of $7.8 million was awarded to 41 state and local health agencies to improve their ability to link different sources of data, such as sales of certain pharmaceuticals, which could be helpful in detecting a covert bioterrorist event.

Rapid identification and confirmatory diagnosis of biological agents are critical to ensuring that prevention and treatment measures can be implemented quickly. CDC was allocated $13 million in fiscal year 1999 to enhance state and local laboratory capacity. CDC has established a Laboratory Response Network of federal, state, and local laboratories that maintain state-of-the-art capabilities for biological agent identification and characterization of human clinical samples such as blood. CDC has provided technical assistance and training in identification techniques to state and local public health laboratories. In addition, five state health departments received awards totaling $3 million to enhance chemical laboratory capabilities from the fiscal year 2000 funds. The states used these funds to purchase equipment and provide training.

CDC is working with state and local health agencies to improve electronic infrastructure for public health communications for the collection and transmission of information related to a bioterrorism incident as well as other events. For example, $21 million was awarded to states in fiscal year 1999 to begin implementation of the Health Alert Network, which will support the exchange of key information over the Internet and provide a means to conduct distance training that could potentially reach a large segment of the public health community. Currently, 13 states are connected to all of their local jurisdictions. CDC is also directly connected to groups such as the American Medical Association to reach healthcare providers.

CDC has described the Health Alert Network as a "highway" on which programs, such as the National Electronic Disease Surveillance System (NEDSS) and the Epidemic Information Exchange (Epi-X), will run. NEDSS is designed to facilitate the development of an integrated, coherent national system for public health surveillance. Ultimately, it is meant to support the automated collection, transmission, and monitoring of disease data from multiple sources (for example, clinician's offices and laboratories) from local to state health departments to CDC. This year, a total of $10.9 million will go to 36 jurisdictions for new or continuing NEDSS activities. Epi-X is a secure, Web-based exchange for public health officials to rapidly report and discuss disease outbreaks and other health events potentially related to bioterrorism as they are identified and investigated.

Upgrading CDC Capacity

CDC is upgrading its own epidemiologic and disease surveillance capacity. It has deployed, and is continuing to enhance, a surveillance system to increase surveillance and epidemiological capacities before, during, and after special events (such as the 1999 World

Trade Organization meeting in Seattle). Besides improving emergency response at the special events, the agency gains valuable experience in developing and practicing plans to combat terrorism. In addition, CDC monitors unusual clusters of illnesses, such as influenza in June. Although unusual clusters are not always a cause for concern, they can indicate a potential problem. The agency is also increasing its surveillance of disease outbreaks in animals.

CDC has strengthened its own laboratory capacity. For example, it is developing and validating new diagnostic tests as well as creating agentspecific detection protocols. In collaboration with the Association of Public Health Laboratories and the Department of Defense, CDC has started a secure Web-based network that allows state, local, and other public health laboratories access to guidelines for analyzing biological agents. The site also allows authenticated users to order critical reagents[8] needed in performing laboratory analysis of samples.

The agency has also opened a Rapid Response and Advance Technology Laboratory, which screens samples for the presence of suspicious biological agents and evaluates new technology and protocols for the detection of biological agents. These technology assessments and protocols, as well as reagents and reference samples, are being shared with state and local public health laboratories.

Preparedness and Response Planning

One activity CDC has undertaken is the implementation of a national bioterrorism response training plan. This plan focuses on preparing CDC officials to respond to bioterrorism and includes the development of exercises to assess progress in achieving bioterrorism preparedness at the federal, state, and local levels. The agency is also developing a crisis communications/media response curriculum for bioterrorism, as well as core capabilities guidelines to assist states and localities in their efforts to build comprehensive anti-bioterrorism programs.

CDC has developed a bioterrorism information Web site. This site provides emergency contact information for state and local officials in the event of possible bioterrorism incidents, a list of critical biological and chemical agents, summaries of state and local bioterrorism projects, general information about CDC's bioterrorism initiative, and links to documents on bioterrorism preparedness and response.

The National Pharmaceutical Stockpile Program maintains a repository of life-saving pharmaceuticals, antidotes, and medical supplies, known as 12- Hour Push Packages, that could be used in an emergency, including a bioterrorist attack. The packages can be delivered to the site of a biological (or chemical) attack within 12 hours of deployment for the treatment of civilians. The first emergency use of the National Pharmaceutical Stockpile occurred on September 11, 2001, when in response to the terrorist attack on the World Trade Center, CDC released one of the eight Push Packages.

Building the National Pharmaceutical Stockpile Program

The National Pharmaceutical Stockpile also includes additional antibiotics, antidotes, other drugs, medical equipment, and supplies, known as the Vendor Managed Inventory, that can be delivered within 24 to 36 hours after the appropriate vendors are notified. Deliveries from the Vendor Managed Inventory can be tailored to an individual incident. The program

---

[8] A reagent is a substance used to detect the presence of another substance.

received $51.0 million in fiscal year 1999, $51.8 million in fiscal year 2000, and $51.0 million in fiscal year 2001. CDC and the Office of Emergency Preparedness (another agency in HHS that also maintains a stockpile of medical supplies) have encouraged state and local representatives to consider stockpile assets in their emergency planning for a biological attack and have trained representatives from state and local authorities in using the stockpile. The stockpile program also provides technical advisers in response to an event to ensure the appropriate and timely transfer of stockpile contents to authorized state representatives.[9] Recently, individuals who may have been exposed to anthrax through the mail have been given antibiotics from the Vendor Managed Inventory.

GAPS IN CDC'S RESEARCH AND
PREPAREDNESS ACTIVITIES FOR BIOTERRORISM

While CDC has funded research and preparedness programs for bioterrorism, a great deal of work remains to be done. CDC and HHS have identified gaps in bioterrorism research and preparedness that need to be addressed. In addition, some of our work on naturally occurring diseases also also indicates gaps in preparedness that would be important in the event of a bioterrorist attack.

Research Activities

Gaps in research activities center on vaccines and field testing for infectious agents. CDC has reported that it needs to continue the smallpox vaccine development and production contract begun in fiscal year 2000. This includes clinical testing of the vaccine and submitting a licensing application to the Food and Drug Administration for the prevention of smallpox in adults and children.[10] CDC also plans to conduct further studies of the anthrax vaccine. This research will include studies to better understand the immunological response that correlates with protection against inhalation anthrax and risk factors for adverse events as well as investigating modified vaccination schedules that could maintain protection and result in fewer adverse reactions. The agency has also indicated that it needs to continue research in the area of rapid assay tests to allow field diagnosis of a biological or chemical agent.

Preparedness Activities

Gaps remain in all of the areas of preparedness activities under CDC's program. In particular, there are many unmet needs in upgrading state and local capacity to respond to a

---

[9] For more information on the National Pharmaceutical Stockpile Program, see *Combating Terrorism: Accountability Over Medical Supplies Needs Further Improvement* (GAO-01-463, Mar. 30, 2001).

[10] Previous plans were for 40 million doses of the vaccine to be produced initially, with expected delivery of the first full-scale production lots in 2004. The department now plans to expand and accelerate production significantly.

bioterrorist attack. There are also further needs in upgrading CDC's capacity, preparedness and response planning, and building the National Pharmaceutical Stockpile.

Upgrading State and Local Capacity

Health officials at many levels have called for CDC to support bioterrorism planning efforts at the state and local level. In a series of regional meetings from May through September 2000 to discuss issues associated with developing comprehensive bioterrorism response plans, state and local officials identified a need for additional federal support of their planning efforts. This includes federal efforts to develop effective written planning guidance for state and local health agencies and to provide on-site assistance that will ensure optimal preparedness and response.

HHS has noted that surveillance capabilities need to be increased. In addition to enhancing traditional state and local capabilities for infectious disease surveillance, HHS has recognized the need to expand surveillance beyond the boundaries of the public health departments. In the department's *FY 2002—FY 2006 Plan for Combating Bioterrorism*, HHS notes that potential sources for data on morbidity trends include 911 emergency calls, reasons for emergency department visits, hospital bed usage, and the purchase of specific products at pharmacies. Improved monitoring of food is also necessary to reduce its vulnerability as an avenue of infection and of terrorism. Other sources beyond public health departments can provide critical information for detection and identification of an outbreak. For example, the 1999 West Nile virus outbreak showed the importance of links with veterinary surveillance.[11] Initially there were two separate investigations: one of sick people, the other of dying birds. Once the two investigations converged, the link was made, and the virus was correctly identified.

HHS has found that state and local laboratories need to continue to upgrade their facilities and equipment. The department has stated that it would be beneficial if research, hospital, and commercial laboratories that have state-of-the-art equipment and well-trained staff were added to the National Laboratory Response Network. Currently, there are 104 laboratories in the network that can provide testing of biological samples for detection and confirmation of biological agents. Based on the 2000 regional meetings, CDC concluded that it needs to continue to support the laboratory network and identify opportunities to include more clinical laboratories to provide additional surge capacity.

CDC also concluded from the 2000 regional meetings that, although it has begun to develop information systems, it needs to continue to enhance these systems to detect and respond to biological and chemical terrorism. HHS has stated that the work that has begun on the Health Alert Network, NEDSS, and Epi-X needs to continue. One aspect of this work is developing, testing, and implementing standards that will permit surveillance data from different systems to be easily shared.

During the West Nile virus outbreak, while a secure electronic communication network was in place at the time of the initial outbreak, not all involved agencies and officials were capable of using it at the same time. For example, because CDC's laboratory was not linked to the New York State network, the New York State Department of Health had to act as an intermediary in sharing CDC's laboratory test results with local health departments. CDC and the New York State Department of Health laboratory databases were not linked to the

---

[11] See *West Nile Virus Outbreak: Lessons for Public Health Preparedness* (GAO/HEHS-00-180, Sept. 11, 2000).

database in New York City, and laboratory results consequently had to be manually entered there. These problems slowed the investigation of the outbreak.

Moreover, we have testified that there is also a notable lack of training focused on detecting and responding to bioterrorist threats.[12] Most physicians and nurses have never seen cases of certain diseases, such as smallpox or plague, and some biological agents initially produce symptoms that can be easily confused with influenza or other, less virulent illnesses, leading to a delay in diagnosis or identification. Medical laboratory personnel require training because they also lack experience in identifying biological agents such as anthrax.

Upgrading CDC Capacity

HHS has stated that epidemiologic capacity at CDC also needs to be improved. A standard system of disease reporting would better enable CDC to monitor disease, track trends, and intervene at the earliest sign of unusual or unexplained illness.

HHS has noted that CDC needs to enhance its in-house laboratory capabilities to deal with likely terrorist agents. CDC plans to develop agent-specific detection and identification protocols for use by the laboratory response network, a research agenda, and guidelines for laboratory management and quality assurance. CDC also plans further development of its Rapid Response and Advanced Technology Laboratory.

As we reported in September 2000, even the West Nile virus outbreak, which was relatively small and occurred in an area with one of the nation's largest local public health agencies, taxed the federal, state, and local laboratory resources. Both the New York State and the CDC laboratories were quickly inundated with requests for tests during the West Nile virus outbreak, and because of the limited capacity at the New York laboratories, the CDC laboratory handled the bulk of the testing. Officials indicated that the CDC laboratory would have been unable to respond to another outbreak, had one occurred at the same time.

Preparedness and Response Planning

CDC plans to work with other agencies in HHS to develop guidance to facilitate preparedness planning and associated investments by local-level medical and public health systems. The department has stated that to the extent that the guidance can help foster uniformity across local efforts with respect to preparedness concepts and structural and operational strategies, this would enable government units to work more effectively together than if each local approach was essentially unique. More generally, CDC has found a need to implement a national strategy for public health preparedness for bioterrorism, and to work with federal, state, and local partners to ensure communication and teamwork in response to a potential bioterrorist incident.

Planning needs to continue for potential naturally occurring epidemics as well. In October 2000, we reported that federal and state influenza pandemic plans are in various stages of completion and do not completely or consistently address key issues surrounding the purchase, distribution, and administration of vaccines and antiviral drugs.[13] At the time of our report, 10 states either had developed or were developing plans using general guidance from CDC, and 19 more states had plans under development. Outstanding issues remained, however, because certain key federal decisions had not been made. For example, HHS had

---

[12] See *Bioterrorism: Review of Public Health Preparedness Programs* (GAO-02-149T, Oct. 12, 2001).

[13] See *Influenza Pandemic: Plan Needed for Federal and State Response* (GAO-01-4, Oct. 27, 2000).

not determined the proportion of vaccines and antiviral drugs to be purchased, distributed, and administered by the public and private sectors or established priorities for which population groups should receive vaccines and antiviral drugs first when supplies are limited. As of July 2001, HHS continued to work on a national plan. As a result, policies may differ among states and between states and the federal government, and in the event of a pandemic, these inconsistencies could contribute to public confusion and weaken the effectiveness of the public health response.

Building the National Pharmaceutical Stockpile

The recent anthrax incidents have focused a great deal of attention on the national pharmaceutical stockpile. Prior to this, in its *FY2002 – FY 2006 Plan for Combating Bioterrorism,* HHS had indicated what actions would be necessary regarding the stockpile over the next several years. These included purchasing additional products so that pharmaceuticals were available for treating additional biological agents in fiscal year 2002, and conducting a demonstration project that incorporates the National Guard in planning for receipt, transport, organization, distribution, and dissemination of stockpile supplies in fiscal year 2003. CDC also proposed providing grants to cities in fiscal year 2004 to hire a stockpile program coordinator to help the community develop a comprehensive plan for handling the stockpile and organizing volunteers trained to manage the stockpile during a chemical or biological event. Clearly, these longer range plans are changing, but the need for these activities remains.

CONTACT AND ACKNOWLEDGMENTS

For further information about this statement, please contact me at (202) 512-7118. Robert Copeland, Marcia Crosse, Greg Ferrante, David Gootnick, Deborah Miller, and Roseanne Price also made key contributions to this statement.

RELATED GAO PRODUCTS

Homeland Security: A Risk Management Approach Can Guide Preparedness Efforts (GAO-02-208T, Oct. 31, 2001).

Terrorism Insurance: Alternative Programs for Protecting Insurance Consumers (GAO-02-199T, Oct. 24, 2001).

Terrorism Insurance: Alternative Programs for Protecting Insurance Consumers (GAO-02-175T, Oct. 24, 2001).

Combating Terrorism: Considerations for Investing Resources in Chemical and Biological Preparedness (GAO-02-162T, Oct. 17, 2001).

Homeland Security: Need to Consider VA's Role in Strengthening Federal Preparedness (GAO-02-145T, Oct. 15, 2001).

Homeland Security: Key Elements of a Risk Management Approach (GAO-02-150T, Oct. 12, 2001).

Bioterrorism: Review of Public Health Preparedness Programs (GAO-02- 149T, Oct. 10, 2001).

Bioterrorism: Public Health and Medical Preparedness (GAO-02-141T, Oct. 9, 2001).

Bioterrorism: Coordination and Preparedness (GAO-02-129T, Oct. 5, 2001).

Bioterrorism: Federal Research and Preparedness Activities (GAO-01- 915, Sept. 28, 2001).

Combating Terrorism: Selected Challenges and Related Recommendations (GAO-01-822, Sept. 20, 2001).

Combating Terrorism: Comments on H.R. 525 to Create a President's Council on Domestic Terrorism Preparedness (GAO-01-555T, May 9, 2001).

Combating Terrorism: Accountability Over Medical Supplies Needs Further Improvement (GAO-01-666T, May 1, 2001).

Combating Terrorism: Observations on Options to Improve the Federal Response (GAO-01-660T, Apr. 24, 2001).

Combating Terrorism: Accountability Over Medical Supplies Needs Further Improvement (GAO-01-463, Mar. 30, 2001).

Combating Terrorism: Comments on Counterterrorism Leadership and National Strategy (GAO-01-556T, Mar. 27, 2001).

Combating Terrorism: FEMA Continues to Make Progress in Coordinating Preparedness and Response (GAO-01-15, Mar. 20, 2001).

Combating Terrorism: Federal Response Teams Provide Varied Capabilities; Opportunities Remain to Improve Coordination (GAO-01- 14, Nov. 30, 2000).

Influenza Pandemic: Plan Needed for Federal and State Response (GAO- 01-4, Oct. 27, 2000).

West Nile Virus Outbreak: Lessons for Public Health Preparedness (GAO/HEHS-00-180, Sept. 11, 2000).

Combating Terrorism: Linking Threats to Strategies and Resources (GAO/T-NSIAD-00-218, July 26, 2000).

Chemical and Biological Defense: Observations on Nonmedical Chemical and Biological R&D Programs (GAO/T-NSIAD-00-130, Mar. 22, 2000).

Combating Terrorism: Need to Eliminate Duplicate Federal Weapons of Mass Destruction Training (GAO/NSIAD-00-64, Mar. 21, 2000).

Combating Terrorism: Chemical and Biological Medical Supplies Are Poorly Managed (GAO/T-HEHS/AIMD-00-59, Mar. 8, 2000).

Combating Terrorism: Chemical and Biological Medical Supplies Are Poorly Managed (GAO/HEHS/AIMD-00-36, Oct. 29, 1999).

Food Safety: Agencies Should Further Test Plans for Responding to Deliberate Contamination (GAO/RCED-00-3, Oct. 27, 1999).

In: Bioterrorism: Prevention, Preparedness and Protection   ISBN 1-60021-180-1
Editor: J. V. Borrelli, pp. 139-161   © 2007 Nova Science Publishers, Inc.

Chapter 5

BIOLOGICAL AND CHEMICAL TERRORISM: A CHALLENGE FOR HEALTH PROFESSIONALS

Flávia Falci Ercole
Universidade Federal de Minas Gerais, Belo Horizonte, Brazil
Tânia Couto Machado Chianca
Universidade Federal de Minas Gerais, Belo Horizonte, Brazil
Marângela Carneiro
Universidade Federal de Minas Gerais, Belo Horizonte, Brazil

ABSTRACT

Among terrorist events in general, those that use chemical and biological weapons disseminate panic among the populations of both developed and in development countries. This fact was evidenced in the bioterrorist events after the fatidical September 11, 2001, especially those that concern letters with anthrax. It also has attracted attention to the fragility and vulnerability of people exposed to the risk of terrorist attacks with chemical and biological weapons. All of the countries, independent of their political and ideological orientations or international relationships, are at risk of a terrorist attack. Some countries are already worried about the formulation of safety protocols, answer programs to disasters caused by man and prevention of terrorism. Terrorism represents a danger for public health and it is a challenge for the epidemic surveillance of the systems of health and for the professionals that work in them. Explosions of bombs as well as chemical or biological attacks resulting in victims produces a great impact in the community and the epidemic data collected after the occurrences of such attacks have great importance in the formulation of prophylactic measures, treatment and control of diseases and others consequences of bioterrorism. The health professionals need to be trained to identify and assist people with diseases caused by biological and chemical agents. The health systems should have effective epidemic surveillance, laboratories prepared to identify noxious biological and chemical agents, trained human resources, medications, materials and equipment adapted to face several types of menaces. This paper offers updated information about epidemiological actions to be taken on the imminence of and/or immediately after biological terrorist attacks. The main goal is to collaborate with health professionals in the formulation of prophylactic protocols and measures of control of diseases through recognition of infections and intoxications. The epidemiological aspects of old and uncommon diseases are also considered, as those caused by *Bacillus anthracis, Clostridium botulinum* toxin, *Yersinia pestis, Variola major and Ferver hemmorráfica*-Ebole which are easily cultivated - as well as the chemical agents, which are easily manipulated and transported. Care precautions, infection control and occupational risk measures are also presented. The nurse's role is well described, because these professionals have special importance in hospital or community attendance of patients and therefore need to be trained to act in different situations. The cooperation among the countries is an important element to improve the knowledge and the information on how to deal with bioterrorism consequences towards world safety.

INTRODUCTION

The terrorist events that took place in the United States of America on the eleventh of September 2001 reached not only the Americans but also other people around the world, showing the vulnerability and the fragility of worldwide defense institutions, regarding the imminent risk of a terrorist attack. What was considered invisible, unthinkable and maybe a distant reality turned out to be a daily concern for families, healthcare professionals and communities in general [1-4].

Maybe, the event of September 11th marks the beginning of a series of disasters that may emerge, intentionally provoked by mankind all over the world.

Although Brazil tries to keep a governmental policy as well as a neutral and mediator international relation, it is not free from the terrorist attacks and their consequences. The globalization has brought people and countries together, and it has made available resources and services that are more modern each day. The aerial transportation is a facilitator, while it works as an efficient and quick disseminator of diseases such as smallpox, hemorrhagic fever and the plague. Other means of dissemination of diseases, which worries the Brazilian authorities nowadays, are the flocks of birds of passage that may be reservoirs and transmitters of viruses and bacteria.

As healthcare professionals, our concern is about these unnoticed issues that occur in our daily practice. Are we ready to react quickly or to prevent bioterrorist or chemical attacks? Will we manage to control a possible epidemic in such a way that we minimize the diseases and deaths that may occur in our community?

We believe that as nurses, among other health professionals, we will be in the front line of the Health System, in the detection as much as in the prevention of epidemics and treatment of diseases resulting from a biological and chemical war [5]. Acquisition of knowledge in this issue is essential through periodic updating and training, establishing mechanisms of national epidemic surveillance that are efficient to gain cooperation among countries so that we may prevent and fight such problems.

In so doing, this paper aims to present a revision of the epidemic aspects of the main agents that are used in the bioterrorism and chemical war. Historical, clinical and therapeutic aspects of the diseases resulting from terrorist acts have been considered, as well as the prevention and the importance of precaution to the worldwide public health.

PROCEDURES DURING LITERATURE RESEARCH

The approach used while searching and selecting publications was a survey on systematized and up-to-date information in order to obtain systematic revision in literature, seeking for the evidence that subsidizes the clinical practice of healthcare professionals, which is based on directives that will lead to actions for preventing, treating and controlling diseases resulting from terrorist acts [6].

With this purpose in mind, articles cataloged from the database of the Electronic Medical Index at the National Library of Medicine (Medline), Latin-American health Literature (Lilacs), books and *online* information from the Center for Disease Control and Prevention (CDC-P) in Atlanta, USA, and from John Hopkins Center for Civilian Bio defense Studies during the period of 1993 to 2005 were used. The great majority of the selected papers was taken from the database of MEDLINE and LILACS.

During the bibliographic research, the following descriptors or key words were used: biological and chemical terrorism, agents, measures of control and precautions. At first, the search limitation considered bioterrorism, chemical terrorism, main agents, precautions and control. The selection of the publications was done considering the themes above which have been quoted in several languages. The request for the publications was made by BIREME – The Caribbean Latin American Center of Information on Health Science and by the library at the Health Campus in UFMG – Federal University of Minas Gerais in Belo Horizonte, Brazil, through the System of Bibliographic Commuting. All the acquired articles and material from secondary sources (03) were printed and filed. Fifty papers were chosen. To be eligible, the papers should consider the themes bioterrorism, chemical terrorism and the epidemiological considerations for each disease. Publications with different levels of evidence, and even those papers about theoretical and philosophical reflections on bioterrorism have been considered.

HISTORICAL PRECEDENTS OF BIOLOGICAL AND CHEMICAL TERRORISM

Historically speaking, the use of infectious agents as weapons in biological war is not new to us [7]. Their use has been described in different periods of history. It is known that the Neanderthal men used to put feces on their war arrows in order to increase their lethal power against their enemies [7-8]. Similarly to what happened in Moses' time, spore powder of the pathogen *Bacillus Anthracis* was spread over the great potency of the Old Age, and there was powder. Out of the ten plagues that God sent to Egypt in order to punish pharaoh, two might have been anthrax [4,7,9].

In 1346, during the second pandemic of plague, corpses of people who had been killed by this disease were thrown by the Tartars within the walls of the surrounded town of Kaffa (the present city of Crimea). Between 1754 and 1767, the British army, which was at war against the French in American territory, sent to the Delaware (north American Indians that were allied with them) blankets and bed sheets that had been previously used in a hospital where patients with smallpox had been treated [4,8].

In far-off time, the use of biological agents in wars was little known. Although the biological manipulation has currently become scientific, during the World War I, Germany developed and used several biological weapons, although the impact caused by the results was not divulged worldwide [4,8].

Since the World War II, countries such as Japan, the USA, the Soviet Union and Iraq have undertaken research in order to manipulate, produce and store, for military use, biological and chemical agents with great power to cause disease and death [10].

Japanese are suspected, during the occupation in China, to have used biological weapons in large scale and with a great number of victims [8,10-11].

During the second half of the XXth century, during the Cold War, the USA as well as the Soviet Union introduced projects for the development of biological weapons, the same was done by Canada and the United Kingdom [11-12].

In 1942, the USA started its production of biological weapons by using missiles carried with *B. anthracis* and the country is accused of using these weapons in the war against Korea. On the other hand, the Soviet Union is accused of using mycotoxins of *Fusarium* in Laos and Afghanistan [2-3,8].

All these events culminated in 1972, at the International Convention for the Prohibition of the Development of Biological Weapons, in which the former president Richard Nixon ordered the destruction the American biological arsenal. Even after the treaty was signed up by many country representatives, it is known that at least ten countries kept and expanded their programmes for the development of biological weapons [2,4,11-15].

In late seventies, the USA destroyed its biological arsenal [14]. However, countries such as the Soviet Union, Iraq and Japan kept programs for the development and production of biological weapons, most of them resistant to antimicrobials and vaccines [14-15]. The Soviets and the Germans would have developed strains of *Francisella tularensis*, the agent that causes tularemia, a disease which is resistant to most kinds of existent antimicrobials [11]. It is also known that the Soviets reached a very high level as far as it concerns the development of biological weapons. It became evident in 1979, during the accident that happened in Sverdlovsk [16]. For unknown reasons, there was accidental but efficient air dispersal of a small amount of *B. anthracis* spores, causing countless cases of the disease and several deaths among humans and animals through digestive-respiratory ways. The Soviet Union also developed the smallpox virus in order to counterattack the USA, in case nuclear weapons were thrown over them [17].

According to information obtained from the database at Monterey Institute of International Studies in the city of Monterey, California, USA, [14] fifty-five events related to biological and chemical terrorism happened in the world in a period of forty years (1960-1999).

Up to that point, biological and chemical weapons had been used with military purpose. Nowadays, incidents involving biological and chemical agents, even limited number, have been supposedly obtained through the so-called black market [10] and have been related with the practice of terrorism and other criminal acts.

A terrorist event can be conceptualized as an act that involves an organization or person that conspires and uses a violent way to reach a political, ideological or religious target [18]. The bioterrorism is an illegal and criminal event, in which biological and chemical agents are thrown deliberately over human beings, animals and plants so that the government institutions or even the civilian population are intimidated and certain aims are reached [19]. The motivation that leads to such practice as well as the kind of groups that carry them out are several. In recent years, terrorist events have abruptly increased in number, and have been attributed to terrorist groups of the left wing. They are groups or people who are extreme nationalists-separatists, *ad-hoc* groups who are involved with retaliation and also religious groups connected with violent sects or apocalyptical prophecies [14].

Among all the terrorist attacks using biological agents, only one reached a large number of victims when it was used, in 1984, the bacterium *Salmonella Typhimurium*, at the Dalles restaurant, in Oregon, USA. This event resulted in seven hundred and fifty-one cases of food poisoning, all of which non-fatal [14].

In 1995, the Japanese ultra nationalist terrorist group Aum Shinrikyo killed twelve people in the Tokyo subway by using Sarin gas [14]. The same group had already used spores of *B. anthracis* fortunately causing no deaths [11].

Before the incidents that happened in the USA involving the bacterium *B. anthracis*, there was a belief that the need for sophisticated and high cost technology, highly skilled labor for the production, storage and transport of biological agents and toxins, represented technical barriers that would impose limits to the terrorist acts with numerous victims. However, these attacks are an indicative that neither technical factors, as the treaties and agreements for weapons control, nor the moral aversion associated with the use of biological weapons, will detain the use of these agents as weapons of mass destruction [1,20].

An attack in which biological or chemical weapons are used (to contrast with a conventional military attack) may happen as an invisible event, in which people will not be aware of their own exposure. It may not be obvious for days and weeks, when the epidemic will be already set up. The illness and/or death will reach a large number of people, even before the right diagnosis of it is given by the health services. The lack of knowledge that most health professionals have related to some of the main diseases caused by biological war, makes it difficult and finally delays the early diagnosis and implementation of control measures [21-22].

Nowadays, while shortening distances, the air transport may also spread quickly and easily some diseases such as the Ebola-hemorrhagic fever, the plague and smallpox, taking them to several places in the world, even those not war prone or that have not been marked by terrorism, such as Brazil. The biological and chemical terrorism is a real threat [20]. How to face this kind of terrorism?

TECHNICAL ASPECTS OF THE BIOLOGICAL AND CHEMICAL TERRORISM

There are many biological and chemical agents with recognized potential for their use in bio and chemical terrorism. They are easily produced and acquired, easily disseminated through aerosol, they are contagious and have potential to cause disease and death [23-24]. Many bacteria, toxins and viruses are known in our midst, although the diseases they cause, their effects and consequences are not usually seen in our daily clinical practice [20].

CDC-P defines three categories of biological agents "A, B and C" (Table 1), and describes chemical agents that would cause great impact on public health if they were used as weapons, in biological and chemical wars [15,24-25]. Nuclear incidents, natural disasters, bombs and incendiary agents are discussed in other papers [18]. At the moment, we will focus and discuss the biological agents and the diseases that are part of category A. Due to the facility of manipulation, dissemination and transmission of the agents, six agents are recognized as having more probability of being used in bioterrorist attacks [23]: *Bacillus anthracis* (anthrax), *Yersinia pestis* (plague), *Smallpox major* (variola), *Clostridium botulinum toxin* (botulism), *Francisella tularensis* (tularemia) and the *Ebola virus* (viral hemorrhagic fever).

Table 1 – Categories of Biological agents with potential to be used in bio terrorism

Categoria A	Categoria B	Categoria C
Bacilllus anthracis	*Vibrio cholerae*	*Yellow fever*
Varíola major	*Salmonella species*	*Tuberculosis pharmacoligical resistent*
Clostridium botulinum toxin	*Escherichia coli O157:H7*	*Hantavírus*
Francisella tularensis	*Burkholderia mallei*	*Viral Hemorrahagic fevers: – ticks*
Yersinia pestis	*Brucella species*	
Viral Hemorrahagic Fever – *Ebola* – *Marburg* – *Lassa*	*Viral encephalitis:* – *Venezuelan equine encephalitis* – *eastern and western equine encephalitis*	
	Coxiella burnetii	
	Cryptosporidium parvum	
	Ricin toxin	

Source: Adaptaded from CDC-P, 2005 [4,24-26]

In order to develop an effective answer to bioterrorism, it is vital to understand why the biological and chemical agents are effective when they are used as war weapons, what they are and how we can recognize them in the community.

BIOLOGICAL AGENTS WITH POTENTIAL FOR MAJOR PUBLIC HEALTH IMPACT

Category "A" Agents (Table 2)

1. TheBbacterium - B. Anthracis - Anthrax

Anthrax is a word originated from Greek and means 'coal'. This bacterium, *Bacillus anthracis*, is a gram-positive bacillus, aerobic and spore-forming, very resistant and able to survive in the environment [21] for many years. It causes an acute infectious disease also known as carbuncles, by provoking a black cutaneous lesion [27]. It usually happens with mammals such as cattle and sheep, which acquire spores by swallowing contaminated soil. Occasionally, human beings may be infected through skin contact, ingestion and inhalation of spores of the *B. anthracis* from infected animals, animal products (fur) and contaminated material [4,11-15, 20-21, 27-30].

The transmission of the inhalant disease does not happen from person to person. The direct exposure to the lesion secretions of the cutaneous anthrax can result in secondary skin infection [21]. In humans, the infection may occur in three forms: pulmonary, cutaneous and gastrointestinal, depending on how the disease was caught. The pulmonary form is associated with bioterrorism due to the facility in which the population may be exposed to aerosol containing spores of the bacterium [27-30]. The incubation period varies from one day to eight weeks, and the initial symptoms appear around seven days after the exposure [30-31].

The pulmonary infection presents two clinical stages. Initially, unspecific symptoms such as fever, dyspnea, cough, headache, vomiting, weakness, abdominal and thorax pain which may be confused with the symptoms of a common cold. The second stage starts abruptly, with high fever, severe respiratory deficiency, shock and death. Half the patients develop hemorrhagic meningitis with meningism, delirium and obnubilation. In these cases, death happens in hours. The inhalant anthrax is usually fatal [21,27-31].

In most cases (95%), the cutaneous form is acquired when there is a continuous lesion on the skin. The infection starts with a pruriginous papule similar to an insect bite. Between one or two days it becomes a three-millimeter vesicle, with clear or serosanguinolent secretions. Then it grows into a lesion, about one to three centimeters, with necrosis in the center and then it becomes a dry eschar with resolution in two weeks [27-31], leaving no scars. The gastrointestinal infection is acquired when food containing spores is consumed, and its characteristic is acute inflammation of the gastrointestinal tract. It starts with unspecific symptoms such as nausea, anorexia, vomit, fever, followed by abdominal pain, hematemesis and severe diarrhea. These symptoms progress quickly to sanguinolent diarrhea, acute abdomen and sepsis. It usually brings the person to death [21,28].

The diagnosis can be reached through quick laboratory tests as antigen-capture enzyme-linked immunosorbent (ELISA), hemoculture, gram and vesicular culture, in case it is cutaneous anthrax [30-31]. The chosen antibiotics for the treatment and prophylaxis of this infection are G Penicillin, Doxiciclin and Ciprofloxacin, administered throughout sixty days [28,30-31]. As a preventive measure, it is indicated the prophylaxis with antimicrobials (up to the confirmation of the exposure, the treatment should be kept for eight weeks) and with immunization through three doses of the vaccine (inactive anthrax), in intervals of fifteen days [21].

2. The Bacterium - Francisella Tularensis - Tularemia

The Tularemia is a zoonosis with a bacterial origin. It is mainly rural, and occasionally takes hold of man. It is found in North America, some regions from North Africa, Europe and Asia [4,11-13,23,30-32].

The bacterium *Francisella tularensis* is an aerobic bacillus, gram-negative, non-spore-forming and highly resistant, able to survive for weeks, under low temperature, in water, humid soil, hay, straw or decomposing animal carcass. This species is divided into two subspecies: *F. tularensis biovar tularensis* (type A), usually found in North America, highly virulent in animals and human beings and *F. tularensis biovar palaearctica* (type B), of low virulence, but it is the cause of all kinds of human tularemia in Europe and Asia [23,30-32]. It is considered a powerful biological weapon, for its high virulence, easy dissemination and great potential of causing illness and death [32]. The natural reservoirs of this bacterium are small rodents (rabbits, beavers and others), wild birds, and some other amphibian and fish. The vectors are hematofaphag flies, ticks (including those of dogs) and rabbit lice [30].

The human infection may occur through the ingestion of water, meat or contaminated soil; infected flies and tick bites; manipulation of infected tissues and fluids of animals; inoculation through the eyes; contaminated air, dust and pollen inhalation; direct contact with the bacterium through the opening of culture plaques [30-32]. Transmission from person to person has not been reported. Incubation period varies from one to fourteen days. The non-specific feverish disease may have, in average, its beginning between the third and fifth day after exposure. [30-31].

The tularemia is presented in six classical forms: Ulceroglandular, glandular, oculoglandular, oropharyngeal, pneumonic and typhoidal or septic [30-31]. The initial clinical symptoms are fever, shivering, linphadenopathy, general malaise, mialgy, diarrhea, fatigue, anorexia, papules or vesicle cutaneous lesions. After the regional lymphatic nodules are involved, organs such as lungs, liver, kidneys and other lymphatic nodules may be also involved. With symptoms progress and without proper treatment, there will be respiratory failure, shock and death [30].

The diagnosis [30-31] can be done through culture and fluorescence direct from the exudates of the wound and blood, ELISA and Polymerase Chain Reaction (PCR). The best way of preventing the disease is not to be exposed to the etiologic agent in its natural environment. The vaccine derived from the non-virulent strain (type B) has been used to protect people who work directly with the bacterium in laboratories.

With proper treatment, the mortality rate in the USA has been around 2% [31]. Treatment is done with antibiotics such as streptomycin and the gentamicin for up to ten days. Other antibiotics like macrolides, chloranfenicol and fluoroquinolone have been used successfully in the treatment of tularemia [32].

3. The Bacterium - YersiniaPpestis - Pulmonar Plague

This illness is an infectious disease that takes hold of animals and human beings. It is caused by the bacterium *Yersinia pestis*, an aerobic rod, gram-negative, non-spore-forming, which has as its natural host some species of rodents. It can be found in many regions of the world (Canada, Europe, the USA, Africa and South America), and it is transmitted to the man through infected fleas (disease vectors), resulting in lymphatic and sanguineous and septic infections (bubonic plague) infections [4,11-15,21,23]. This disease has had a strong impact in the history of mankind since 541 a. C, when the first pandemic of plague took place in Egypt.

An outbreak related to the bioterrorism is done through air, through aerosols dispersion, causing a variant of the disease, the pulmonary epidemic. When the *Y. pestis* infects the lungs, the first signs and symptoms are fever, headache, weakness, purulent or sanguinary pulmonary mucus. The bronchopneumonia gets worse around two to four days, and it may cause septic shock and, if there is no proper and quick treatment, it may cause death. The transmission from person to person is through saliva droplets and nasal secretions [21,23,28].

The diagnosis can be done through clinical, epidemiological and laboratorial data as serological tests (agglutination and immunofluorescence). In case of pulmonary epidemic, the culture of the oropharynx secretions is made [21,23,28].

Recommended antibiotics for the treatment are streptomycin, tetracycline and chloranfenicol. The antibiotic prophylaxis, throughout seven days, is recommended in the contacts [28]. The vaccine for the plague exists, but its effectiveness has not been confirmed for the pulmonary type of the disease. The mortality for non-treated cases of the pulmonary epidemic is 100% [33].

4. The Variola Virus – Smallpox

There are evidences that show the first cases of the disease happened before the Christian era [31]. The smallpox has been eradicated all over the world since 1977 [4,11-15,23,28,34]. The disease is caused by a virus that belongs to the *Poxvirus* group. They are very resistant if kept under low temperatures, and may remain viable in skin scabs and secretions, in clothes and surfaces for many years. However, they are not very resistant to heat [30].

It is transmitted through close contact among people, through oropharyngeal secretions or cutaneous lesions of infected people, or through aerosol [23,28,34]. The smallpox is more infectious during the first week, when a great number of the virus is present in the saliva, but there is the risk of catching it before all the crusts and scabs have come off [26,28]. The first symptoms start to appear around twelve days after the person is exposed, and they include high fever, fatigue, headache, pain on the nape, along abdominal pain and delirium. Around two or three days after the beginning of the symptoms, a typical eruption appears first on the mouth and the pharyngeal mucous, then face, trunk, arms and legs. Initially, the lesions are flat and reddish, then they change into vesicular lesions full of pus that, in two weeks, get dry and create crusts that come off while the person evolutes to the cure. Most smallpox patients recover from the disease, but death occurs in 30% of the cases [21,23, 28, 34].

The treatment of the smallpox is done through hidric support and medicines to control fever and pain, but there are no specific medications. Antibiotics may be used in case of secondary infections [4,23,28,34]. Routine vaccination was suspended in 1972. Immunity level is not known precisely the among the people who received the vaccine. There is a belief that the immunization effects last from three to five years, therefore, the people who previously received the vaccine are susceptible to the disease [34]. After exposure to the smallpox virus, the vaccine is recommended to decrease the severity of disease or to prevent it, if taken within four days [28].

5. The Ebola Virus – Ebola Hemorrhagic Fever

The *Ebola hemorrhagic fever* is a severe illness, often fatal in humans and primates. The disease has appeared sporadically since its initial recognition in 1976, in Africa, where confirmed cases were reported in Congo, Gabon, Ivory Coast and Uganda. The disease is caused by the *Ebola virus,* a RNA virus family member, called Filoviridae [4,11-15,23,35]. Three out of the four identified Ebola viruses trigger the disease in humans: *Ebola-Zaire, Ebola-Sudan e Ebola-Ivory Coast.*

The fourth species, the *Ebola-Reston,* has caused the disease in primates, although there are no reported human cases. The natural reservoir of the *Ebola* virus and the existence of arthropod vectors are not well known yet. Researchers, however, believe, based in other similar viral diseases, that it might have an animal host native to the African continent [35].

The virus transmission occurs in the direct contact with the infected person, with corpses, and, indirectly, through direct contact with objects that have been contaminated with infected body secretions such as, blood, urine, feces, saliva, and oral-tract secretions and sperm. Because of that, family and healthcare providers are under greater risk to be infected (Table 2). The transmission via air was not identified in the human outbreaks, but the subject is still in dispute. The virus entry to the body are the soft tissues and the wounded skin which is continuous lesioned [23,35-36].

Signs and symptoms of Ebola hemorrhagic fever in the onset are not the same for all patients. The most reported symptoms in the acknowledged cases are fever, headache, joint and muscle aches, stomach pain, weakness and diarrhea. Sorethroat, skin rash, petechias, red eyes with edemas, epistaxes, internal and external bleeding, difference in blood color were also seen in some patients. After a week, the patient can show chest pain, blindness, severe hemorrhage, anuria, hypo blood pressure and shock followed by death. Its initial stage can be confused with Typhoid Fever or Malaria [36].

There are neither vaccines nor specific treatment against Ebola Hemorrhagic fever. The patient receives hidric support with electrolyte reposition, oxygen-therapy, antibiotics for the secondary infections, transfusions, etc. The diagnosis can be given by using ELISA testing, IgG ELISA, PCR and virus isolation on the onset of the illness [35-36].

6. The Botulism Toxin - Clostridium Botulinum Toxin - Botulism

Botulism is a non-person-to-person-transmissible illness that causes muscle paralysis. It is caused by a nerve toxin called *Clostridium botulinum* that is produced by a grand-positive anaerobic sporific bacterium. Botulism cases are rare and usually caused by the absorption of the toxin by the wounded skin or the gastro-intestinal mucous, as contaminated food is eaten, making the person ill in just a few hours. There is also the airborne botulism and is closely related to bioterrorism [4,11-12,23,39].

The *foodborne botulism* is followed by gastrointestinal symptoms such as nausea, vomiting, dry mouth, blurred vision or double vision, drooping eyelids, difficulty swallowing, muscle paralysis (first noticed on shoulders, arms, thighs and lower legs). Symptoms generally begin twelve to thirty-six hours after eating a contaminated food. Respiratory muscle paralysis can lead to death unless respiratory support is given, in time, to the patient [4,21,28,39]. An effective reduction on the severity of symptoms can be seen if an antitoxin is precociously used, during course of illness [21].

CDC-P often categorizes the most important chemical agents or the ones with greater possibility of use in a terrorism attack according to their damage effectiveness in people that are exposed to them. Taking into account the numberless agents found in each category/type presented by CDC–P, only the ones that could easily cause greater impact to public health are going to be mentioned.

Table 2. Characteristics of the Bioterrorism Agents

Disease	Clinic	Transmission	Diagnosis	Isolation	Profilaxy after-exposure	Treatment
Anthrax Inhalation	Fever, shivering, weakness, nausea, vomiting, difficult breathing	Spores inhalation	Bacteria Culture, blood and saliva, PCR, Immunoflorescence in tissues or secretions	Standard Precautions	Ciprofloxacin for 60-100 days or Doxaciline	Ciprofloxacin 500 mg IV every 12 hrs or Doxaciline 100 mg every 12 hrs.
Gastrointestinal Anthrax	Fever, abdominal pain, nausea, vomiting, anorexia, hematemese, diarrhea with bleeding.	Eating of contaminated food	Blood and/or feces Culture	Standard Precautions	Ciprofloxacin during 60-100 days or Doxaciline	Ciprofloxacin 500 mg IV every 12 hrs or Doxaciline 100 mg every 12 hrs.
Cutaneous Anthrax	Pruritic papule that evolves into a ulcerated wound and a necrotic eschar	Direct contact with spore or infected tissue	Lesion Culture, lesion biopsia	Standard Precautions	Ciprofloxacin during 60-100 days or Doxaciline	Ciprofloxacin 500 mg IV every 12 hrs or Doxaciline 100 mg every 12 hrs.
Smallpox	Fever, headache, initial Exanthem in mouth and Pharynx, and rest of body afterwards	Direct contact with respiratory droplets or secretions	Electron Microscopy of lesion secretions, ELISA, PCR	Airborne and Contact Precautions	Any vaccine?	Support Treatment. Ciclovir?
Tularemia	Fever, adenomegalies, skin lesions	Inoculation of contaminated secretion, contact with contaminated animals, arthropod bites	Blood culture, spit, PCR, inmunobloting, Electrophoresis of pulsatile fields	Standard Precautions	Oral Doxaciline 100 mg or IV Ciprofloxacin 500 mg oral or IV every 12 hrs for 10 days.	Estreptomicine 1 g IM every 12 hrs during 10 days or Gentamicin 5mg/Kg IM/IV for 10 days
Botulism	Flaccid Paralysis (non-fever), Ptosis of the eyelids, blurred vision, Dysarthria, Dysphonia	Droplet Contaminated food or contamination by wounds	Blood, feces, gastric aspiration for toxin detection. ELISA-Ag	Standard Precautions	Pentatoxoid	Anti-toxine, clinical support as mechanical ventilation.
Plague	High Fever, Hemoptysis, vomiting, headache, respiratory difficulty	Rodent fleas	ELISA in urine, Sorology for IgM, IgG and immunoflorescence	Droplets Precautions	Oral Doxaciline 100 mg or IV Ciprofloxacin 500 mg oral or IV each 12 hrs for 10 days.	Estreptomicine 1 g IM every 12 hrs for 10 days or Gentamicin 5mg/Kg IM/IV for 10 days
Viral Hemorrhagic Fever	Intravascular Fever, disseminated coagulation, low blood pressure, increased vascular permeability	Differs for each viral agent. Contact with contaminated secretions. Contact with arthropod?	Blood Culture, ELISA-Ag, PCR	Airborne and Contact Precautions	Patient in total Isolation	Clinical Support Therapy. For Arenavirus, Ribavirin initial dose 30mg/Kg IV, followed by 15 mg/Kg every 6 hrs.

Source: Adapted from Franco-Paredes, C, Rodriguez Morales, AJ, 2004 [4]

CHEMICAL AGENTS WITH GREATER POTENCIAL TO BE MANIPULATED IN CHEMICAL TERRORISM

Chemical Agents

Biotoxins are venoms found in plants and animals. *Digitalis* and *Strychnine* are found among them. Signs and symptoms of intoxication by digitalis caused by high doses of *Digoxin* include primarily gastrointestinal signs such as nausea and vomiting, hypercalemia, severe cardiovascular effects such as bradiarrithmy, ventricular tachycardia and atrial fibrillation [40].

Digoxin therapeutic levels differ from one lab to another and also from one patient to another, because of that, laboratorial diagnosis done by the seric concentration of *Digoxin* should be correlated with the clinic signs found in the patient. As for *Strychnine,* it is a powerful venom used to kill rats and mice. Its origin is found in the *Strychnos nux vomica* plant, often found in India, Sri Lanka and Australia. It can be inhaled, directly vein injected, taken with food, diluted or mixed in water or drugs such as cocaine, heroin e LSD.

Signs and symptoms can be seen in between fifteen to sixty minutes, agitation being one of the first, followed by spasms on legs and arms until respiratory failure followed by death. The person must be taken to hospital immediately and even with treatment, this person bear few chances of survival [41-42].

Mustard gas (H) appears among the *Blister Agents/Vesicants* and is a non-smell gas as in its pure and colorless state. When mixed to oils and other solvents, this gas acquires the yellow color along with odors similar to garlic, onion or mustard. Exposure to this irritating gas can be accidental, as when it is used in military training areas and as it is used as a chemical war agent, as it was in World War I. Symptoms appear in between two to twenty-four hours after exposure. *Mustard gas* can penetrate skin and eyes, as well as causes vesicles or blisters in soft tissues and skin, its effects can be seen in the respiratory tract (bronchitis) and also can reach the gastrointestinal tract, causing diarrhea, pain, nausea e vomiting. It is not usually fatal but in high levels can lead to death, depending on time and extension of exposure. There is no antidote. Basic clinic support should be given to the victim and m*ustard gas* [43] should be removed from body (Table 3).

Among the *Blood Agents* that can attack the blood, we find *Arsine (SA)* that is a toxic gas that is easily accumulated in poorly ventilated areas. It is colorless, non-irritating and acquires a garlic-like smell when in greater levels in the environment. After inhaled, its symptoms can be noticed from two to twenty-four hours after exposure and are fatigue, weakness, headache, drowsiness, confusion, nausea, vomiting, abdominal pain, dark urine, hemolisys, yellowish skin and eyes, taquypnea or bradypnea, muscle cramps until respiratory failure followed by death. There are no antidotes for the Arsine victim. The person should be taken to an open-air area, bathed with water and soap; the impregnated clothes should be taken off, ventilatory and hemodynamic support offered in the shortest time possible [44].

Caustics Agents (Hydrofluoric acid) can cause corrosion and ulcers in skin, eyes, soft tissues of the nose, mouth, throat, esophagus, stomach, lungs (edema), bone loss and blindness. Depending on the concentration of the chemical agent and extension of time exposure, the damaged skin can cause severe pain. Visible symptoms can be noticed in between 12 to 24 hours after exposure. The victim of intoxication should be removed from the site where the gas can be found, as well as his/her clothes whilst the body should be washed with soap and water. If the person is still alert and able to swallow, one to two glasses of water or milk with calcium, magnesium and antiacids should be given. The victim should be quickly given medical attention [45].

Among *Pulmonary Agents, Ammonia* was selected as a chemical agent that causes irritation and severe edema in the respiratory tract. Nose, throat and alveolus membrane are severely damaged taking the victim to a pulmonary edema condition. Effects from exposure occur in between 2 to 24 hours. Rapid onset of symptoms is an indication of a bad prognosis. Clinic treatment should start with oxigenotherapy, ventilatory support and hemodynamic monitoring. Antibiotics are used in secondarily in cases of infection from inhaling. Patients with asthma history should undergo corticotherapy treatment [46].

Three-Quinuclidinil Benzilate (BZ) and the *Opioids-Fentanyls* are among the *Incapacitating Agents.* They are all classified as stimulating and/or depressor that not necessarily kill, but interfere inhibiting the victim production metabolism of acetilcolin, thus, lethal agents can be used with no resistance. If inhaled, swallowed or absorbed by skin, they produce symptoms similar to high doses of atropine.

BZ toxicity trigger an anticolinergic syndrome that triggers a combination of signs and symptoms including hallucination, agitation, mydriatics, blurred vision without tearing, reddishness, urine retention, tachycardy, hypertension, hyperthermia. These effects are dose-dependent. Symptoms can start from one hour after exposure till 48 hours after. Diagnosis is given by detection of toxin in urine. Physostigmine is known as an antidote to BZ. Exposure to opioids typically occurs by ingestion, but can potentially be the result of inhalation if the opioids are pulverized. Clinic effects from intoxication by opioids result in the central nervous and respiratory systems depression manifesting lethargy or comma, respiratory depression, miosis and possible apnea. Opioids [46-47] are detected in urine (Table 3).

After a non-intentional ingestion of Long-Acting Anticoagulants (Super Warfarin), most patients can be asymptomatic. Nevertheless coagulopathy signs can appear in between 24 to 72 hours after exposure. Coagulopathy can be shown as nasal and gum bleeding, hematury, echimoses, hemorrhagic petechiae, cerebral hemorrhage or uncontrollable bleeding. Diagnosis can be done by seric level of the anticoagulation of plasma, urine, prothrombin time, abnormal factor level II and VII [48].

Arsenic and *Mercury* are examples of M*etal agents* that can cause intoxication. Arsenic ingestion causes severe gastrointestinal signs and symptoms such as abdominal pain, nausea, vomiting e diarrhea that can quickly lead to dehydration and hypovolemic shock, cardiac arrhythmia, mental disarray, systemic failure and death. The diagnosis can be done by measuring levels of venom in urine (>50µg total for urine in 24 hours) [49].

Exposure to *Mercury* can cause signs and symptoms that include vomiting e diarrhea with bleeding, hypovolemic shock, oliguria, kidney failure and death. In survival cases of poisoning by mercury, it is possible the victim to develop neurological, dermatological (flaking hands and feet) and renal symptoms. Hypertension, shivering, paresthesia can also be present. The diagnosis is done by measuring mercury levels in urine or blood (>10µg/l) [49-50].

Among *Nerve agents, Sarin gas (GB)* is well known as the agent of the human produced chemical war. It was made up in Germany, in 1938, as a pesticide. They are similar to the ones called organofosforade, though much more powerful. It is highly toxic and has rapid results [51-53]. At first, Sarin is an insipid, colorless and odorless liquid in its pure form, being able to evaporate becoming gas and rapidly spreading itself in the environment. People are exposed to *Sarin* by having contact with eyes or skin, inhaling the gas itself, drinking contaminated water (it can be easily mixed with water), eating contaminated food and dressing clothes which were exposed to gas vapor. The extension of poisoning caused by *Sarin* depends on how was the person exposed and time exposure. Symptoms appear in after a few seconds from the initial exposure to the Sarin vapor and till 18 hours after exposure to *Sarin* liquid form (Table 3).

Being Sarin quite volatile, people can be repeatedly exposed to it without noticing, accumulating its effects. Those exposed to lower or moderate doses of Sarin, by inhaling contaminated air, or eating contaminated food, or drinking contaminated water, or even by contact with contaminated surfaces, can experience some symptoms such as: rhinorrhea, tearing, myosis, aching eyes, blurred vision, tachypnea, involuntary muscle cramps, mental confusion, headache, nausea, vomiting and/or abdominal pain, diarrhea, bradycardia or tachycardia, high or low blood pressure, cough, chest pressure, sudoresis, excessive salivation, increasing of diuresis, loss of consciousness, convulsions, paralysis, respiratory failure followed by death. Treatment (Table 3) consists in taking the person away from contaminated area, wash his/her body with water and soap, undress contaminated clothes, give ventilatory support, give antidote (atropine and 2-Pan Cl) [51].

Representing the *Organic Solvents, Benzene* is a natural chemic product that part of unblended oil, gasoline and other. It is widely used and produced by the plastic, resin, nylon, synthetic fiber, lubricant, detergent, paint, glue, drug and pesticide industry. Indoor air generally contains levels of benzene higher than those in outdoor air. Benzene, in that case, comes from paints, glues, furniture wax, and detergents. Gas stations can contain higher levels of benzene than in other areas. People working in industries that use benzene may be exposed daily to the highest levels of intoxication. A major source of benzene exposure is tobacco smoke. Those breathing high benzene levels may develop signs and symptoms such as headache, drowsiness, dizziness, rapid or irregular heartbeat, tremors, mental confusion, unconsciousness and death. People that eat or drink high-level benzene contaminated food may develop signs and symptoms such as vomiting, irritation of the stomach, dizziness, drowsiness, convulsions, rapid and irregular heartbeat and death. Benzene direct exposure to the eyes, skin or lungs may cause irritation and tissue damage. Long-time exposure to benzene brings damage to blood and bone marrow causing harmful anemia, leukemia and liver and splinter cancer [54].

Treatment consists in moving victim away from the suspected area of contamination, wash body with water and soap, remove clothing, place person under ventilatory and homodynamic support. No antidote is known for benzene poisoning [54].

Riot Control Agents/Tear Gas are chemical compounds usually a combination of different chemical agents. Most common compounds are known as *chloroacetophenone (CN)*, *chlorobenzylidenemalononitrile (CS)* and other. They are used by law enforcement officials for crowd control and by individuals and the general public for personal protection (for example, pepper spray). CS is also used in military settings to test the speed and ability of military personnel to use their gas masks. These agents can be liquid, solid and volatile so that particles and droplets will be in contact with through people's skin, eyes and respiration. Effects of these agents usually last from 15 to 30 minutes, after removing the person from source and being decontaminated. People exposed to riot can experience several symptoms after exposure: red shot eyes, blurred vision, tearing, burning eyes and nose, rhinorrhea, edemas in the eyes and nose, mouth irritation and intense burning, sialorrhea, difficulty in swallowing, chest tightness, asthma, coughing, shortness of breath, choking sensation, wheezing, red and burning skin, nausea e vomitings. Long lasting exposure or exposure to a large dose of tear gas, especially in a closed setting, can cause severe effects such as blindness, glaucoma, failure respiratory and possible death [55].

Treatment consists in removing person from contaminated area to a fresh aired area, wash body affected parts with water and soap, remove contaminated clothing, rinse eyes with fresh water, provide ventilatory support, use medications such as steroids and bronchodilators, and bangage should be used in skin. No antidote exists for poisoning from tear gas [55].

Ethylene glycol and Propylene glycol are two examples of *Toxic Alcohols*. They are clear, colorless, slightly syrupy liquids at room temperature. Both compounds are used to make antifreeze and de-icing solutions for cars, airplanes, and boats; to make polyester compounds; and as solvents in the paint and plastics industries. *Ethylene glycol* is also an ingredient in photographic developing solutions, hydraulic brake fluids and in inks used in stamp pads, ballpoint pens, and print shops. High exposure to *Ethylene glycol* can damage kidney, heart, and the nervous system. Eating or drinking very large amounts of Ethylene glycol can result in symptoms such as nausea, cerebral edema, convulsions, slurred speech, disorientation, and heart and kidney problems and death. *Ethylene glycol* affects the body's chemistry by increasing the amount of acid, resulting in metabolic problems [55-56].

Propylene glycol is an alcohol, usually used as an additive that works as food stabilizer. It is used to absorb extra water and maintain moisture in certain medicines (vitamins), cosmetics, or food products. Both exist in air in the vapor form, although propylene glycol must be heated or briskly shaken to produce a vapor. In the environment, both compounds break down within several days to a week in water and soil. Similar to *Ethylene glycol* effects, *Propylene glycol* increases the amount of acids in the body. Effective treatment consists in respiratory and hemodynamic support, hemodialysis, and use of specific antidote (Charcoal 1 mg/kg) and a sodium bicarbonate solution to balance acidosis [55-56].

Adamsite (Diphenylaminechloroarsine or DM) is a *Vomiting Agent* able to induce vomiting. Most exposures occur by inhalation and typically lead to symptoms as nasal, ocular and respiratory tract irritation. There are no biologic markers available for Adamsite exposure [57].

EPIDEMIOLOGIC EVIDENCE THAT LEADS TO THE RECOGNITON OF A TERRORIST BIOLOGICAL AND CHEMICAL ATTACK

- Increase of cases with signs and symptoms of similar illness;
- Increased occurrence of non-explainable illnesses or deaths;
- When a person shows signs of a illness caused by a not very common agent;
- Uncommon appearance of illnesses in a community or population in a set period of time;
- When non-usual, non-typical and genetic modified agents are identified;
- Increase of illnesses in an endemic form;

Table 3. Pharmacologic Management of Chemical Exposure

Drug	Indication	Action	Adult Dose	Pediatric Dose
Atropine	Nerve	Blocks cholinomimetic effects of organophosphates	1-6 mg I.V. May reapet every 5-60 minutes until atropinization. Also administer pralidoxime	0.05mg/Kg I.V. May repeat every 10-30 minutes until atropinization. Also administer pralidoxime
Pralidoxime	Nerve	Reactivates cholinesterases that		
Amyl Nitrite (Cyanide Kit)	Cyanide (Step 1)	Converts hemoglobin to methemoglobin, which reacts with cyanide to form cyanmethe-moglobin.	0.3 ml by inhalation for 15-30 seconds; repeat every 60 seconds until sodium nitrite and sodium thiosulfate available.	0.3 ml by inhalation for 15-30 seconds; repeat every 60 seconds until sodium nitrite and sodium thiosulfate available
Sodium Nitrite (Cyanide Kit)	Cyanide (Step 2)	Combines with hemoglobin to form methemoglobin	300 mg in 10ml solution given IV over 10 min. If symptoms reappear ½ the dose may be repeated in 2 hours.	Hemoglobin (Hgb) Dependent Hgb 7 – 5.8 mg/Kg Hgb 8 – 6.6 mg/Kg Hgb 9 – 7.5 mg/Kg Hgb 10 – 8.3 mg/Kg Hgb 11 – 9.1 mg/Kg Hgb 12 – 10.0 mg/Kg Hgb 13 – 10.8 mg/Kg Hgb 14 – 11.6 mg/Kg
Sodium Thiosulfate (Cyanide Kit, Versiclear)	Cyanide (Step 3)	Provides extra sulfur group to rhodanase, increasing the rate of detoxification of cyanide.	12.5 g in 50 ml solution given over 10 min. May repeat one-half the dose in 2 hours if symptoms reappear.	Hemoglobin (Hgb) Dependent Hgb 7 – 0.95mg/Kg Hgb 8 – 1.10 mg/Kg Hgb 9 – 1.25 mg/Kg Hgb 10 – 1.35 mg/Kg Hgb 11 – 1.50 mg/Kg Hgb 12 – 1.65 mg/Kg Hgb 13 – 1.80 mg/Kg Hgb 14 – 1.95 mg/Kg
Physostigmine salicylate (Antilirium) Physostigmine sulfate (Eserine, Isopto Eserine)	Incapacitant ing	Inhibits destruction of acetylcholine by acetylcholinesteras e	0.5-2 mg IV slowly over 2-3 minutes. Repeat every 20 minutes as needed. Repeat 1-4 mg dose if life-threatening symptoms reappear.	0.01-0.03 mg/Kg/dose slow IV over 2-3 minutes. May repeat in 15 minutes. Maximum dose 2 mg.
British Anti-Lewisite (BAL, dimercaprol)	Vesicants	Combines with lewisite ions to form extractable chelates	3mg/Kg IM every 4 hours x 2 days, then every 6 hours on the 3rd day, and every 12 hours for 10 days.	3mg/Kg IM every 4 hours x 2 days, then every 6 hours on the 3rd day, and every 12 hours for 10 days.

Source: Adapted from Stokes, E, Gilbert-Palmer D, Skorga P, Young C, Persell D., 2004 [57]

- Co-existence of multiple illnesses that are non-defined, in a single person with no explanation;
- When there are illnesses or deaths among animals that precede or follow human illnesses or deaths;
- When people working or living in places with air-conducting central systems fall ill;
- When there is non-typical transmission by aerosols, food or water [58].

RECOMMENDED CARE FOR INFECTIONS
AND INTOXICATIONS CONTROL

Standard-precaution measures should be taken as a routine [10] so that assistance can be given to all hospitalized patients. Among standard-precaution measures are included hand-washing (water, soap and glycerin alcohol 70%); use of personal protection equipment (EPI) such as gloves, mask, hat, gown, and safety glasses; vaccination; prevention of cut and puncture accidents; use of occlusive healing on the exudative wound. Those measures are intended to reduce transmission risk of microorganisms, knowing or not its source of infection, to all and any hospitalized patient and to minimize working risk for the professional who manipulate contaminated material or any body secretion that can be suspected of contamination [38]. With some infect-contagious illnesses, those measures are used along specific additional precautions for contact-, air- and droplet- transmission.

Healthcare for patients with symptoms that lead to suspicion or confirmation of infection associated to *B. anthracis*, with *cutaneous and/or pulmonary Tularemia and Botulism,* CDC-P recommends the use of standard precautions for infection control [21]. As no person-to-person transmission occurs in the three before mentioned illnesses there is no need of respiratory isolation, private room and special air system. Cleaning, desinfection and sterilizing of room, equipment, instruments, as well as patient transport, and clothing manipulation should be done with the use of standard precautions which recommended by CDC [21] to any and all hospitalized patient.

Patients suspected or confirmed for *Yersinia pestis* infection, mainly for P*ulmonary Plague* type, CDC-P recommends precautions measures for droplets be taken along with standard precautions [21]. A private room must be used; contact with patient must be done using a surgical mask while in a distance shorter than a meter. Transmission precautions via droplets must be kept until seventy-two hour completion of antibiotic therapy.

Patients suspected or confirmed for *Smallpox*, contact and airborne precautions are recommended by CDC-P and must be used in addition to standard-precautions [21]. Among them, they should be kept in an isolated room; special air-filtration system with six to twelve air-changes per hour (keeping negative air pressure in relation to corridor and adjacent areas); air-filtration system monitoring; sealed doors; use of HEPA (high-efficiency particulate air respirator) mask with filter.

Healthcare for the suspected or confirmed cases for *Ebola virus hemorrhagic fever,* CDC-P recommends the use of standard precautions along with contact precautions [38]. Among them, patient should be isolated in a private room, with air-conditioning system. If not at all possible, windows should bear mosquito nets; use of EPI, double gloves, plastic gowns over clothing, HEPA masks and rubber boots. Medical equipment must be exclusive to patient. Also important is the need to limit invasive procedures, injectable medication and number of professionals and visitors to the room. Family and visitors should be orientated as for the use of protective clothing and hand-washing techniques. Furniture surface and equipment cleaning must be done with water and soap, followed by the use of a chlorine solution at 0,05% (1:100 dilution). For body secretions which have been splashed on the floor, paper towels should be used for removal, and then, water and soap, followed by a chlorine solution at 0,5% (1:10 dilution). Patient-care equipment and other items should be disposable, and being incinerated after use. Special care should be taken by the healthcare professional to avoid its own contamination during EPI removal.

As far as clinical assistance is concerned, CDC-P recommendations, in general, for suspected or confirmed cases of intoxication by *chemical agents*, are that (Table 3):

- First, victim should be removed from locale of exposure to a higher environment with fresh air, since possibility of death is reduced effectively as most gases are heavier than air;
- Victim must be decontaminated;
- Contaminated clothing must be quickly removed and wrapped up in two plastic bags;
- Body must be washed in water and soap;
- In cases of venom ingestion, vomitings must not be induced;
- Victim must receive immediate clinical respiratory and hemodynamic support, be given antidotes (whenever possible) and any other necessary medications;
- Laboratory tests to measure seric levels of venom.

CONCLUSION

Can earth still be considered a paradise? Nature has been continuously and increasingly destroyed by man. More and more, man has interfered in the environment by deforestating vast areas, polluting waters, overwarming the planet and resorting to terrorism which have all been a contribution to unknown virus and bacteria proliferation, allowing them to spread globally [37].

Modern life pictures a global super population (over six billion people). Nowadays, there are 25 agglomerations in the world, each with more than 10 million people. Traveling and commuting are both becoming gradually quicker and easier which facilitate the propagation of old diseases as well as the emerging of new ones such as Marburg Hemorrhagic Fever, WNV (West Nile Virus), *Bartonella bacilliformis*, Ebola hemorrhagic fever, Plague and Spanish Flu.

The general feeling is that public health systems of several countries, as Brazil, should also invest in programs of response to bioterrorism. These countries have no previous experiences that support the prophylactic actions taken so far to deal with this serious problem, one more added up to the many others already in existence among the health of its population. Maybe actions have been more theoretical than practical.

Brazilian and world health institutions must be prepared, along with their healthcare professionals, to deal, in an efficient way, with the problem of biological and chemical weapons. We, as healthcare professionals, are extremely concerned about that. We believe that, as professionals that take care of the population's health, we should be prepared for this invisible, nevertheless real, threat. Our responsibilities are many and education should be one of the priorities [63]. In case of a terrorist attack, population will be pushed to panic. How can we deal with all of these issues at the same time? Nurses and teams should be emotionally prepared, but most of all, they will have to be prepared technically and scientifically to identify beforehand symptoms of each illness. To this end, it is important that professionals be updated and given the opportunity to be trained in a practical way, through courses, talks, workshops, and debates on the subject of infect-contagious diseases, as well as their control measures.

Hospitals equipped with an epidemiological hospital service are not enough. They should have a well infrastructured infection control program, in which healthcare professionals are skilled and up-to-date and an advanced microbiology laboratory should be present. Even like that, unexpected experiences will happen during an epidemic catching us unprepared. Early diagnosis, treatment and control of isolated possible cases of biological and chemical can mean less stress, even though it seems to me that it will not be easy. Equipping professionals technically and scientifically is fundamental so that patients are properly cared for, preparation and emotional support are essential to minimize anxiety upcoming from the nursing during assistance, concerning potential risk of auto-contamination of their families.

In each country, a national system of epidemiology watching must be alert for the presence of any unusual event that may occur within its borders. It must establish guidelines, emergency plans and priority programs for the development of actions to reduce disasters in the whole country, as well as to supply emergential aid and assistance to the population that has been affected by disasters and bioterrorist and chemical attacks [59].

In this new perspective of the national public health, a dream has come true. There is no previous experience for anybody. An unavoidable period of learning will have to take place. We should make an effort to make it shorter with as little disagreeable consequences as possible. We should prepare ourselves to the hidden, invisible and unimaginable.

International policy may be the best prophylaxis against biological and chemical terrorist attacks so that lives can be saved. Policies that favor the individual, eradicating hunger, through education, freeing the stressed mind and applying action that dignify the man in poverty.

Are we prepared? Do we have the necessary technology?

REFERENCES

[1]   Varkey P, Poland GA, Cockerill, F, et al. Confronting bioterrorism Physicians on the front line. *Mayo Clin Proceed* 2002; 77:661-672.

[2]   Lane CH, Fauci AS. Bioterrorism on the home front: a new challenge for American Medicine. *JAMA 2001;* 286(20):2597-2599.

[3]   Del-Rio C, Franco-Paredes C. Bioterrorism: an intentional release of a biologic agent. *Salud Publica Mexico 2001;* 43(6): 585-588.

[4]   Franco-Paredes C, Morales AJR. Bioterrorismo: preparándose para lo impensable. *CIMEL 2004;* 9(1):31-40.

[5]   Barajas K, Stewart WA, Combs EW. The army chemical/biological SMRT (SMART-CB) team: the nurse rule. *Crit Care Nurs Clin N. Am.* 2003; 15:257-264.

[6]   Castro, A. Revisão Sistemática com ou sem Metaanálise. São Paulo: AAC 2001. [online]. [accessed aug 2005]. Available in URL: http://www.metodologia.org/meta 1.pdf

[7]   Mondy C, Cardenas D, Avila M. The Role and Advanced Practice Public Health Nurse in Bioterrorism Preparedness. *Public Health Nursing* 2003; 20(6): 422-431.

[8]   Jacinto da Silva L. Guerra biológica, bioterrorismo e saúde pública. *Cad Saúde Pública.* 2001; 17(6):1519-1523.

[9]   Christopher Gw, Cielak TJ, Pavlin JA, Eitzen Jr EM. Biological warfare: a historical perspective. *JAMA* 1997; 278:412-417.

[10]   Marr JS, Malloy CD. An epidemiologic analysis of the ten plagues of Egypt. *Caduceus* 1996; 12:7-24.

[11]   Stillsmoking K. Bioterrorism-Are you Ready for the Silent Killer? *AORN Journal* 2002; 76(3):434-450.

[12]   Gwerder LJ, Beaton R, Daniel W. Bioterrorism: implications for the occupational and environment health nurse. *AAOHN Journal* 2001:49(11):512-518.

[13]   Center for Civilian Biodefense Studies. Threat of bioterrorism. [online]. [accessed oct 2005]. Available in URL: http://www.hopkins-biodefense.org/pages/center/threat.html

[14]   Osterholm MT. Bioterrorism: a real modern threat. In: Scheld WM, Craig WA, Hughes JM, editors. Emerging Infections. 5^a ed. Whashinton, DC: ASM Press; 2001. p.213-222.

[15]   Bioterrorism: safeguarding the public's health. Lancet 2001; 358:1283.

[16]   Van Courtland Moon JE. The Korean war case. *Ann NY Acad Sci* 1992; 666:53-83.

[17]   Tucker JB. Historical trends related to bioterrorism: an empirical analysis. *Rev Biomed* 1999 julio-septiembre; 10(3):185-93.

[18]   Center for Disease Control. Disease. Recognition of illness associated with the intentional release of a biological agent. *MMWR* 2001; 50(49):893-7.

[19]   Meselson M, Gulilemin J, Hugh-Jones M, Langmuir A, Popova I, Shelokov A, et al. The Sverdlovsk anthrax outbreak of 1979. *Science* 1994; 266:1202-1208.

[20]   Woodall J. The Soviet bioweapons program: an insider's new. *Lancet* 1999; 354: 1568-1569.

[21]   Cangemi CW. Occupational response to terrorism. *AAOHN Journal* 2002; 50(4):190-198.

[22]   Sawyer PP. Bioterrorism: are we prepared? *Home Healthcare Nurse* 2003; 21(4):220-223.

[23]   Ercole FF, Costa RS. Protocolos de cuidados frente a doenças decorrentes de bioterrorismo. *Rev Latino-Am Enfermagem* 2003; 11(4):516-524.

[24]   APIC-Bioterrorism Task Force and CDC-Hospital Infections program Bioterrorism Working Group. Bioterrorism readiness plan: a template for healthcare facilities. [online]. [accessed oct 2005]. Available in URL: http://www.cdc.gov/ncidod/hip/Bio/bio.htm

[25]   Center for Civilian Biodefense Studies. A New Form of Terrorism. [accessed oct 2005]. [online]. Available in URL: http://www.hopkins-biodefense.org/pages/center/form.html

[26]   Altman GB. Invisible threats. *Nurs. Management* 2002; 33(1):43, 45-47.

[27] Salazar MK, Kelman B. Planning for Biological Disasters: occupational Health Nurses as "First Responders". *AAOHN Journal* 2002; 50(4):174-181

[28] Center for Civilian Biodefense Studies. Agent Fact Sheet Info. [accessed oct 2005]. [online]. Available in URL: http://www.hopkins-biodefense.org/pages/agents/agent. html

[29] Center for Disease Control. Recognition of illness associated with the intentional release of a biological agent. *MMWR* 2001; 50(49):893-7.

[30] Center for Disease Control. Agent/Disease. [accessed oct 2005]. [online]. Available in URL: <http://www.bt.cdc.gov/Agent/ Agentlist.asp>

[31] Center for Civilian Biodefense Studies. Agents/Anthrax. [accessed oct 2005]. [online]. Available in URL: http://www.hopkins-biodefense.org/pages/agents/agentanthrax.html

[32] Center for Disease Control. Facts About: Anthrax, Botulism, Pneumonic Plague, and Smallpox. [accessed oct 2005]. [online]. Available in URL: http://www.bt.cdc. gov/DocumentsApp/FactsAbout/FactsAbout.asp

[33] Pile JC, Malone JD, Eitzen EM, Friedlander AM. Anthrax as a potential biological warfare agent. *Arch Intern Med* 1998;158:429-34.

[34] Amstrong D, Colten J, editors. *Infectious Diseases.* Philadelphia: Mosby; 2001.

[35] Mandell GL, Bennett JE, Dolin R, editors. Principles and practice of infectious diseases. 5^a ed. New York: Churchill Livinstone; 2000.

[36] Center for Civilian Biodefense Studies. Agents. [accessed oct 2005]. [online]. Available in URL: http://www.hopkins-biodefense.org/pages/agents/agenttularemia. html

[37] Center for Civilian Biodefense Studies. Agents. [accessed oct 2005]. [online]. Available in URL: http://www.hopkins- biodefense.org/pages/agents/agentplague.html

[38] Center for Civilian Biodefense Studies. agents. [accessed oct 2005]. [online] Available in URL: http://www.hopkins- biodefense.org/ pages/agents/agentsmallpox.html

[39] Center for Disease Control. Disease. Fact Sheets: Ebola Hemorragic Fever. [accessed oct 2005]. [online]. Available in URL: http://www.cdc.gov/ncidod/dvrd/spb/mnpages/ dispages/ebola.htm

[40] Camara FP. O vírus ebola e sua infection. Folha Médica 1995 julho/setembro; 111(1):47-51.

[41] Centers for Disease Control and Prevention and World Health Organization. Infection Control for Viral Hemorrhagic Fevers in the African Health Care Setting. Atlanta; 1998.

[42] Center for Civilian Biodefense Studies. Agents. [accessed oct 2005]. [online]. Available in URL: http://www.hopkins- biodefense.org/ pages/agents/agentbotox.html

[43] Martins MP. Manual de infection hospitalar: epidemiologia, prevenção e controle. 2^a ed. Rio de Janeiro: Medsi; 2001.

[44] Centers for Disease Control and Prevention. Case Definition: Digitalis. [accessed nov 2005]. [online]. Available in URL: http://www.bt.cdc.gov/agent/gigitalis/casedf.asp

[45] Centers for Disease Control and Prevention. Facts About Strychnine. [accessed nov 2005]. [online]. Available in URL: http://www.bt.cdc.gov/agent/strychnine/basics/ facts.asp

[46] Centers for Disease Control and Prevention. Facts About Sulfur Mustard. [accessed nov 2005]. [online]. Available in URL: http://www.bt.cdc.gov/agent/sulfurmustard/ basics/facts.asp

[47]   Agency For Substances And Disease Registry. ToxFaQs [TM] Blister Agents: Sulfur Mustard Agent H/HD, Sulfur Mustard Agent HT. [accessed nov 2005]. [online]. Available in URL: http://www.atsdr.cdc.gov/tfactsd3.html

[48]   Centers for Disease Control and Prevention. Facts About Arsine. [accessed nov 2005]. [online]. Available in URL: http://www.bt.cdc.gov/agent/arsine/facts.asp

[49]   Agency For Substances And Disease Registry. Medical Management Guidelines (MMGs) for ARSINE (AsH$_3$). [accessed nov 2005]. [online]. Available in URL: http://www.asdr.cdc.gov/MHMI/mmg169.html

[50]   Centers for Disease Control and Prevention. Facts About Hydrogen Fluoride (Hydrofluoric Acid). [accessed nov 2005]. [online]. Available in URL: http://www. bt.cdc.gov/agent/hydrofluoricacid/basics/facts.asp

[51]   Centers for Disease Control and Prevention. Ammonia. [accessed nov 2005]. [online]. Available in URL: http://www.bt.cdc.gov/agent/ammonia/casedef.asp

[52]   Centers for Disease Control and Prevention. Case Definition: 3-Quinuclidinyl Benzilate (BZ). [accessed nov 2005]. [online]. Available in URL: http://www.bt.cdc.gov/agent/bz/casedef.asp

[53]   Centers for Disease Control and Prevention. Case Definition: Opioids(Fentanyl, Etorphine or others). [accessed nov 2005]. [online]. Available in URL: http://www.bt.cdc.gov/agents/opioids/casedef.asp

[54]   Centers for Disease Control and Prevention. Case Definition: Long-Acting Anticoagulant (Super Warfarin). [accessed nov 2005]. [online]. Available in URL: http://www.bt.cdc.gov./agent/superwarfarin/casedefinition.asp

[55]   Centers for Disease Control and Prevention. Arsenic (inorganic). [accessed nov 2005]. [online]. Available in URL: http://www.bt.cdc.gov./agent/arsenic/casedef.asp

[56]   Centers for Disease Control and Prevention. Mercury (inorganic). [accessed nov 2005]. [online]. Available in URL: http://www.bt.cdc.gov./agent/mercury/mercinorgcasedf. asp

[57]   Centers for Disease Control and Prevention. Mercury (organic). [accessed nov 2005]. [online]. Available in URL: http://bt.cdc.gov/agent/mercury/mercorgcasedef.asp

[58]   Centers for Disease Control and Prevention. Mercury (organic). [accessed nov 2005]. [online]. Available in URL: http://bt.cdc.gov/agent/sarin/basics/facts.asp

[59]   Agency For Substances And Disease Registry. ToxFaQs [TM] for Nerve Agents (GA, GB, GD, VX). [accessed nov 2005]. [online]. Available in URL: http://www. atsdr.cdc.gov/tfacts166.html

[60]   Centers for Disease Control and Prevention. Facts About Benzene. [accessed nov 2005]. [online]. Available in URL: http://www.bt.cdc.gov/agent/benzene/basics/ facts.asp

[61]   Centers for Disease Control and Prevention. Facts About Riot Control Agents Interin document. [accessed nov 2005]. [online]. Available in URL: http://www.bt.cdc.gov/ agent/riotcontrol/factsheet.asp

[62]   Centers for Disease Control and Prevention. Riot Control Agent Poisoning. [accessed nov 2005]. [online]. Available in URL: http://www.bt.cdc.gov/agent/riotcontrol/ agentpoisoning.asp

[63]   Agency For Substances And Disease Registry. ToxFaQs [TM] for Ethylene Glycol and Propylene Glycol. [accessed nov 2005]. [online]. Available in URL: http://www.atsdr.cdc.gov/tfacts96.html

[64]   Centers for Disease Control and Prevention. Case Definition: Adamsite (DM). [accessed nov 2005]. [online]. Available in URL: http://www.bt.cdc.gov/agent/ adamsite/casedef.asp

[65]   Stokes E, Gilbert-Palmer D, Skorga P, Young C, Persell D. Chemical Agents of Terrorism: Preparing Nurse Practioners. *The Nurse Practioner* 2004; 29(5):30-39.

[66]   Ministério De Salud. Secretaria Nacional de Defesa Civil. Informacíon Básica Sobre Bioterrorismo. [accessed oct 2001]. [online]. Disponível em URL: http://www. defesacivil.gov.br.

[67]   Organização Pan-Americana de Saúde. Preparativos para Riscos de Bioterrorisno e Terrorismo Químico. [accessed oct 2001]. [online]. Disponível em URL: http:// www.cetesb.sp.gov.br/

[68]   Steed CJ, Howe I.A, Pruitt R H, Sherrill WW. Integrating Bioterrorism Education into Nursing Scholl Curricula. *Journal of Nursing Education* 2004; 43(8):362-367.

In: Bioterrorism: Prevention, Preparedness and Protection   ISBN 1-60021-180-1
Editor: J. V. Borrelli, pp. 163-172   © 2007 Nova Science Publishers, Inc.

Chapter 6

BIOTERRORISM: PUBLIC HEALTH PREPAREDNESS*

Robin J. Strongin and C. Stephen Redhead

ABSTRACT

The September 11th attack and subsequent intentional release of anthrax spores via the U.S. postal system have focused policymakers' attention on the preparedness and response capability of the nation's public health system. The anthrax attacks put a tremendous strain on the U. S. public health infrastructure, an infrastructure that many experts argue has been weakened by years of neglect and under-funding. To better understand the preparedness gaps that exist, as well as the disparate functions and agencies that define public health in this country, the Congressional Research Service (CRS), in conjunction with George Washington University's National Health Policy Forum (NHPF), convened a seminar on October 26, 2001, entitled, *The U.S. Health Care System: Are State and Local Officials Prepared for Bioterrorism? How Should the Federal Government Assist?* This report was supported, in part, by a grant from the Robert Wood Johnson Foundation.

Speakers included William L. Roper, M.D., M.P.H., Dean, School of Public Health at the University of North Carolina; Georges C. Benjamin, M.D., Secretary, Maryland Department of Health and Mental Hygiene; Amy Smithson, Ph.D., Director, Chemical and Biological Weapons Non-Proliferation Project, the Henry L. Stimson Center; and Janet Heinrich, Dr. P.H., R.N., Director, Health Care–Public Health, U.S. General Accounting Office. The panelists presented a detailed overview of public health and the difficult choices the country faces in preparedness planning and rebuilding. The speakers made clear in their remarks that while immediate needs must be met, the importance of planning for the longer-term must not be overlooked. They suggested the need to recognize the multitude of returns on initial investments in public health. For example, if some drug-resistant bacteria were to emerge, independent of any terrorist activity, the capabilities developed to combat bioterrorism would be invaluable.

Based upon their varied experiences, there was general consensus among all the speakers that public health preparedness, while dependent upon federal financial and other assistance, was largely a local matter. They argued that mending the gaps in the current public health fabric will require significant long-term commitments from the federal government, including investments and improvements in: laboratory capacity, regional planning, workforce training, epidemiology and surveillance systems, information systems, communication systems, and media relations.

The panelists stressed that as priorities are set and resources committed, it is imperative that all preparedness efforts be coordinated at all levels of government–federal, state, and local.

INTRODUCTION

The anthrax events that occurred in the wake of the September 11th terrorist attacks (see box on p. 2) triggered a heightened state of alert and a series of questions related to the ability of the United States public health system to adequately meet the challenges associated with anthrax as well as smallpox, plague and other possible bioterror threat agents. In response to those questions and concerns, CRS, in conjunction with George Washington University's National Health Policy Forum, sought to provide a forum for congressional staff to hear from leading experts in the field.[1] Speakers for the session included: William L. Roper, M.D., M.P.H., Dean, School of Public Health at the University of North Carolina; Georges C. Benjamin, M.D., Secretary, Maryland Department of Health and Mental Hygiene; Amy Smithson, Ph.D., Director, Chemical and Biological Weapons Non-Proliferation Project, the Henry L. Stimson Center; and Janet Heinrich, Dr. P.H., R.N., Director, Health Care–Public Health, U.S. General Accounting Office.

Over the years, experts have been calling for a more robust public health infrastructure,[2] for a closer working relationship between the medical and public health communities, and for a broader research and development agenda in this area. Preparing for attacks that might take a number of very different forms has taken on greater urgency since September 11th. Priorities have shifted, and the importance of the public health and safety infrastructure has become a much greater concern.

The existence of significant gaps in the country's emergency preparedness was made clear by the speakers. Examples of the inadequacies in the public health system that emerged during the anthrax crisis included: the lack of laboratory capacity and the rapidity with which they became overwhelmed, the problems in communicating accurate information to the public, the lack of coordination and timely information exchange among the various components of the health care system, and the lack of coordination and seamless integration

---

[*] Excerpted from *Bioterrorism Reader*, by Arthur P. Rogers, New York: Nova Science Publishers, Inc., 2002.

[1] Originally conceptualized as two separate sessions, the first one focusing on the federal role in preparedness and the second on the state and local response capabilities, the meeting that ultimately took place was collapsed into one session due to the Capitol Hill closures associated with the anthrax contamination. When the meeting was finally held, it addressed both the federal as well as the state and local perspectives.

[2] The seminal 1988 Institute of Medicine (IOM) report, *The Future of Public Health* (Washington, DC: National Academy Press), identified three prongs that define public health and its infrastructure: (1) The Mission of Public Health: the fulfillment of society's interest in assuring the conditions in which people can be healthy [p. 40]; (2) The Substance of Public Health: organized community efforts aimed at the prevention of disease and promotion of health. It links many disciplines and rests upon the scientific core of epidemiology [p. 41]; and (3) The Organizational Framework of Public Health: encompasses both activities undertaken within the formal structure of government and the associated efforts of private and voluntary organizations and individuals [p. 42].

between public health, public safety, law enforcement, and the media. The clash of cultures – particularly around information sharing – between law enforcement (keeping information under wraps for security purposes) and public health investigations (broadly disseminating information in order to contain epidemics) was cited as having the potential to undermine the integrity and the ability of public health to accomplish its goals.

U.S. Anthrax Attacks

Twenty-two cases of anthrax occurred as a result of the intentional dissemination of *Bacillus anthracis* spores through the U.S. postal system: 11 cases of inhalation anthrax and 11 cases of cutaneous anthrax. Five of those with inhalation anthrax died. The remaining 17 patients have made a full recovery. The majority of cases occurred in persons working at postal facilities in New Jersey and Washington, DC, where contaminated letters were handled or processed by high-speed sorting machines, or at media companies in New York City or Florida, where the letters were delivered. At least 300 postal and other facilities were tested for the presence of *B. anthracis* spores, and more than 32,000 potentially exposed persons were given antibiotics, none of whom subsequently developed anthrax.

Federal officials confirmed that the bacterial spores used in the attacks belong to the Ames strain, a variant of the anthrax bacterium that was first isolated from a cow in Texas in 1981. Because of the strain's virulence, it was studied for years by the U.S. Army's biological weapons program and distributed to several labs in the United States and abroad to help them test vaccines. The spores sent to Capitol Hill were processed into a highly concentrated and very fine, dry powder. In this form, the tiny spores, each about 1-3 microns in diameter, readily aerosolize and are capable of being inhaled deep into a person's lungs where they can trigger the most serious, inhalational form of the disease.

Though the recent anthrax attacks are small in scale compared to the scenarios envisioned by bioterrorism experts and played out in recent government exercises (e.g., Deep Winter), they exposed weaknesses in the public health system and showed that it is ill-prepared to deal with a large-scale bioterroist attack.

The speakers provided an overview of the current state of emergency preparedness at all levels of government, by identifying both the gaps that exist and the steps being taken to close them. A recurring theme underscored by all the presenters throughout the seminar was that closing the preparedness gaps by shoring up the public health system will help protect against the growing threat both from natural events – increasing because of global travel, ubiquitous imported food, and antibiotic resistant pathogens – as well as intentional attacks.

Key among the discussions was how to design the best preparedness "game plan." The speakers believe the plan should be: one that is well coordinated among all levels of governments and among all the various players; one that spends dollars wisely and efficiently without duplicating efforts already underway; one that depoliticizes public health and one that understands that public health is a local need dependent upon federal dollars; one that recognizes both the short and long-term needs and the fact that rural areas have even less capacity than suburban or urban areas; one that is given immediate priority.

PUBLIC HEALTH PREPAREDNESS: THIS ONE IS FOR REAL

For many years, issues pertaining to public health have seldom been given priority attention. This changed with the first case of inhalation anthrax in Florida in early October. That first case of anthrax, the index case in public health parlance, propelled the public health system into the spotlight and commanded the attention of the entire nation. Public health, explained Dr. William L. Roper,[3] is all about protecting the public against threats to their health. At the time this seminar was held, public health had become front-page news, headline information on the 24-hour news shows. But the U.S. public health infrastructure, after years of languishing was described as fragile, thin, and in need of repair. According to Dr. Roper, the nation directs most of its health resources towards medical care (e.g., physicians, hospitals) and biomedical research. The public health system receives only "crumbs," as compared to other components of the health care system.

He believes the longstanding problem of the lack of attention to and underinvestment in public health has been compounded by recent events, including pressures brought on by the current economic slowdown and state budget shortfalls. At the same time, the public health system faces increased demands and heightened expectations in the wake of September 11 and the anthrax attacks.

According to Dr. Roper, the public's expectations, not surprisingly, called for 100% protection with no risks. The goal of public health is to minimize health risks. This was a particularly challenging aspect of the anthrax events because of the unfamiliarity of the disease among medical professionals. While the science was evolving on an almost daily basis, the learning curve was steep, and public health officials and personnel – at the federal, state, and local levels – were working around the clock to try to contain the anthrax outbreaks and ease the public's fear. Dr. Roper cautioned against carping about and criticizing the Centers for Disease Control and Prevention (CDC), the lead public health agency at the federal level, and other health officials as they made their way through the nation's first major bioterror attack. While he praised the dedication of all involved, Dr. Roper voiced his concern over the inevitable emotional and physical burn-out that would ultimately occur among the front-line workers. Adding to the growing list of challenges, Dr. Roper asserted that not only would workers grow weary, but supplies of protective clothing and other gear could be depleted, further endangering health officials and first responders.

In order to meet the current public health challenges and to be better prepared for future events (which include both deliberate and naturally occurring public health threats), Dr. Roper stressed the importance of continuing the efforts already underway. Building upon existing training programs[4] (such as the Public Health Grand Rounds and the Public Health Training Network), improving existing communication systems, and strengthening existing information systems (such as the Health Alert Network[5]) will ultimately upgrade the public

---

[3] William L. Roper, M.D., Ph.D., is Dean of the School of Public Health at the University of North Carolina. He was director of CDC from 1990–1993.

[4] For additional information, go to the University of North Carolina's School of Public Health Web site, [http://www.sph.unc.edu] and click on "bioterrorism."

[5] A nationwide program, developed by the CDC in partnership with the National Association of County and City Health Officials, the Association of State and Territorial Health Officials, and other health organizations, to establish the communications, information, distance-learning, and organizational infrastructure that will link local health departments to one another and to other relevant organizations.

health system and infuse it with the resources, tools, and personnel that will be necessary to protect the public now and in the long-term.

PUBLIC HEALTH PREPAREDNESS:
ONE STATE'S (MARYLAND) EXPERIENCE

Dr. Georges C. Benjamin[6] opened his presentation by reviewing the various types of public health concerns (organisms causing morbidity and organisms causing mortality) and the various ways in which these organisms could present, including natural events, overt events, covert events, high-risk events such as the Olympics or a presidential inaugural, and police actions that discover a risky site (e.g., finding a bioterror lab during a routine drug bust). The challenge facing public health officials is knowing when an attack has occurred, particularly in a bioterror scenario which can take days or even weeks to become obvious.

The key to preparing for such an event is surveillance – finding unprecedented numbers of cases or unusual circumstances, signs that raise the index of suspicion. The impact of surveillance on survivability is huge; Dr. Benjamin cited studies conducted by researchers at the Johns Hopkins University confirming that early warning systems save lives.

Early warning systems are one of many components necessary for successful preparedness. Disasters, Dr. Benjamin maintained, overwhelm health care systems that are already stretched thin. "One of our objectives is to shorten the time from absolute chaos to controlled disorder." Maryland has taken the following steps to better prepare for public health events, whether a naturally occurring outbreak or the result of a covert release of a dangerous pathogen.[7] These activities include:

- advance planning;
- ongoing surveillance and pre-incident intelligence gathering;
- establishing a predetermined chain of command and authority (medical personnel are not comfortable working in command and controlled environments);
- building relationships with law enforcement personnel ("have lunch with your FBI agent");
- establishing rapid, broad communication capabilities (that can identify sentinel events and enhance communications); and
- training personnel (public health staff, laboratory staff, medical providers, medical examiners, as well as mail room and office staff).

In order to minimize the chaos associated with a public health crisis, Dr. Benjamin noted that his priorities included the development of policies concerning decontamination of people and facilities, prophylaxis and vaccination, quarantining and isolation, and the monitoring of rescue workers. Other issues that Dr. Benjamin has planned for in order to minimize confusion during a public health crisis include: capacity building (planning for surge capacity

---

[6] Georges Benjamin, M.D., is Maryland's Secretary of Health and Mental Hygiene.
[7] For additional information, go to Maryland's Dept. of Health and Mental Hygiene Web site [http://www.dhmh.state.md.us].

– a sudden, often unexpected increase in service demand – among hospitals and nursing homes), preauthorization for payment (linking to managed care and other payers), community mental health needs, pest and rodent control, waste control, mortuary needs, disease follow-up, and access to vital health records.

Preparedness funding priorities for the state of Maryland center around increasing laboratory capacity (in terms of resources and personnel), strengthening communication and information systems, as well as improving training and education programs for health care workers, the public, and the media. These state set priorities mirror those articulated by Dr. Roper in his remarks. The call for better coordination, better planning, better training, as well as a greater investment in and commitment to those agencies that make up the vast network known as public health was the major theme of all four speakers.

PUBLIC HEALTH PREPAREDNESS: LESSONS FROM THE FIELD

Dr. Amy Smithson[8] drew on the research and findings from her Henry L. Stimson Center Report #35, *Ataxia: The Chemical and Biological Terrorism Threat and the U.S. Response*[9] which contained information based on the combined wisdom of front line operatives interviewed in 33 cities across the country. According to Dr. Smithson's research, most cities reported being better prepared to handle a chemical, rather than a biologic attack because cities have a sizeable number of HAZMAT (hazardous materials) teams as compared with the necessary resources that would be needed to handle a bioterror incident.

Although all those surveyed indicated an uneasiness in the level of preparedness on the "medical side of the house" for both chemical and biologic attacks, the primary concern repeatedly raised by the experts was the ability – or inability – of the cities' public health officials to be able to figure out something was wrong and to isolate the responsible organism quickly enough to be able to contain an outbreak and successfully treat the victims of such an attack.

According to experts interviewed by Dr. Smithson, disease reporting is the first critical step in determining a suspicious cluster of events. Dr. Smithson noted that the current system is reliant upon physicians who are "only human" and given the new awareness of bioterror threats, are going to be asked to identify diseases they have never seen before.

In trying to overcome this obvious hurdle, New York City (NYC) has broken new ground by monitoring all of its emergency services calls (911 calls). Analysts have developed software that can identify disease markers or sentinel events, flagging unusual outbreaks of diseases, for example during unusual seasons. If for instance, a cluster of flu-like cases were to occur during a non-peak flu season time period, this would trigger a red flag that public health officials could investigate. It is the equivalent of a digital early warning system. Over-the-counter drug products are also monitored in New York City, again to spot unusual purchasing patterns during atypical seasons. This effort requires that the resources and capacity to harness and crunch the data are available at the local level. Similarly, New York City has also selected sentinel hospitals that are *always* on alert, always looking for the exotic

---

[8] Amy Smithson, Ph.D., is Director of the Chemical and Biological Weapons Non-Proliferation Project at the Henry L. Stimson Center, Washington, DC.
[9] For a full copy of the report, go to [http://www.stimson.org/cwc/ataxia.htm].

disease first (an approach not typically utilized in classic diagnostic work-ups). All of these initiatives allow New York City to take the pulse of the system on a continuous basis.

Once an unusual situation is uncovered, notices can be sent out to other hospitals, laboratories, and medical personnel alerting them to a potential outbreak while at the same time seeking additional input from the field. This system is useful not just for covert criminal attacks, but is also vitally important in containing naturally occurring public health disasters such as influenza outbreaks and food-borne related illnesses. This is particularly critical given the global nature of the world today and its effect on the spread of disease.

The New York City surveillance system is unfortunately the exception and not the rule. Dr. Smithson stressed that this level of sophistication is desperately needed across the country. But, this alone is not sufficient. Dr. Smithson noted that a second tool that must be used in tandem with a sophisticated early warning surveillance system involves what a physicist at Sandia National Labs has developed. This tool is in many ways a mirror-image of the NYC system in that the capability to access data from a central data bank is placed directly in the hands of the physicians. If a patient or group of patients present with suspicious symptoms, the doctor can type data (e.g., from diagnostic tests) directly into a hand held device and retrieve information from a central data repository. Together, according to Dr. Smithson, these two tools – which would provide a rolling temporal and diagnostic map in the physician's geographic area – would arm the front line medical professionals, potentially providing enough time to jumpstart a prophylaxsis program that could save lives. The science and technology exist today to implement these capabilities. Up until very recently, however, the resources and commitment were lacking. Dr. Smithson believes that the window of opportunity to put these programs in place has never been greater.

Another largely ignored but critical component of emergency preparedness that must be improved upon is regional hospital planning. Again, according to Dr. Smithson's research, bona fide regional planning where regular disaster drills are practiced is the exception rather than the rule. During her interviews with hospital administrators, Dr. Smithson learned that the inability to charge medical personnel time to a reimbursable health service largely explained the lack of regular disaster planning and drills. Given the financial disincentives associated with these planning efforts, coupled with the relatively low level threat potential (until recently), it was not surprising that these efforts were deemed low priorities. Respondents said that most plans were drawn up using medical personnel who volunteered their time. Dr. Smithson pointed out, however, that most health professionals volunteering their time tend to work with the uninsured.

Dr. Smithson stressed that in the absence of these regional "game plans," entire local health care systems could collapse. These plans must allow for the maintenance of maternity wards, burn and trauma centers, and critical care units, services which will continue to be in demand regardless of whether a bioterror or other public health crisis ensues. Likewise, the plan must insure an adequate level of supplies (i.e., not assuming that there will be sufficient suppliers for all hospitals but actually conducting the research and mapping out the logistics of which hospital will receive what quantity of which specific supplies.) Other considerations pointed out by Dr. Smithson that warrant attention include figuring out, ahead of a crisis, precisely how the national stockpile of prescription drugs and other medical supplies will be distributed. (This aspect of planning would necessitate the provision of security in the case of mass panic.) In addition, there must be a regional plan regarding prophylaxis strategies; deciding for example, who gets vaccinated when. Another dimension requires local regions to define what assistance they can expect from the federal government, how long it will take until it arrives, and what it will take to fill the gaps until federal assistance arrives. Dr. Smithson strongly stated the opinion that while table-top exercises such as *Dark Winter* are important, they do not go nearly far enough and that it is imperative that real drills be practiced on a regular basis.[10]

Dr. Smithson made a plea to the audience that any preparedness package include adequate, well coordinated state and local public health and front line preparedness capacity building. She stressed that this does not necessarily mean more money, but money spent more wisely. She then raised the question of the role of the federal government.

PUBLIC HEALTH PREPAREDNESS: THE FEDERAL ROLE

Dr. Janet Heinrich[11] summarized the recent findings of a September 28, 2001 U.S. GAO study she directed, *Bioterrorism: Federal Research and Preparedness Activities*,[12] which found that over 20 federal agencies have a role in emergency preparedness. While the role and responsibilities of these agencies cut a wide swath, from detection of disease to the provision of vaccines, from research and development to prevention, coordination at the federal level is severely fragmented. While there are many efforts to coordinate these activities, the outlook so far, according to Dr. Heinrich, is bleak.

Pointing to the vast increase in dollars allocated to preparedness efforts (a 310% increase since FY1998) Dr. Heinrich stressed the need to establish priority spending for these monies. Her call, which was echoed by all those on the panel, was to include training, communication and information systems enhancement, and capacity building at the top of the priority list. Another important aspect of priority setting involves getting the money from the federal purse into the state and local coffers where it is needed most, in other words, deciding which priorities should be funded with federal dollars. The question was raised whether directing federal preparedness money to vaccines and prescription drug stockpiles was the most judicious use of these funds given that state and local public health entities do not rate these items high on their priority lists. GAO found that vaccine and drug stockpiles are seen by many public health officials in the trenches as a short-term "band-aid" fix for a limited number of biologic threats, and not the crucial longer-term commitment needed to shore up the thinly stretched basic public health infrastructure of today. It was pointed out that one key contribution the new office of homeland security could make would be to assist in coordinating the transfer of federal dollars to local level needs.

---

[10] Dark Winter was an exercise designed to simulate possible U.S. reaction to the deliberate introduction of smallpox in 3 states during the winter of 2002. The exercise itself was conducted at Andrews Air Force Base on June 22–23,2001. Former senior government officials played the roles of National Security Council members responding to the evolving epidemic. For more information on Dark Winter, go to [http://www.hopkins-biodefense.org].

[11] Janet Heinrich, Dr. P.H., R.N., is Director of Health Care and Public Health issues at the U.S. General Accounting Office.

[12] A copy of the report in its entirety can be found by going to the GAO Web site [http://www.gao.gov], clicking on "Find GAO Reports" and entering report number "GAO-01-915."

QUESTIONS FROM THE AUDIENCE

Questions from the audience covered several themes, most of which revolved around the division of labor and responsibility among the federal, state, and local governments. One audience member questioned whether today's decentralized public health system is the most appropriate structure for fighting the war on terrorism. It was pointed out that the recent terror attacks were really national attacks, akin in many ways to the attack on Pearl Harbor (in which a national response ensued). The consensus among the panelists was that these issues are local and that a national superstructure would ultimately create a false sense of security and would undermine the ability of an already fractured local public health system to rebuild. The panelists were of the strong opinion that this is *the* opportunity for shoring up and bolstering a permanent state and local capacity and that there was a definite role for the federal government, one that was not solely centered on finances. An example cited was that while the CDC is only one component of the U.S. public health enterprise, it is a vital resource to state and local officials. If, however, experts at the CDC are prohibited from sharing information, the integrity and the ability of the entire public health infrastructure could be at stake. So too might be the health of the public.

Another area that received attention from the audience involved states' capacities to effectively use additional funds that would make their way from the federal coffers into state and local budgets. Concern was expressed among many in the audience that there be adequate accountability as to how the new federal dollars would be spent in the name of bioterror and emergency preparedness. Monies should not be diverted to oncology wards, for example, at the expense of decontamination units.

The issue of incorporating professional standards for front line and medical personnel into education programs was raised in a related round of questions and answers. The panel agreed that where the power of Washington could be brought to bear was in institutionalizing professional standards into existing programs that could be modified to incorporate bioterrorism training. They said it would not be enough for the federal government to dictate exactly how to conduct a particular preparedness related activity. Rather, the states should be given maximum flexibility and control, but at the same time, they must be held accountable.

There seemed to be agreement that while most of the day to day action would continue to take place at the state and local levels, there were several important ways the federal government could enhance preparedness (e.g., financing and conducting technical research and development, financing and maintaining the national pharmaceutical stockpile and coordinating and sharing clinical expertise through the CDC). But to be successful, such commitment must not waver when the anthrax crisis comes to a close. An example of "yo-yo public health funding" commitments cited was the U.S. experience with tuberculosis (TB). When the country faced a serious TB epidemic, monies were provided with the express purpose of ridding the country of TB. But as soon as TB was largely eradicated, the monies were cut. The lack of public health funds for education and prevention contributed to the return of TB, only this time it came back in an antibiotic-resistant form. More monies had to be infused into the system, and eradicating antibiotic-resistant TB remains a public health challenge. The message from the speakers was clear: fighting disease – whether naturally occurring or manmade – will require a consistent, coordinated, long-term commitment.

CONCLUSION

The distinction between bioterrorism and chemical terrorism, as well as that between radiologic and nuclear terrorism, is critical, for in the differences between them lie the unique requirements for preparedness. While many of the issues and challenges are the same, regardless of the type of terror attack (for example, the ability of the health care system to deal with mass casualties and the "worried well," short and long-term mental health needs, and panic), the nature of an attack will determine the needed response and ultimately the level of preparedness. In the end, while the initial responses may start out differently, all emergency responses ultimately rely on the same health and safety infrastructure. An infrastructure that has fallen into a critical state of disrepair after years of neglect and budget cuts, according to the speakers at the seminar. As federal and state lawmakers debate and devise strategies for becoming better prepared, there was consensus among all the panelists that whatever form the final plans take, they should be well coordinated, well funded, and long-term.

In: Bioterrorism: Prevention, Preparedness and Protection   ISBN 1-60021-180-1
Editor: J. V. Borrelli, pp. 173-194   © 2007 Nova Science Publishers, Inc.

Chapter 7

DEVELOPING AND VALIDATING DIAGNOSTIC ASSAYS FOR BIODEFENSE

Nick M. Cirino, Maureen Shail, Christina Egan

Wadsworth Center, New York State Department of Health, Albany, New York, USA

"It is possible to fail in many ways...while to succeed is possible only in one way".

Aristotle

ABSTRACT

Throughout history, humankind has battled infectious microorganisms that cause outbreaks of disease and death. As if the microbes weren't formidable enough in themselves, man has often employed some of these pathogens as weapons against other humans. The use of biological organisms or toxins to incapacitate or kill (biological warfare), or to cause civil disruption, chaos, and terror (bioterrorism), is documented to have occurred over the past several hundred years, all building to the anthrax mailings in the United States in 2001. The new paradigm of protecting the public from natural and man-made biological threats has rapidly transformed the public health and national security infrastructures in the United States. The nexus between basic research and applied research focused on protecting humans from pathogenic organisms has been termed biodefense. Biodefense is not a discipline *per se*, but a concerted application of other disciplines (immunology, biochemistry, pharmacology, microbiology) to the protection of human health and the enhancement of national security. One major component of biodefense is the rapid detection and identification of pathogenic or toxic materials that may be the etiological agents of a biological attack. The public health infrastructure must be able to rapidly detect (i.e., rule-in) these agents, as well as agents that cause more common, natural diseases with similar clinical presentations. This rule-in/rule-out algorithm is essential for an effective, rapid response, enabling initiation of appropriate medical intervention. An optimal diagnostic test would be able to rule-in any causative agent, while simultaneously ruling-out (i.e., determine not to be present) all of the others. Validating assays that are used to identify pathogens like anthrax- or plague-causing microorganisms are complex and costly, but absolutely necessary to ensure a quality diagnostic with near-zero false-positive and false-negative results. A rigorous, quality-controlled, and statistically robust process must be followed, to validate these methods. As an initial development of a broad-spectrum diagnostic platform, we have employed a real-time PCR (rtPCR) array detection approach to rule-in or rule-out many of the NIAID categories A and B priority pathogens. Parameters for assay sensitivity, specificity, accuracy, and robustness are defined and established prior to assay development, to ensure the quality of the method. Approaches, achievements, and obstacles encountered along the path to assay validation will be discussed.

INTRODUCTION

Our objective is to produce a validated rtPCR screening assay capable of detecting and discriminating many different pathogens on the select agent list. While there are many rtPCR chemistries and platforms available [1], we have chosen 5'-nuclease assay chemistry (i.e., TaqMan) and detection on the Applied BioSystems instruments, so as to be consistent with methodologies used by other public health laboratories. Before we present our assay development data, several components of bioanalytical assay development and validation must be defined and described. Once a researcher has acquired these basic concepts, the general process by which diagnostic assays are measured will become readily understandable, as will the specific process that we have undergone to develop our rtPCR multiplex assay.

Assay Development Versus Assay Validation

The main objective in method development is the establishment of performance criteria which, if unbiased, are accurate measures of assay quality. Performance criteria should take into account any applicable federal or state regulations as well as clinical considerations (e.g., the concentration of analyte in the proposed sample matrix). Assay development requires continuous evaluation and refinement; it is clearly distinct from the validation phase, which is a final, statistically meaningful appraisal of assay performance. Integration into the assay development of rigorous performance metrics that are consistent with International Conference on Harmonization (ICH) guidelines will expedite the bioanalytical method validation process. ICH performance parameters include specificity, accuracy, linearity, precision, range, sensitivity (e.g., the limit of detection, or LOD, and the limit of quantitation, or LOQ) and robustness[3,4]. It must be remembered that assay development is an iterative process of assessments and improvements versus the pre-established performance metrics whereas validation is a proof that the assay can meet all performance metrics when performed in a defined protocol. By understanding the differences between development and validation phases, assay developers can more expeditiously proceed through the development phase and transition to the validation phase.

Diagnostic Assay Development

A diagnostic assay is a test used to indicate the presence (rule-in) or absence (rule-out) of a specific target analyte. A diagnostic assay can be qualitative, semi-quantitative (qualitative results based on a quantitative assay), or fully quantitative. For this discussion, we will focus on qualitative or quantitative assays only. A qualitative assay indicates only the presence or absence, at or above a defined threshold, of the target analyte. A quantitative assay yields a measurement of how much of a target analyte is present. One optimization strategy for fully quantitative and semi-quantitative assays is the use of a calibration curve. Another common optimization technique for semi-quantitative assays involves the use of receiver operating characteristic (ROC) curves. For most clinical diagnostic assays, the desired results are a rule-in/rule-out of the etiologic agent so that appropriate medical intervention can be initiated. For environmental diagnostics and forensics, quantitative assays are more critical so as to assess risk of exposure or spread.

An assay's evolution begins with the identification of a clearly defined goal. Whether the assay is for basic research or diagnostic purposes, the intended use becomes the driver by which development and validation criteria are established. The qualitative rtPCR assays that we have developed for forensics and environmental samples can be employed for clinical samples as well. Performance metrics can further be broken down into two categories: measurement and variability. Measurement parameters include specificity, accuracy, and linearity, while variability parameters include precision, range, sensitivity, and robustness. The overall impact of each parameter depends on whether the assay being developed is to be used as a qualitative assay (e.g., clinical diagnostics) or as a quantitative one. Each of the performance criteria will be defined and discussed below.

Analytical Specificity

An assay's ability to generate a negative result when the specific target analyte is not present. Specificity is often confused with selectivity, which is very different. Selectivity is a measure of an assay's ability to detect 'indistinguishable' analytes (e.g., all strains of a pathogenic bacterium). For discussion of this and other assay quality parameters, a simple table serves as a guideline (Table 1).

Table 1. Assay performance evaluation table for a known absolute standard (i.e., target DNA spiked into known negative samples)

	Analyte present	Analyte absent	Total
Test positive	a = true positive	b = false positive	a+b
Test negative	c = false negative	d = true negative	c+d
Total	a+c	b+d	a+b+c+d

From the above table, many assay performance metrics can be estimated:

- Specificity = $100 \times d/(b+d)$
- Sensitivity = $100 \times a/(a+c)$
- Positive predictive value = $100 \times a/(a+b)$

- Negative predictive value = 100 x d/(c+d)
- Accuracy = 100 x [(a+d)/(a+b+c+d)]

These are estimates for sensitivity, specificity, etc, because they are based only on a representative sample set; if another subset of specimens were to be tested, the estimates of performance would probably be numerically different. However, if the sample set is closely representative of specimens from the target patient population, the estimates will be statistically unbiased, and the estimates will equal the true values. For example, if a nucleic acid test (NAT) specific for *Bacillus anthracis* were run on 25 near-neighbor *Bacillus* species, and if one positive result were generated, the Specificity of the assay (100 x 24/(1+24)) would be 96%. For most NATs, like rtPCR, specificity panels are critical to the evaluation of assay performance. Specificity panels should include genetic near neighbors, host or patient extracts, common flora found in the particular matrix, and other organisms that would be included in a diagnostic assay.

Analytical Sensitivity

The degree to which a low level of a target analytes can be detected with some level of certainty, when present. When an assay result is compared to a known clinical status or to a perfect standard (known positive or negative), the sensitivity of the assay is estimated as the proportion of specimens for which the test is positive (Table 1). The LOD is the level at which the positive predictive value is above a predefined threshold and the results are therefore considered to be accurate and precise. The LOQ is the minimum amount of analyte that, when measured, gives a precise and accurate measurement. For example, for our rtPCR assay, we want to show sensitivity above 20 gene copies of the target analyte in a reaction. The theoretical LOD for any PCR-based assay is one intact copy of the target sequence, however, due to stochastic and partitioning issues, one copy cannot be reproducibly detected. In addition, the LOQ for quantitative PCR assays, including rtPCR is typically above 25 copies, due to first-hit kinetics and inconsistent quality (i.e., percent fragmented) of the target nucleic acid sequences. We therefore set the threshold of detection at the LOQ.

Accuracy

The degree to which the assay test result and the true value (i.e., presence or absence) agree. Accuracy is typically a qualitative measure of whether an assay generates correct positive and negative results (Table 1); it can be defined as the percentage of true results (positive or negative) divided by the total number of tests run.

Precision

The degree to which individual results of multiple measurements of a series of standards agree. There are three classes of precision:

- *repeatability- one location, one operator, short time frame*
- *intermediate precision- one location over a number of weeks*
- *reproducibility- precision between two or more locations*

Precision is determined through calculation of the mean, the standard deviation (S.D.) with a 95% confidence interval, and the coefficient of variation (CV) of the data. Although the CV has been widely utilized, it is not useful in all cases. For example, in negative analyte cases in which the signal approaches zero, the mathematical result will be an infinitely large CV that does not correctly reflect the assay's precision. Presentation of the S.D. and its corresponding 95% confidence interval is preferred. The pass-fail criteria for this type of precision analysis involve assessing whether or not the S.D. of the estimate exceeds the precision goal. Precision is a quantitative metric that is used to assess operator, instrument, facility, and temporal effects on assay performance. In simple terms, if an assay is precise, 1000 gene copies of a target analyte will repeatedly and reproducibly generate a result of 1000 gene copies, regardless of variations in analyst, location, or instrument. In reality, a range of measurements will be found centered around 1000 gene copies, but within a defined confidence interval.

Linearity

An assay's ability to elicit a result that is directly, or by means of defined mathematical transformation, proportional to the concentration of analyte within a given range.

Linearity of a quantitative assay is intrinsically linked to the physical property that is being generating the result. Linearity analysis involves use of an assay to test approximately 5-10 samples, preferably with multiple replicates of each specimen. This type of analysis assesses three assay performance metrics: accuracy, linearity, and reportable range (LOQ). The acceptance criteria for these parameters should be defined before an experiment is begun. Real-time PCR assays have a broad inherent linearity, typically 6-8 logs, dependent only on the optical sensitivity of the detection platform used. For the assay's reportable range, the acceptable parameters should reflect the assay's analytical range. The degree of linearity of the assay results can be predefined by an acceptable goodness-of-fit statistical test range. In the case above, rtPCR is linear over 6-9 orders of magnitude because the detection platform monitors when a fluorescent signal becomes detectable, reported as a cycle threshold or Ct, and does not directly correlate fluorescent intensity to amplification. For rtPCR assays, the amplification efficiency (ε) can be determined directly from the linearity parameter data. The efficiency corresponds to:

$$\varepsilon = \left(10^{(-1/m)} - 1\right) \times 100.$$

For example, if the slope (m) of a log10 dilution standard curve is -3.4193, the efficiency of that assay is 96.1%.

Range

The interval between the upper and lower levels that have been demonstrated to be determined with accuracy, precision, and linearity. The lower limit of the range is typically the LOQ; analytical results outside this range cannot be quantified precisely, even though they may be accurate (i.e., positive above LOD but below LOQ). From our example above, if an rtPCR assay detected *B. anthracis* at 10 gene copies, a level below our LOQ, in two of four replicates, the sample would be called positive but below LOQ; accordingly, the number of gene copies of *B. anthracis* DNA could not be quantitated precisely.

Robustness

An assays ability to withstand the effects of operational parameters and to generate an accurate and precise result. The main factors that can affect assay performance are temperature, humidity, matrix affects, sample contaminants, and reagent composition. Assay developers should study these factors alone and in combination, to assess their effects on the assay's accuracy, precision, repeatability, and cross-reactivity.

Diagnostic Assay Validation

After successful completion of the development phase, an assay must undergo a thorough validation study, prior to implementation. For the validation phase, a SOP, or standard operating procedure, should be defined and accepted. The SOP must also include predefined acceptance criteria for each of the assay parameters. A validation plan is typically established by the regulatory or oversight entity, in order to assure assay quality and to confer confidence in the assay results. Validation studies typically include analyses that confirm accuracy, precision, sensitivity, and specificity. If an assay passes and becomes validated, a report should be prepared to document all phases of the development and validation.

The assay validation must be performed in a comparable specimen matrix to that which will eventually be used for diagnosis (e.g., blood or serum for bacteremia diagnosis). This validation study should include a study performed in a blinded fashion to ensure that there is no up weighting of samples containing target, relative to the negative controls. The blinded validation study should include at least 25-30 seeded samples and at least 10 negative control samples. The seeded samples should include samples with a target organism concentration that is at or near the LOD. In the draft FDA guidelines for validation of molecular assays for the detection of microbial pathogens, seeding of target organisms into the specimen at a concentration 2-3 times the LOD is recommended [2]. The sensitivity assays and initial characterization of the assay that are performed in the development phase can be utilized as guidelines for the validation study. Ideally, the validation should utilize actual specimens containing the target of interest. Unlike assays being developed for *E. coli* or *Salmonella,* for which stool specimens containing these organisms are readily available in the clinical laboratory, assays designed to detect biothreat agents are not readily available in laboratories. Various specimen types should be seeded with target organism if clinical specimens are not available. The assay to be validated must be tested for each specimen type to which it will be applied, since there are differences in physical properties, inhibitors present, and pathogen load among various different specimen types. An assay designed to detect *Yersinia pestis* on an environmental swab can have very different parameters from the same assay designed to use sputum specimens. While a comparison of the validated assay against another available assay can be performed, the validation study should ideally be compared against a gold standard assay, usually culture-based testing. In addition, since most rtPCR assays are performed on extracted or purified DNA, the validation study must account for the potential loss of nucleic acid during the isolation process; thus, the validation study is normally performed using an initial concentration that is higher than the LOD.

Unlike the statistical and experimental methods for assay development, which are not well defined, the statistical methods for assay validation have been established and widely published. As part of its Harmonized Tripartite Guideline, the ICH released the following two documents: "Text on Validation of Analytical Procedures" and "Validation of Analytical Procedures: Methodology" [3,4]. These documents provide the metrics to be used for assay performance, as well as essential validation parameters and evaluation methods. Validation parameters include not only the numerical result of a test (e.g., the mean or median value), but also the variability of the test measurements (e.g., the S.D. or CV). The parameters outlined above directly influence the test result (accuracy, linearity, and specificity), while precision, robustness range, and LOD influence the test variability.

REAL-TIME PCR ASSAY DEVELOPMENT

Real-time PCR Basics

Real-time PCR is a method by which fluorescence is utilized to measure specific amplicon production after each cycle of the polymerase chain reaction. Every rtPCR assay contains a fluorescent molecule that is attached to a reported probe. This fluorescent molecule either can be a non-specific intercalating fluorophore (e.g., SYBR Green™) or it can be covalently attached to an oligonucleotide probe such as a TaqMan™, Molecular Beacon™, Scorpion™, or Hyb™ probe. The latter type of probe is utilized in a fluorescent resonance energy transfer (FRET), resulting in specific monitoring of the accumulation of the target sequence amplicon. SYBR Green™ fluorophore allows monitoring of any amplicon accumulation, since the dye intercalates into double-stranded DNA indiscriminately and is not target-specific. A recent review highlights rtPCR assays designed for detection of biothreat agents, as well as instrumentation available for rtPCR [1]. Newer instrumentation has been developed that can simultaneously detect more than one fluorescent wavelength, so that multi-target or multi-organism detection is now possible in a single reaction tube. Our current assay development for biothreat agent analysis employs TaqMan chemistry with ABI 7000 detection equipment, although the other chemistries and detectors possess directly comparable quality parameters. Our validated assays have also undergone rigorous testing on other real-time platforms and can be performed on other instrumentation. It is important to validate real-time assays on each type of instrumentation, if the assays are going to be run on several different rtPCR platforms. In certain cases, modifications have to be made in particular assay parameters.

PCR has revolutionized diagnostics and in particular, infectious disease testing and analysis. The technology, developed in 1985, facilitated the detection of nucleic-acid sequences and enabled sequencing of large DNA fragments, leading ultimately to sequencing of the human genome and the genomes of many pathogens [5]. In addition, PCR has expedited the development and validation of exquisitely specific and sensitive diagnostic tests. There are now many commercially available PCR kits for analysis of common enteric and respiratory bacterial and viral organisms that have been validated, and several have undergone the FDA approval process for use as diagnostic assays for human clinical illness. Detection of biothreat agents using rtPCR assays had not been a big market for commercial development until the bioterrorist release of anthrax through the mail system in 2001. There are now some diagnostic PCR tests commercially available; however due to the restrictions placed on the possession, use, and transfer of these bacteria, viruses, and toxins that are classified as select agents, many companies have shied away from developing tests for these pathogens, leaving a critical gap in the diagnostic capability for infectious disease biothreat agents.

Through the utilization of the new instrumentation, the simultaneous amplification and fluorescent detection of two or more target DNA or RNA sequences can be monitored in a single reaction. With the use of sets of specific primers and probes, as many as 4-6 different targets can be detected in a single well or reaction tube. Multiplex PCR was reported in 1988 soon after the original uniplex technique had been invented [6]. Since the 1980s, the technology has experienced vast improvements ranging from novel strategies for heating and cooling units that reduce the overall length of the PCR run, to machines that have the ability for high-throughput, to reduction of amplicon contamination through capture of the data in a real-time, closed tube system. This technology is extremely well-suited to the identification of biothreat agents because it is rapid, highly sensitive and specific, and reproducible [7].

Not only is the rapidity of result availability extremely valuable in infectious disease diagnostics, but because this technique is so sensitive and specific for the target analyte PCR also offers tremendous benefit over traditional culture-based methods and protein-based assays such as immunoassays. In traditional culture methods for bacterial and viral agents, results are obtained usually days to weeks after the receipt of the specimen. The testing is often complicated by the presence of other bacteria and viruses, and identification is hampered by the similar morphologies and similar biochemical results of many bacteria and viruses. While immunoassays offer the advantage that testing is often quicker than culture analysis, results are not as sensitive and can be compromised by improper transport or low numbers of organisms. PCR analysis is more sensitive than immunoassays and has a larger range for transport conditions, since the target is the analyte and not the viable organism. In addition, no other methodology offers comparable ease of assay development through the use of available genomic databases, thereby allowing simple *in silico* evaluation of assay components (i.e., primers and probes) even before the assay is performed. This PCR method can be carried out within minutes to hours, depending on the chosen format and platform [1].

Real-time PCR has benefits over conventional PCR when there is a need to identify of multiple targets in one reaction tube. Multiplex conventional PCR assays have been developed that can detect nine targets in a single amplification reaction [8,9]. In order to obtain confirmation of these results, the amplicons produced should be either sequenced or confirmed by hybridization. Often reporting of results is delayed significantly, due to the sequencing requirement for confirmation. Often, amplified products must be sent to a different laboratory for confirmatory testing if sequencing capability is not available on-site. Also, this process increases the possibility of laboratory contamination [10]. Highly trained individuals are essential for post-PCR processing, if laboratory contamination is to be minimized. Real-time PCR analysis removes the possibility of post-amplification processing, since reaction tubes do not have to be opened; rtPCR as this analysis utilizes a hybridization probe and thereby avoids the requirement for additional sequencing or hybridization analysis. Real-time PCR greatly reduces the turnaround time for reporting of results, as well as minimizing the number of highly trained personnel. The potential for post-amplification contamination is greatly reduced. A minimum level of training is nevertheless needed in the overall PCR workflow, to avoid other areas of potential contamination. While sequencing of amplicons for confirmation is not necessary for rtPCR, amplification of more than one target is important in the determination of a positive result. Newer platforms and generations of real-time instruments have resulted in a great decrease in assay time, from 2 ½ hours down to as little as 30 minutes. This is a great advantage over classical culture, recognition element-based, or array-based assays, which typically take 4-24 hours to produce a result.

Another benefit of probe-based rtPCR assays is the ability to incorporate the use of DNA melt curve analysis. Typically multiplex rtPCR can detect 2-4 targets in one reaction, but the use of double-stranded DNA melting analysis in the assay design can further increase the number of targets that are discriminated in one reaction. This results in the capability of strain or species differentiation using temperature discrimination [11, 12]. For example, Panning and co-workers utilized melting curve analysis to discriminate various orthopox viruses in a single amplification reaction [13]. This technique uses a universal primer set to amplify sequences of members of the *Orthopoxvirus* genus; differences in melting temperatures due to mismatches between the fluorescent probe and the amplicon indicate which species of *Orthopoxvirus* is present. For clarity, the focus of this chapter will be the validation of a single target analyte, but the same principles apply to the validation of a multi-analyte rtPCR assay.

As in other types of testing, sample processing is a key critical component of a good diagnostic PCR assay. Extraction of DNA is an important, initial step in the performance of multiplex PCR on biothreat samples. There are many commercially available reaction components (e.g., mastermixes) for rtPCR that include additives to reduce the effects of the potential PCR-specific inhibitors commonly found in environmental and clinical sample matrices associated with biothreat events. There is significant research on inhibition in various sample matrices. Inhibition controls should be included in every assay run. Some laboratories do not include this important control into their assay design, due to the increased cost of validating and using the assay. Only after the assay has been thoroughly evaluated, and after a statistically significant number of samples have been tested, can it be concluded that the assay procedures used successfully remove all traces of inhibitory substances from the sample. Even an extensive study of inhibition in one sample type does not preclude the possibility that a sample submitted for testing may vary slightly and contains inhibitors. Therefore, it is advisable to retain inhibition controls in the assay.

Some laboratorians and researchers are proponents of testing unprocessed samples. In the developmental assay process, it must be proven that the specimen type to be tested can be assayed without potential loss of sensitivity, and that this specimen type does not show substantial inhibition. Only for assays that have been thoroughly evaluated with statistically significant numbers of a single sample type and that have been found to show no loss of sensitivity (compared to the singleplex assay) should this non-processing approach be used.

However, the approach may also be suitable for samples with minimal volume [14].

Definition of Method End-user

For the purposes of this assay development description, we propose that the end-user is trained technician or laboratorian doing sample analysis in an appropriate fixed facility (i.e., a BSL3 laboratory, or a BSL2 laboratory with BSL3 practices). We wish to develop an assay that can be used as either a quantitative method (for suspicious material testing and environmental site characterization) or a semi-quantitative method (for clinical diagnosis). In either case, the assay is to be used strictly as a screening tool, with results being reported only after independent confirmation by an alternative test modality (i.e., culture). Because we are developing a screening method, we emphasize sensitivity, selectivity, and negative predictive value of the test.

Definition of Probable Assay Matrix and Processing Method

The ultimate goal of this assay development phase is to develop a test that can be used on a wide range of sample types, ranging from blood, to cutaneous lesion swabs, to environmental white powders. Because of the broad spectrum of potential sample matrices, the assay and upstream processing methods, such as nucleic acid extraction, must be very robust, and appropriate scientific controls must be integrated into the process to monitor inhibition or sample matrix effects. Nucleic acid isolation and extraction have both been well studied, and there are commercial kits available. The most time- and cost-effective approach for our method development was to compare several of the kits, to see which yielded the highest quality and most consistent nucleic acid products for subsequent rtPCR analysis. Nucleic acid extraction methods previously employed by our laboratory have included many extraction kits. Experience indicated that the MasterPure™, AquaPure™, and Qiagen™ kits were the most likely to be amenable to the sample matrices selected.

Assay Quality Parameters

Specificity
Specificity testing is comprised of the use of a broad panel of nucleic acids that can include human DNA, potential biothreats/biological weapons, avirulent or vaccine strains of target pathogens, common clinical sample flora, and common products that can be used as hoax materials for biothreats (e.g., flour). Table 3 in the Results section shows the specificity panel used for the *Francisella tularensis* rtPCR assay. The table is broken into three sections: a subset of nucleic acids that have special significance to the *Francisella tularensis* assay, a subset of nucleic acids that can be found in various clinical specimen types, and a general specificity panel for biothreat agents. The first group contains near-neighbors and various strains of the target organism, as well as morphologically similar organisms often confused with the target organism upon microscopic analysis. The first and second groups are modified from assay to assay, and they vary from target analyte to target analyte, whereas while the third group is consistent for most biothreat rtPCR assay developments.

Sensitivity
The power of rtPCR is the exquisite sensitivity that can be achieved through amplification. For this reason, the rtPCR method is well suited as a screening method when it is desired to rule-out as many pathogens as possible, in as few tests as possible. A positive result would will the analyst to do further directed testing, to rule-in the suspected pathogen. For a screening assay, we want to minimize false-negative results. For confirmatory testing methods, we want to minimize false-positive results. While PCR-based methods can theoretically detect a single intact copy of a target nucleic acid, we propose that 25 copies is a

more realistic and achievable LOD with non-detection (i.e., a false-negative result) of duplicate samples <1% of the time, assuming a Poisson distribution of signatures in a small sample volume of 5 μl. Since this is a screening method only, the positive predictive value can be relatively low, since we will continue to analyze all non-negative samples.

In addition, if we consider a broad sampling of individual rtPCR assays, it becomes apparent that a clear and consistent break in cycle threshold values occurs between detect and non-detect results at around cycle 40, for most of the commercially available laboratory rtPCR systems (i.e., ABI7000, ABI 7500, Rotorgene, Mx3000, BioRad iCycler, Cepheid SmartCycler). If we assume that this split corresponds to target DNA presence (i.e., ≥ 1 amplifiable copy) or absence (i.e., <1 amplifiable copy), then we can back-calculate the equipment sensitivity to amplicon accumulation-dependent fluorescence change. In general, assuming greater than 95% amplification efficiency, this sensitivity corresponds to detection of approximately 10^{11}-10^{12} amplicons. This amount of amplicon would be readily visible on an agarose gel if post-amplification analysis were performed.

Robustness

As indicated above, we will need to develop a robust sample processing method, which can be used for a diverse set of sample matrices, as well as a robust analytical method that can consistently detect target analytes. For this reason, we will use (1) validated, commercially available extraction kits upstream of our rtPCR analytical method, and (2) PCR mastermix that we know to be insensitive to some of the common PCR inhibitors found in the pre-established matrix types.

Accuracy

Diagnostic accuracy is defined as the ability of the test system to obtain the correct result [15]. Due to the fact that one application of the assay being developed is clinical diagnostic use, we must have a highly accurate test. The typical clinical assay accuracy criterion is >95%, so that false negative results are minimized to <5%. While accuracy represents balance between minimizing false negative results (i.e., maximizing sensitivity) and maximizing true positive results (i.e., high specificity), the proposed use of this assay as a screening method allows us to down-weight false positives with respect to the false negatives.

Precision

Because the assay being developed is for screening of samples, the criteria for precise measurement are not weighted strongly. Neither medical intervention nor environmental remediation is dependent on the analyte concentration; only the presence or absence of the analyte matters. That being said, an internal assay positive control is invaluable in assessing assay quality, and in interpreting unexpected data. Therefore, as we develop our screening assay, we will integrate a known concentration of a positive control into each analytical run, in order to confirm reagent and amplification quality. Besides assuring mastermix quality and PCR cycling, the use of a positive control allows the baseline and threshold settings to be adjusted so as to effectively normalize the analysis from run to run, thereby minimizing inter-operator and/or inter-equipment variability.

Range

Most rtPCR assays have an excellent linear dynamic range of minimally 6 logs (10^2 to 10^8 target sequence copies per reaction). The range can be extended to include higher concentrations of the target sequence but the cost is a broad baseline range so it is not recommended. For quantitative measurement, a dilution series of a known stock of target DNA should be included in the rtPCR analysis, and subsequent conversion to a physical measurable quantity can be achieved. For these purposes, we typically convert the concentration of target nucleic acid from grams to target copies. This is done using the following assumptions:

Average Molecular Weight (MW) of deoxyribonucleotide bases:

dAMP 331.2, dCMP 307.2, dGMP 347.2, dTMP 322.2.

Therefore, the Average MW = 327 per base *or* 654 per base pair (bp).

1 OD_{260} in water $\approx 5*10^4$ ng/ml dsDNA.

Therefore, for dsDNA:

Total bp dsDNA = ng dsDNA$*(1$ bp$/654)*(1/1.6606*10^{-15}$ ng)

Copies of target dsDNA = total bp dsDNA in solution / genome or plasmid size.

For example, for a 1 OD_{260} solution of a 10,000-bp plasmid,

Total bp dsDNA = $5*10^4$ ng/ml $* (1$ bp$/654)*(1/1.6606*10^{-15}$ ng) = $4.60*10^{16}$ bp/ml

So

Copies of Target dsDNA = $(4.60*10^{16}$ bp/ml) $*$ $(1$ copy/10,000 bp) = $4.60*10^{12}$ copies/ml

And,

$(4.60*10^{12}$ copies/ml) / $(5*10^4$ ng/ml) = $9.2*10^7$ copies/ng.

Similar calculations can be made for ssDNA and ssRNA, where the two changes are the average nucleotide MW for ssDNA (327/base) or ssRNA (340/base) and the OD conversion (1 OD_{260} in water $\approx 4*10^4$ ng/ml) for both single-stranded species.

Additional Quality Controls

For all rtPCR assays, a negative control or no template control (NTC) is used to establish baseline and threshold criteria by which the samples are analyzed. NTCs typically consist of water or buffer added to rtPCR reactions, although any sample that does not show amplification can be used as a NTC. As discussed above, a positive control of a known concentration should also be included in each analytical run. This control has many purposes: besides acting as a qualitative assessment of assay performance, it can serve as a monitor for inhibition, and can be used to reduce assay-to-assay variability (see Precision, above). One potential problem with inclusion of positive controls in the method is the risk of sample cross-contamination.

In most diagnostic labs where PCR-based methods are being used, there is a well-defined workflow and decontamination process that must be strictly adhered to, in order to minimize the potential for sample cross-contamination, especially from positive control material or post PCR-amplified products. In order to minimize contamination, it is advisable to maintain separate areas for individual steps of the PCR workflow. A three- or four-step unidirectional PCR set-up helps to minimize cross contamination of samples and reagents. The first step or area is the PCR clean area/PCR reagent set-up, which is used for PCR mastermix reaction set-up. This area is only entered once and cannot be re-entered after completion of the PCR assay. The second step/area is a space in which DNA addition to the PCR mastermix occurs. It is advisable to have another area (if space allows) where positive control material can be added; this space is physically separated from the space where unknown samples are added, to avoid cross- contamination of unknown samples with known positive material. If this is not possible, unknown samples should always be set up and capped before positive control material is opened. Positive control material should always be added at or near the LOD to avoid cross- contamination. Again, complete decontamination of these areas should be performed after each set-up. The third or fourth step (again, depending on space constraints) is the area in which the PCR machines are located. This should be physically separated from the space where mastermix is set up and where DNA is added to reaction tubes. Once this area has been entered, the other PCR areas cannot be re-entered. Each of these areas should contain devoted equipment such as pipettes and PPE such as lab coats and gloves, and these supplies should not be moved from area to area. This sequestration helps to minimize the potential for contamination.

While rtPCR mitigates much of the risk resulting from post-amplification analysis, 'tagging' of positive control material is also essential, so that target analyte detection can be differentiated from positive control sample contamination. For our rtPCR assay, we have chosen a simple approach: inclusion of several target sequences into a single plasmid [16]. In this way, the positive control material generates positive signals for disparate targets, which would not normally all be present in a single sample. This positive control can then be utilized for multiplex PCR reactions that are currently being developed in our laboratory for the simultaneous detection of multiple biothreat agents in a single tube.

An extraction control should also be used each time that a PCR assay is run. The use of an extraction control assures that the extraction reagents have adequately lysed the cells, and that high-quality DNA was obtained. This extraction control can serve also as an inhibition control. While the current chapter focuses on the process of validation of the PCR assay, it is important to keep in mind that DNA is, in most cases, extracted from various sample types; thus, inhibition and extraction are also key components into the validation process.

Quality Assurance Program

Of paramount importance to the validation of any laboratory assay is the development of a solid quality assurance (QA) and quality control (QC) program. Although this is crucial to any assay and to the overall functioning of a laboratory, it is particularly critical for PCR assays, since the slightest deviation from a SOP can produce unintended amplification of a target not from the sample or specimen of interest. Lack of a high-quality QA program can lead to serious problems, in efforts to validate a new assay.

The QA program should include a regularly scheduled monitoring of areas in which PCR is performed, to ensure that there is no amplicon contamination. This monitoring should include swipes of the areas and performance of PCR assays utilizing these survey samples, to assure that no contamination is present. Also, areas in which target DNA is used such as the extraction area or area where the positive control is added should always be cleaned before and after every use. There are commercially available products that remove DNA contamination from surfaces; the use of bleach to destroy DNA is highly recommended as an additional decontamination method.

Not only are the reagents and supplies part of the QA/QC program, but the equipment that is utilized for PCR assays-whether it is a convention PCR machine or a real-time instrument- should have routine maintenance performed, to ensure the integrity of each run. The machine should be included in a monthly surveillance program that monitors any amplicon contamination. As well, routine background checks and dye calibrations should be performed as recommended by rtPCR manufacturer. Documentation of such maintenance should be maintained in the laboratory. Often, it serves as a valuable troubleshooting reference when machine malfunctions occur.

Another critical component of the QA program is the competency of the analysts performing the assays. During each assay validation process, multiple analysts should verify the robustness and precision of the assay. Proficiency testing programs should be set up and documented in order to maintain the level of competency. For some PCR assays, external PCR proficiency testing programs are available; if not, there are available internal proficiency testing programs should be initiated and documented. By maintaining competency of the analysts who perform the assays you will help to ensure reliable, high-confidence testing.

RESULTS AND DISCUSSION

Data from an assay designed to detect the biothreat agent *F. tularensis* will be used to illustrate the necessary validation performance metrics. This is a single-analyte target assay. Table 2 shows the assay performance estimates. In the blinded validation, a total of 40 specimens will be tested. We hope to achieve the result that all 30 seeded specimens will be positive while the 10 negative unseeded specimens will produce negative results yielding a 0% false-positive and false-negative rate.

Table 2. Assay performance estimation for Francisella tularensis real-time PCR assay.

	Analyte present	Analyte absent	Total
Test positive	30	0	30
Test negative	0	10	10
Total	30	10	80

This assay was designed to detect *F. tularensis* DNA from environmental swab samples.

Table 3. Specificity Panel for *Francisella tularensis*

Genetically and Morphologically Similar Organisms	Common Flora Found in Various Specimen Types	Biodefense Panel
Francisella tularensis LVS	*Moraxella catarrhalis*	*Bacillus subtilis*
F. tularensis WC1*	*Cornybacterium diptheriae*	*Ba. cereus*
F. tularensis WC2*	*Co. aquatica*	*Ba. anthracis* Sterne
F. tularensis WC 3*	*Staphylococcus epidermidis*	*Ba. anthracis* Pasteur
F. tularensis WC 4*	*S. aureus*	*Ricinus communis*
F. philomiragia	*Proteus mirabilis*	*Yersinia pestis*
Legionella pneumophila	*E. coli* (6 strains)	*Clostridium botulinum* Type B
Pseudomonas aeruginosa	*Streptococcus pyogenes*	*Cl. botulinum* Type E
Pasturella multocida	*St. agalactiae (group B)*	*Cl. botulinum* Type F
Haemophilus influenzae	*St. pneumoniae*	WR Vaccinia extract
Acinetobacter lwoffi	*Neisseria meningitidis*	*Brucella abortus*
Oligella ureolytica	*Mycobacterium tuberculosis*	*Br. canis*
Bordetella pertussis	*Vibrio cholera* nonO:1	*Br. melitensis*
Bo. pertussis	*Shigella dysenteriae* (2 strains)	*Br. suis*
Bo. parapertussis	*Sh. flexneri* B	Non-dairy Creamer
Bo. bronchiseptica	*Sh. boydii* (3 strains)	Flour
	Sh. sonnei D	Human DNA
	Salmonella typhi	
	Sa. arizoniae	
	Sa. Typhimurium	
	Enterococcus faecalis	
	Serratia marcescens	
	Yersinia enterocolitica (3 strains)	
	Klebsiella pneumoniae	
	Morganella morganii	
	Enterobacter cloacae	

* denotes strains of the Wadsworth Center Laboratory Culture Collection.

Specificity

Table 3 gives a comprehensive list of organisms, toxins, and viruses (in boldface) that were used to determine the specificity of our assay. Organisms that are highlighted produced a positive result in specificity testing. Only strains of the target organism, *F. tularensis,* produced a positive result, indicating that the assay is 100% specific for this target. It is extremely important to do a thorough specificity test on the assay being developed. Especially critical, when dealing with assays detecting biothreats in environmental samples such as white powders, is the inclusion of common skin flora and organisms that may be found in the environment; this will minimize false-positive results. A false negative can lead to serious consequences for patient care, while a false positive can lead to significant expenditure of resources, and serious public health consequent management issues. An *in silico* analysis using sequences from a source such as the GenBank® database is a good starting point, for determining what organisms should be included in the study. It must be noted that, whereas this database contains a vast number of sequences, it in reality represents only a small percentage of microorganisms, despite the great strides that have been made in recent years in microbe sequencing.

Sensitivity

As stated in the first portion of this chapter, the assay developed was designed to be able to detect 25 gene copies of the target analyte, a value which is in line with the reported infectious dose of *F. tularensis* agent [17]. Table 4 shows sensitivity data from the assay. The assay can detect 4.2 CFUs or 6.67 gene copies of the target organism; this is an excellent sensitivity that is comparable with the gold standard culture methods, which can detect a single CFU.

Table 4. Sensitivity study for the *Francisella tularensis* assay

CFUs/reaction	Gene Copies/reaction	PCR result (Ct)
4,200,000	6.67×10^6	17.9
420,000	6.67×10^5	20.4
42,000	6.67×10^4	24.2
4,200	6.67×10^3	26.9
420	6.67×10^2	30.7
42	66.7	34.0
4.2	6.67	37.2
0.42	0.67	>45
0.042	0.067	>45

The data from the assay were generated using the LVS attenuated strain of *F. tularensis*. A 1 McFarland standard was made and then serially diluted 1:10. The serial dilutions were extracted, and DNA was interrogated using the rtPCR assay. Each dilution was tested in duplicate. This sensitivity study was repeated in triplicate. Data shown are the averages from one study.

Table 5. Limit of detection study for *Francisella tularensis* real-time PCR assay

	Test #1 (Ct value)	Test #2 (Ct value)	Test #3 (Ct value)	Test #4 (Ct value)	Test #5 (Ct value)
6.67 gene copies (Replicate 1)	38.5	38.6	37.2	36.6	37.3
6.67 gene copies (Replicate 2)	37.1	38.6	38.3	38.2	39.4
6.67 gene copies (Replicate 3)	39.0	38.4	39.6	36.6	38.0
Mean 6.67 gene copies	38.2	38.5	38.4	37.1	38.3
Standard Deviation	1.00	0.15	1.18	0.92	1.06
Coefficient of Variation	2.60%	0.41%	3.07%	2.50%	2.80%
3.34 gene copies (Replicate 1)	39.8	37.5	45	37.4	45
3.34 gene copies (Replicate 2)	40.4	37.8	38.0	37.4	40.1
3.34 gene copies (Replicate 3)	42.9	45	45	37.1	39.0
Mean 3.34 gene copies	41.1	37.6	N.A.	37.3	39.6
Standard Deviation	1.66	0.16	N.A.	0.19	0.79
Coefficient of Variation	4.10%	0.45%	N.A.	0.52%	2.00%

In order to determine the LOQ or LOD in this assay, we performed a more detailed analysis (Table 5). In Table 4, the lower limit of detection was found to be 6.67 gene copies. This concentration was serially diluted 1:2 in order to determine the true LOD. In 3 out of 5 experiments, there were replicates that did not detect the lower of the two concentrations of DNA, 3.34 gene copies; however, in all 5 experiments the assay could detect 6.67 gene copies. The LOD for this assay is 6.67 gene copies, a value which is well below the 25 gene copies that was set as the sensitivity parameter before the validation of this assay began.

Precision

Table 5 shows the results of 5 different experiments performed on separate days. Note that the mean and S.D. for the replicates and experiments on different days are very consistent, while the lower of the two concentrations of DNA shows a great deal of fluctuation. The assay is extremely precise down to 6.67 gene copies. Data have been generated to show that this assay is extremely reproducible at each concentration within the dynamic range (not shown). This is evident from the 6.67 gene copies data point values. At low concentrations in a PCR assay or any diagnostic assay, slight differences between replicates become amplified. In this assay the standard deviation (S.D.) and coefficient of variation (CV) are small. The data show that this assay is highly precise, since the fluctuation in Ct values from experiment to experiment was minimal.

Several different experiments tested the precision of this assay. Table 5 displays the results of five separate experiments performed on several days. Note that the mean and S.D. for the replicates and experiments on different days are very consistent at the 6.67 gene copy level, while the lower concentration of DNA (3.34 gene copies) shows a great deal of fluctuation. The S.D. and C.V. are also very small at the 6.67 gene copy level but both the S.D. and C.V. become much larger at the lower testing concentration (3.34 gene copies) leading to the loss of statistically significant results at the lower level. The assay is therefore precise down to 6.67 gene copies. Reproducibility of results has also been tested using the positive control, which is included in every run. The positive control utilized in this assay remained consistent during the validation process for each experiment (data not shown).

Linearity

A linearity analysis performed on a rtPCR assay can provide a great deal of useful information about the performance of the test. The LOD, sensitivity, and range can all be obtained through this analysis. A linear analysis was performed using 10 dilutions of *F. tularensis* assayed in duplicate. The resulting linear analysis of this assay (Fig. 1) produced a straight line with an R^2 value of 0.998 over 7 orders of magnitude. This value provides a comparison of the fit of the actual data to the hypothetical straight line. The data generated produced a good fit to the predicted values. The data produced a line with a slope of -3.27, the amplification efficiency (ε) is 102% over the range of data points. This predictive value indicates that the PCR assay has been sufficiently optimized. A low efficiency value for the assay e.g. 80%, would indicate that some component of the reaction was limiting the reaction. Optimization of primer or probe concentration, $MgCl_2$ concentrations, or additional components would then have to be re-evaluated, in order to obtain an acceptable linear dynamic range. The sensitivity and LOD that were given in Table 5 were confirmed by this analysis to be 6.67 gene copies.

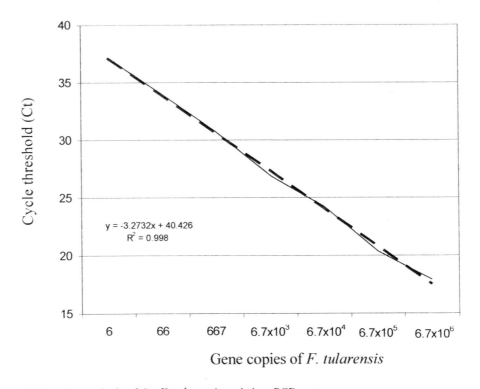

Figure 1. Linearity analysis of the *F. tularensis* real-time PCR assay.

A 1 McFarland concentration *of F. tularensis* was serially diluted 1:10 and then extracted using the Epicentre Masterpure DNA extraction kit. The extracted DNA was assayed in duplicate.

Range

From the data presented in Figure 1, the range of our assay can be calculated to be from 6.67×10^6 gene copies to 6.67 gene copies. These data indicate that the assay can detect the target analyte over a range of concentrations broad to encompass the organism loads that are likely to occur in environmental swab samples.

Accuracy

The purpose of our assay is to serve as a screening tool for the presence of *F. tularensis* in the environment, in the event of an intentional release similar to the 2001 release of *Bacillus anthracis* through the U.S. Postal Service. For such screening purposes, the need for a highly sensitive assay that minimizes false negatives is critical. In order that the initiation of a rapid public health response is possible, in a real biothreat event, it is essential to have the capability of detecting even a minute release of a biothreat agent. While there is a need to be able to determine actual background levels of the biothreat agents that can occur naturally in the environment (as opposed to those of intentional releases) that issue is beyond the scope of the present chapter. As stated earlier, a diagnostic assay should be at least 95% accurate. To validate the accuracy of this assay, a panel was created that contained 10 samples at a low concentration of organism, 10 samples at a medium concentration of organism and 10 containing a high concentration of *F. tularensis* as well as 10 negative control samples (saline mixed with the environmental matrix) The swab samples were all prepared in a blinded fashion by one analyst, to be tested by a second analyst. Non-dairy creamer was used as the matrix. In biothreat hoax situations, common household powders such as creamer, flour, or detergent have been submitted for analysis.

As shown in Table 6, our assay is 100% accurate, with no false positives or false negatives. There was no inhibition present in any of the samples tested. Table 6 is in accordance with the recommendations of both the FDA interim suggested guidelines for molecular assays as well as the CLSI guidelines for molecular diagnostic testing [2]. But, for illustrative purposes, if this assay had failed to detect 5 samples that were seeded with target organism, the resulting accuracy would be 87.5%. This level of accuracy would not be acceptable for a diagnostic assay.

Blinded Validation Study for the *Francisella Tularensis* Real-time PCR Assay

Serial 10-fold dilutions were made of a 1 McFarland suspension of *F. tularensis LVS* ATCC 6223. Three concentrations were evaluated in this study: high (1,345,000 gene copies), medium (181,000 gene copies), and a low concentration of organism (15,800 gene copies). These concentrations were used so that final concentrations of 79 gene copies (low concentration), 905 gene copies (medium concentration), and 6725 gene copies (high concentration) of *F. tularensis* would be added to the PCR reaction tube. Ten microliters containing each of these concentrations were seeded into 10 mg of non-dairy creamer.

Negative samples consisted of 10 ul of saline mixed into 10 mg of non-dairy creamer. Powder was swabbed and placed into 2 ml of Trypticase Soy Broth. The samples were then blinded, and 200 ul were removed and extracted following a using the Epicentre Masterpure DNA extraction kit. Each sample was assayed in duplicate.

Table 6. Results of Blinded Validation

Blindedsample	Final concentration of *F. tularensis* seeded into sample (Gene copies)	Ct (Replicate #1)	Ct (Replicate #2)	Result	Expected Result
1	6725	27.07	27.12	Positive	Positive
2	905	31.55	31.55	Positive	Positive
3	79	35.33	35.72	Positive	Positive
4	Neg	>45	>45	Negative	Negative
5	Neg	>45	>45	Negative	Negative
6	79	36.36	34.78	Positive	Positive
7	905	31.38	31.31	Positive	Positive
8	6725	26.86	27.03	Positive	Positive
9	Neg	>45	>45	Negative	Negative
10	79	34.07	34.24	Positive	Positive
11	905	31.17	31.17	Positive	Positive
12	6725	27.37	26.94	Positive	Positive
13	Neg	>45	>45	Negative	Negative
14	6725	27.35	27.35	Positive	Positive
15	905	31.20	30.80	Positive	Positive
16	79	33.36	33.21	Positive	Positive
17	Neg	>45	>45	Negative	Negative
18	79	36.63	35.21	Positive	Positive
19	905	31.01	30.75	Positive	Positive
20	6725	28.40	28.40	Positive	Positive
21	6725	26.58	26.68	Positive	Positive
22	905	30.37	30.47	Positive	Positive
23	79	34.23	33.93	Positive	Positive
24	Neg	>45	>45	Negative	Negative
25	Neg	>45	>45	Negative	Negative
26	79	33.66	34.13	Positive	Positive
27	905	29.53	29.52	Positive	Positive
28	6725	26.53	26.67	Positive	Positive
29	Neg	>45	>45	Negative	Negative
30	79	33.40	33.21	Positive	Positive
31	905	30.47	30.54	Positive	Positive
32	6725	27.21	26.89	Positive	Positive
33	Neg	>45	>45	Negative	Negative
34	6725	27.07	27.30	Positive	Positive
35	905	31.05	30.49	Positive	Positive
36	79	34.11	33.26	Positive	Positive
37	Neg	>45	>45	Negative	Negative
38	79	35.01	34.23	Positive	Positive
39	905	30.18	30.24	Positive	Positive
40	79	27.06	27.46	Positive	Positive

Robustness

In order to achieve a full validation of this assay, we conducted numerous other tests. Thorough testing of the extraction process, reagents, and matrix was performed, to challenge and to determine the robustness of this assay. Several of these parameters were tested in the initial developmental stage, such as the collection and transport of the sample; detailed studies were also carried out to determine the extent of the presence of inhibitors in environmental samples. These areas, as well as the effects of the testing environment, should be challenged, to complete the validation process.

CONCLUSION

The assay that was developed by our laboratory for the detection of *F. tularensis* underwent a rigorous developmental phase, followed by a thorough validation process. Before the validation stage of any assay commences, the performance metrics of the assay should already have been determined. Through performance of detailed studies of the developmental phase, many problems can be avoided in the validation phase. For example, determination of the sensitivity of an assay utilizing extracted DNA in the development phase produces important information that can be used when the same study is performed in a real-world specimen. Through determination of the LOD of the assay for extracted DNA, an appropriate concentration of the bacterial organism can be chosen, thus avoiding a failure in the validation stage.

The data presented in this chapter reveal that the *F. tularensis* assay is sensitive, specific, precise, and accurate, and thus a highly suitable tool for screening for the presence of this biothreat agent. This chapter has highlighted the most critical components of the validation process. Although the process of development and validation of an assay to be used as a screen for biothreat agents presents unique challenges, the information presented in this chapter can help researchers reach the goal of an appropriately and fully characterized and validated assay.

The methods presented here obviously do not represent an exhaustive review of the available techniques, but rather a general guide to the governing principles in assay development and validation. Consultation with a statistician may offer a more customized approach to user-defined assay development. The use of sound statistical methodologies during the assay validation process will likely lead to reduced development time and reduced overall cost. Utilization of the approaches described in this chapter for the design, development, and validation of a rtPCR assay should result in a reliable, efficient, and reproducible test that can be utilized for detection of biothreat agents.

REFERENCES

[1]   Cirino, NM, Musser KA and Egan C. (2004). Multiplex diagnostic platforms for detection of biothreats agents. Expert Rev. Mol. Diagn. 4:841-857.

[2]   Draft Guidance for Industry and FDA Staff-Nucleic Acid Based In Vitro Diagnostic Devices for Detection of Microbial Pathogens. (HFA-305) Food and Drug

Administration, 5630 Fishers Lane, Rm 1601, Rockville, Maryland, 20852, USA, 2005.

[3]   International Conference on Harmonization. (1995). Guidance for Industry: Validation of Analytical Procedures. Document Q2A. [Online.] http://www.fda.gov/cder/ guidance/ichq2a.pdf.

[4]   International Conference on Harmonization. (1996). Guidance for Industry: Validation of Analytical Procedures. Document Q2B. [Online.] http://www.fda.gov/cder/ guidance/ichq2b.pdf.

[5]   Saiki RK, Scharf S, Faloona F, Mullis KB, Horn GT, Erlich HA, Arnheim N. (1985).

[6]   Enzymatic amplification of beta-globin genomic sequences and restriction site analysis for diagnosis of sickle cell anemia. *Science* 230, 1350-1354.

[7]   Chamberlain JS, Gibbs RA, Raneir JE, Nguyen PN, and Caskey, CT. (1988). Deletion screening of the Duchenne Muscular Dystrophy Locus via Multiplex DNA Amplification. *Nucleic Acids Res.* 16, 11141-11156.

[8]   Peruski AH, Johnson H III, Peruski LF Jr. (2002). Rapid and sensitive detection of biological warfare agents using time resolved fluorescence assays. *J Immunol Methods* 263, 35-41.

[9]   Chamberlain, JS, Gibbs, RA, Raneir, JE, Nguyen, PN, and Caskey, CT. (1988). Deletion screening of the Duchenne Muscular Dystrophy Locus via Multiplex DNA Amplification. *Nucleic Acids Res.* 16, 11141-11156.

[10]   Henegariu O, Heerema NA, Dlouhy SR, Vance GH, Vogt PH. (1997). Multiplex PCR: critical parameters and step-by-step protocol. *Biotechniques.* 23, 504-511.

[11]   Markoulatos P, Siafakas N, Moncany M. (2002). Multiplex polymerase chain reaction: a practical approach. *J. Clin. Lab. Anal.* 16, 47-51.

[12]   11)Wittwer CT, Herrmann MG, Gundry CN, Elenitoba-Johnson KS. (2001). Real-time multiplex PCR assays. *Methods* 25, 430-442.

[13]   Espy MJ, Uhl JR, Mitchell PS, Thorvilson JN, Svien KA, Wold AD, Smith TF. (2000). Diagnosis of herpes simplex virus infections in the clinical laboratory by LightCycler PCR. *J Clin Microbiol.* 38, 795-799.

[14]   Panning M, Asper M, Kramme S, Schmitz H, Drosten C. (2004). Rapid detection and differentiation of human pathogenic orthopox viruses by a fluorescence resonance energy transfer real-time PCR assay. *Clin. Chem.* 50, 702-708.

[15]   Peruski LF Jr, Peruski AH. (2003).Rapid diagnostic assays in the genomic biology era: detection and identification of infectious disease and biological weapon agents. *Biotechniques.* 35, 840-846.

[16]   Clinical and Laboratory Standards Institute. (2005). Molecular Diagnostic methods for Infectious Disease: Proposed Guidelines-Second Edition. CLSI Document MM03-P2 [ISBN 1-56238-568-2]. Clinical and Laboratory Standards Institute, 940 West valley Road Suite 1400, Wayne, Pennsylvania, 19087, USA.

[17]   Inoue S, Noguchi A, Tanabayashi K, and Yamada A. (2004). Preparation of a positive control DNA for molecular diagnosis of *Bacillus anthracis*. Jpn. J. Infect. Dis. 57:29-32.

[18]   Dennis DT, Inglesby TV, Henderson DA et. Al. (2001). Tularemia as a biological weapon: medical and public health management. JAMA. 285: 2763-2773.

In: Bioterrorism: Prevention, Preparedness and Protection
Editor: J. V. Borrelli, pp. 195-202

ISBN 1-60021-180-1
© 2007 Nova Science Publishers, Inc.

Chapter 8

FEDERAL AND STATE RESPONSES TO BIOLOGICAL ATTACKS: ISOLATION AND QUARANTINE AUTHORITY[*]

Angie A. Welborn

ABSTRACT

In the wake of the September 11 attacks, federal, state and local governments have become increasingly aware of the need for an effective response to future terrorist activities. Of significant concern is the government's ability to respond to a biological attack, including the introduction of an infectious or contagious disease into a population. An effective response could include the isolation of persons exposed to infectious biological agents or infected with a communicable disease as a result of the attacks, as well as the quarantine of certain states, cities, or neighborhoods.

Currently, state and local governments have the primary authority to control the spread of dangerous diseases within their jurisdiction, with the federal government's role limited to interstate and foreign quarantine. However, many states have inadequate procedures in place for isolating individuals who are infected or believed to be infected and quarantining areas that are or may be infected. Generally, the laws currently in effect do not address the spread of disease resulting from a biological attack, and for the most part only address specific diseases that were the cause of past epidemics. In light of recent events, many states are reevaluating their public health emergency response plans and are expected to enact more comprehensive regulations relating to isolation and quarantine in the event of a biological attack. Public health experts have developed a Model State Emergency Health Powers Act to guide states as they reevaluate their plans.

This report provides an overview of federal and state quarantine laws as they relate to the isolation or quarantine of individuals, as well as a discussion of the relevant case law. The Model State Emergency Health Powers Act is also discussed.

---

[*] Excerpted from *Bioterrorism Reader*, by Arthur P. Rogers, New York: Nova Science Publishers, Inc., 2002.

INTRODUCTION

In the event of a biological attack, the public health system may respond by taking measures to prevent those infected with or exposed to a disease causing biological agent from infecting others. The terms used to describe these measures generally apply to distinct groups of persons, but are often used interchangeably. Isolation typically refers to "the separation of a known infected person or animal from others during the period of contagiousness in order to prevent the direct or indirect conveyance of the infectious agent."[1] Quarantine refers to "the restriction of movement of a healthy person who has been exposed to a communicable disease in order to prevent contact with unexposed persons."[2] There are varying degrees of quarantine and the authority to order quarantine or isolation is generally very broad.

> First, both complete quarantine and isolation usually involve the confinement of contagious individuals to their residences pursuant to orders from the state health department. Health officials post a public notice forbidding anyone from entering or exiting the dwelling. Alternatively, health authorities may confine an infected person to either a hospital or a prison. Second, health authorities may order a modified quarantine, which selectively restricts an individual from participation in certain activities, e.g. jobs involving food preparation, school attendance, or particularly hazardous activities. The quarantine power also includes the authority to place a contagious individual under surveillance to insure strict compliance with quarantine orders. Finally, the health department may issue segregation orders that require the separation of an entire group of people from the general population. Quarantine orders may extend to any persons who come into contact with the infected individual.[3]

State health departments or health officials typically have primary quarantine authority, though the federal government does have jurisdiction over interstate and foreign quarantine. Both federal and state statutes and regulations will be discussed *infra*.

FEDERAL QUARANTINE AUTHORITY

Under the Public Health Service Act, the Secretary of Health and Human Services has the authority to make and enforce regulations necessary "to prevent the introduction, transmission, or spread of communicable diseases from foreign countries into the States or possessions, or from one State or possession into any other State or possession."[4] While providing the Secretary with broad authority to promulgate regulations "as in his judgement may be necessary," the law places limitations on the Secretary's authority to enact regulations providing for the "apprehension, detention, or conditional release of individuals."[5] Such apprehension, detention, or conditional release may be authorized for the purpose of

---

[1]   See Edward A. Fallone, Preserving the Public Health: A Proposal to Quarantine Recalcitrant AIDS Carriers, 68 B.U.L. Rev. 441, n24 (1988).

[2]   Id at n23.

[3]   Id at 460 - 461.

[4]   42 U.S.C. 264. Originally, the statute conferred this authority on the Surgeon General; however, pursuant to Reorganization Plan No. 3 of 1966, all statutory powers and functions of the Surgeon General were transferred to the Secretary.

[5]   42 U.S.C. 264.

"preventing the introduction, transmission, or spread of such communicable diseases as may be specified from time to time in Executive orders of the President upon the recommendation of the National Advisory Health Council and the Surgeon General."[6]

Generally, regulations authorizing the apprehension, detention, examination, or conditional release of individuals are applicable only to individuals coming into a State or possession from a foreign country or a possession.[7] However, on recommendation of the National Advisory Health Council, the regulations may provide for the apprehension and examination of "any individual reasonably believed to be infected with a communicable disease in a communicable stage and (1) to be moving or about to move from a State to another State; or (2) to be a probable source of infection to individuals who, while infected with such disease in a communicable state, will be moving from a State to another State."[8] If found to be infected, such individuals may be detained for such time and in such manner as may be reasonably necessary.[9] During times of war, the authority to apprehend and examine individuals extends to any individual "reasonably believed (1) to be infected with such disease [as specified in an Executive order of the President] in a communicable stage and (2) to be a probable source of infection to members of the armed forces of the United States" or to individuals engaged in the production or transportation of supplies for the armed forces.[10]

Regulations promulgated pursuant to the Public Health Service Act addressing interstate quarantine primarily restrict travel for persons infected with a communicable disease.[11] Following a transfer of authority from the Secretary of Health and Human Services to the Director of the Centers for Disease Control and Prevention (CDC) in 2000, the Director of the CDC is authorized to take measures as may be necessary to prevent the spread of a communicable disease from one state or possession to any other state or possession if he or she determines that measures taken by local health authorities are inadequate to prevent the spread of the disease.[12] In an effort to prevent the spread of diseases between states, the regulations prohibit infected persons from traveling from one state to another state without a permit from the health officer of the state, possession, or locality of destination, if such permit is required under the law applicable to the place of destination.[13] Additional requirements apply to persons who are in the "communicable period of cholera, plague, smallpox, typhus or yellow fever, or who having been exposed to any such disease, is in the incubation period thereof."[14]

---

[6] 42 U.S.C. 264(b). H.R. 3448, as passed by the House, would eliminate the provision relating to the National Advisory Health Council's recommendation being required prior to the issuance of a quarantine rule or a rule providing for the apprehension of individuals during wartime.

[7] 42 U.S.C. 264(c).

[8] 42 U.S.C. 264(d).

[9] Id.

[10] 42 U.S.C. 266.

[11] The regulations apply to the apprehension, detention, or conditional release of individuals for the purpose of preventing the introduction, transmission, or spread of the following diseases: anthrax, chancroid, cholera, dengue, diphtheria, granuloma inguinale, infectious encephalitis, favus, gonorrhea, leprosy, lymphogranuloma venereum, meningococcus meningitis, plague, poliomyelitis, psittacosis, relapsing fever, ringworm of the scalp, scarlet fever, streptococcic sore throat, smallpox, syphilis, trachoma, tuberculosis, typhoid fever, typhus, and yellow fever. 42 CFR 70.6.

[12] 42 CFR 70.2. Effective September 15, 2000, the Department of Health and Human Services transferred authority for interstate quarantine to the Centers for Disease Control and Prevention, with the Food and Drug Administration retaining authority over animals and other products that may transmit or spread communicable diseases. 65 FR 49906, August 16, 2000.

[13] 42 CFR 70.3.

[14] 42 CFR 70.5.

STATE POLICE POWERS AND QUARANTINE AUTHORITY

The preservation of the public health has historically been the responsibility of state and local governments.[15] While the federal government has the authority to authorize quarantine under certain circumstances, the primary authority exists at the state level as an exercise of the state's police power. The Supreme Court alluded to a state's authority to enact quarantine laws in 1824, *Gibbons v. Ogden.*[16] In *Gibbons*, the Court noted that while quarantine laws may affect commerce, they are, by nature, health laws, and thus under the authority of state and local governments. Courts have noted that the duty to insure that the public health is preserved is inherent to the police power of a state and cannot be surrendered.[17]

While every state has acknowledged the authority to pass and enforce quarantine laws, these laws vary widely by state. Generally, quarantine is authorized through public health orders, though some states may require a court order before an individual is detained.[18] For example, in Louisiana, the state health officer is not authorized to "confine any person in any institution unless directed or authorized to do so by the judge of the parish in which the person is located."[19] Diseases subject to quarantine may be defined by statute, with some statutes addressing only a single disease, or the state health department may be granted the authority to decide which diseases are communicable and therefore subject to quarantine.[20] States also employ different methods for determining when the quarantine or isolation period shall end. Generally, "release is accomplished when a determination is made that the person is no longer a threat to the public health, or no longer infectious."[21]

One common characteristic of most state quarantine laws is their "overall antiquity," with many statutes being between forty and one hundred years old.[22] The more antiquated laws "often do not reflect contemporary scientific understandings of disease, [or] current treatments of choice."[23] State laws were often enacted with a focus on a particular disease, such as tuberculosis or typhoid fever, leading to inconsistent approaches in addressing other diseases.[24] Despite the inconsistencies and perceived problems with such laws, state legislatures have not been forced to reevaluate their quarantine and isolation laws due to a decline in infectious diseases and advances in medicine.[25] However, in light of recent biological terror threats, many states are likely to reconsider their laws in coming legislative sessions.[26]

---

[15] People ex rel. Barmore v. Robertson, 134 N.E. 815, 817 (Ill.1922).

[16] 22 U.S. 1, 25 (1824).

[17] 134 N.E. at 817.

[18] Paula Mindes, Note, Tuberculosis Quarantine: A Review of Legal Issues in Ohio and Other States, 10 J.L. & Health 403, 409 (1995).

[19] La. R. S. 40:17(A).

[20] 10 J.L. & Health at 409. See e.g., Md. Code Ann. 18-324, which addresses only quarantine in tuberculosis cases.

[21] Id. at 410.

[22] Lawrence O. Gostin, et. al., The Law and the Public's Health: A Study of Infectious Disease Law in the United States, 99 Colum. L. Rev. 59, 102 (1999).

[23] Id. at 106.

[24] Id.

[25] 10 J.L. & Health at 413, citing Wendy E. Parmet, AIDS and Quarantine: The Revival of an Archaic Doctrine, 14 Hofstra L. Rev. 53, 54-55 (1985).

[26] States Weighing Laws to Fight Bioterrorism, by Justin Gillis, Washington Post, November 19, 2001, p. A01. See section infra on the Model State Emergency Health Powers Act.

MODEL STATE EMERGENCY HEALTH POWERS ACT

The Model State Emergency Health Powers Act was drafted by The Center for Law and the Public's Health at Georgetown and Johns Hopkins Universities.[27] The purpose of the Model Act is to "facilitate and encourage communications among the various interested parties and stakeholders about the complex issues pertaining to the use of state emergency health powers."[28] It is important to note that this is intended to be a model for states to use in evaluating their emergency response plans, and passage of the Model Act in its entirety is not required. In fact, many states will likely use parts of the Model Act, but tailor their statutes and regulations to respond to unique or novel situations that may arise in their jurisdiction. To date, ten states have introduced legislation based upon the recommendations set forth in the Model Act.[29] Other states are expected to consider similar legislation during their current legislative sessions.

The Model Act provides a comprehensive framework for state emergency health powers, including statutory authority for isolation[30] and quarantine.[31] Section 604 of the model act authorizes the isolation or quarantine of an individual or groups of individuals during a public health emergency.[32] The Model encourages the public health authority to adhere to specific conditions and principles when exercising isolation or quarantine authority. These conditions and principles include insuring that the measures taken are the least restrictive means necessary to prevent the spread of the disease; monitoring the condition of isolated and quarantined individuals; and providing for the immediate release of individuals when they no longer pose a substantial risk of transmitting the disease to others.[33] The Model Act provides that a failure to obey the rules and orders concerning isolation and quarantine shall be treated as a misdemeanor.[34]

The Model State Emergency Health Powers Act sets forth procedures for isolation and quarantine under two different sets of circumstances. Section 605(a) addresses procedures for temporary isolation and quarantine without notice if a "delay in imposing the isolation or quarantine would significantly jeopardize the public health authority's ability to prevent or limit the transmission of a contagious or possibly contagious disease to others." The isolation or quarantine must be ordered through a written directive specifying the identity of the

---

[27] A copy of the Model Act can be found at [http://www.publichealthlaw.net].

[28] [http://www.publichealthlaw.net/MSEHPA/MSEHPA_letter_2.pdf].

[29] The ten states are California, Illinois, Kentucky, Minnesota, Missouri, Nebraska, New York, Pennsylvania, Tennessee and Utah. [http://www.ncsl.org/programs/health/snapshot.htm].

[30] For the purposes of the Model Act, isolation is defined as "the physical separation and confinement of an individual or groups of individuals who are infected or reasonably believed to be infected with a contagious or possibly contagious disease from non-isolated individuals, to prevent or limit the transmission of the disease to non-isolated individuals."

[31] Quarantine is defined as "the physical separation and confinement of an individual or groups of individuals, who are or may have been exposed to a contagious or possibly contagious disease and who do not show signs or symptoms of a contagious disease, from non-quarantined individuals, to prevent or limit the transmission of the disease to non-quarantined individuals."

[32] A public health emergency is defined to include "an occurrence or imminent threat of an illness or health condition" that is believed to be caused by bioterrorism or the appearance of a novel or previously controlled or eradicated infectious agent or biological toxin, and poses a high probability of a large number of deaths, a large number of serious or long-term disabilities, or a significant risk of substantial future harm to a large number or people.

[33] For a complete list of the conditions and principles, see Section 604(b) of the Model Act.

[34] Section 604(c).

individuals subject to the order, the premises subject to the order, the date and time at which the isolation or quarantine are to commence, the suspected contagious disease, and a copy of the provisions set forth in the Act relating to isolation and quarantine.[35] The public health authority is required to petition within ten days after issuing the directive for a court order authorizing the continued isolation or quarantine if needed.[36]

Apart from the emergency procedures outlined above, the public health authority may petition a court for an order authorizing the isolation or quarantine of an individual or groups of individuals, with notice of the petition given to the individuals or groups of individuals in question within twenty-four hours.[37] The public health authority's petition must include the same information as required in the emergency directive discussed above, in addition to "a statement of the basis upon which isolation and quarantine is justified in compliance with this Article."[38] A hearing must be held within five days of the petition being filed, and the court "shall grant the petition if, by a preponderance of the evidence, isolation or quarantine is shown to be reasonably necessary to prevent or limit the transmission of a contagious or possibly contagious disease to others."[39] An order authorizing isolation or quarantine may not do so for a period exceeding thirty days, though the public health authority may move to continue isolation or quarantine for additional periods not exceeding thirty days.[40]

The Model Act provides procedures which allow individuals subject to isolation or quarantine to challenge their detention and obtain release, and provide remedies where established conditions were not met.[41] Individuals subject to isolation or quarantine would be appointed counsel if they are not otherwise represented in their challenge.[42]

Though not yet enacted, the Model Act is being challenged by groups asserting that model legislation is unnecessary and that this particular legislation is "unjustifiably broad."[43] Others have expressed concern that the Model Act "grants unprecedented and....unconstitutional power."[44] Courts will likely be asked to review any version of the Act passed by the states.

LEGAL CHALLENGES TO STATE QUARANTINE AUTHORITY

As noted above, the Supreme Court in *Gibbons v. Ogden* alluded to a state's authority to quarantine under the police powers. In 1902, the Court directly addressed a state's power to quarantine an entire geographic area in *Compagnie Francaise de Navigation a Vapeur v. Louisiana State Board of Health*, where both the law and its implementation were upheld as valid exercises of the state's police power.[45] The petitioners in the case - a shipping company

---

[35] Section 605(a)(2).
[36] Section 605(a)(4).
[37] Section 605(b).
[38] Section 605(b)(2).
[39] Section 605(b)(5).
[40] Section 605(b)(6).
[41] Section 605(c).
[42] Section 605(e).
[43] Review of The Model State Emergency Health Powers Act, by Edward P. Richards, et. al., [http://www.plague.law.umkc.edu/blaw/bt/MSEHPA_review.htm].
[44] See "Quarantine Proposal Sparks Debate," Legal Times, November 5, 2001.
[45] 186 U.S. 380 (1902).

- challenged an interpretation of a state statute that conferred upon the state Board of Health the authority to exclude healthy persons, whether they came from without or within the state, from a geographic area infested with a disease.[46] The petitioner alleged that the statute as interpreted interfered with interstate commerce, and thus was an unconstitutional violation of the commerce clause. The Court rejected this argument, holding that although the statute may have had an affect on commerce, it was not unconstitutional.[47]

Courts have recognized an individual's right to challenge his or her isolation or quarantine by petitioning for writ of *habeas corpus*.[48] While the primary function of a writ of habeas corpus is to test the legality of the detention,[49] petitioners often seek a declaration that the statute under which they were quarantined is unconstitutional or violative of due process. Due process is a concern, though courts are reluctant to interfere with a state's exercise of police powers with regard to public health matters "except where the regulations adopted for the protection of the public health are arbitrary, oppressive and unreasonable."[50] The courts appear to give deference to the determinations of state boards of health and generally uphold such detentions as valid exercises of a state's duty to preserve the public health and not violative of due process. However, some courts have refused to uphold the quarantine of an individual where the state is unable to meet its burden of proof concerning that individual's potential danger to others.[51]

In *People ex rel. Barmore v. Robertson*, the court refused to grant the petition for writ of *habeas corpus* of a woman who ran a boarding house where a person infected with typhoid fever had boarded.[52] The woman was not herself infected with the disease, but she was a carrier and had been quarantined in her home. She argued that her quarantine was unwarranted because she was not "actually sick," though the court noted that "[i]t is not necessary that one be actually sick, as that term is usually applied, in order that the health authorities have the right to restrain his liberties by quarantine regulations."[53] In providing justification for quarantine under these circumstances, the court explained that since disease germs are carried by human beings, and as the purpose of an effective quarantine is to prevent the spread of the disease to those who are not infected, anyone who carries the germs must be isolated.[54] The court found that in the case of a person infected with typhoid fever, anyone who had come into contact with that person must be isolated in order to prevent the spread of the disease to others.[55]

The Florida Supreme Court upheld a quarantine statute that was challenged on due process grounds, denying the petitioners petition for writ of *habeas corpus*. In *Moore v. Draper*, the court stated that, "[t]he constitutional guarantees of life, liberty and property, of

---

[46] 186 U.S. at 384.

[47] Id at 387.

[48] Ex parte Hardcastle, 208 S.W. 531(Tex. Crim. App. 1919).

[49] Habeas corpus is "the name given to a variety of writs, having for their object to bring a party before a court or judge. In common usage, and whenever these words are used alone, they are usually understood to mean the habeas corpus ad subjiciendum." Specifically, habeas corpus ad subjiciendum is "a writ directed to the person detaining another, and commanding him to produce the body of the prisoner, or person detained. This is the most common form of habeas corpus writ, the purpose of which is to test the legality of the detention or imprisonment; not whether his is guilty or innocent." Black's Law Dictionary, 6th Edition, 1990.

[50] People ex. rel. Barmore v. Robertson, 134 N.E. 815, 817 (citations omitted) (Ill.1922).

[51] See State v. Snow, 324 S.W.2d 532 (Ark. 1959).

[52] 134 N.E. 815 (Ill.1922).

[53] Id at 819.

[54] Id at 819 - 820.

which a person cannot be deprived without due process of law, do not limit the exercise of the police power of the State to preserve the public health so long as that power is reasonably and fairly exercised and not abused."[56] In addition to the due process claim, the petitioner had challenged the statute as discriminatory against "all persons other than those of a certain religious faith and belief."[57] The court rejected both arguments finding that the statute was a proper exercise of the state's police power and not violative of the petitioner's constitutional rights.

---

[55] Id at 820.

[56] 57 So.2d 648, 650 (Fla. 1952), citing Varholy v. Sweat, 15 So.2d 267 (Fla. 1943).

[57] 57 So.2d at 648. The court's opinion did not indicate the basis for petitioner's claim regarding religious discrimination and did not reprint the text of the statute. The statute in question was later repealed.

INDEX

D

G

Q

R

S

T

Y

Z